HALL
CTIONS PRESENTE

SBY
LS
6H

MUSIC IS LOVE

by Francesco Lucarelli

CROSBY, STILLS & NASH

This edition © This Day In Music Books 2022
Text ©This Day In Music Books 2022

ISBN: 978-1-7392049-1-4

Artistic directors Neil Cossar and Liz Sánchez

Cover and book design by Gary Bishop
Front cover photo by Henry DIltz
Additional images and background photography by Ian T Cossar

This Day in Music Books, Unit 6 Swindells Yard, Arden Street, New Mills SK22 4NS

www.thisdayinmusicbooks.com

Email: editor@thisdayinmusic.com

Exclusive Distributors: Music Sales Limited 14/15 Berners St London W1T 3JL

Printed and bound by CPI Group (UK) Ltd, Croydon, CR0 4YY

This is a wonderful collection of information about Crosby, Stills & Nash, and the photographs bring the reader even closer to the band. This information has been collected over years and years and is a 'must read' for anyone interested in the band. I've enjoyed reading and looking at these stories for a while now and I'm pleased that you get a chance to do the same.

The greatest thrill a writer/performer can experience is seeing, with your own eyes, the look on people's faces when you have 'connected' with them. For many years now I have been blessed to have fans that treat me with respect, as I respect them.

I hope to be creating for years to come and I hope my fans will come along with me for this ride.

Graham Nash

June 20th, 2022 New York City

PREFACE

Los Angeles, Blackpool, Dallas. Music bridges distances and turns geographical maps into three-dimensional scenarios in which visions and destinies intertwine. David Crosby (California), Graham Nash (England), Stephen Stills (Texas): music brought them together.

'The physiology of our voices made the combination of the three of us so unique,' Stephen Stills said during an interview with Dutch magazine *Oor* in 1992. 'But how it came that we matched so perfectly together was as much a mystery to us, since we had three totally different voices,' David Crosby added. 'And three very different personalities as well,' Graham Nash wrapped it up.

Passion, art and friendship. Music not only as a communion of intentions through a creative process but also as a moment of meeting and sharing ideas, feelings, weaknesses and dreams. In many ways, the story of Crosby, Stills & Nash is also our story.

My discovery of CSN, Neil Young, Joni Mitchell, Jackson Browne, and The Eagles dates back to a summer in the mid-Seventies, thanks to my friend Marco, who taught me my first guitar chords. Playing and singing together the songs of the artists we admired so much became a huge passion, but I could not have imagined how those records and six strings would have marked my life in such a profound way.

As soon as I could, I bought all the albums these Laurel Canyon habitués had released. Freeing them from their cellophane wrap was a kind of ritual. I got carried away by the covers, scrolled through the song titles and looked for more information on the back and on the inner sleeves. Then I put the vinyl on the turntable, put the needle down, and started reading lyrics and notes related to the musicians involved. I spent whole evenings listening to music with headphones on, playing side A and side B of those wonderful records, until every single note was indelibly etched in my memory. Even the rustle of the grooves became an integral part of that listening experience, and I could recognise a record with my eyes closed just by listening to the crackle between the tracks.

It was then that my desire to know more grew. The official discography wasn't enough. Their tours did not touch Italy. The only opportunity to listen to CSN live in an 'official' way came in November 1979, when the triple album taken from the famous *No Nukes* concerts in New York was released. On the day of the release, I went to Millerecords (a Mecca for those who bought records in Rome in those years), walked out with the album tucked into the store's orange envelope, and ran home as fast as I could. I perfectly remember the cardboard smelling of the freshest print, and that rich package full of photographs, which in a second catapulted me into the crowd filling Madison Square Garden.

In the meantime, I had discovered the existence of bootlegs. An exciting period of research began as I tracked down that pirate-recorded vinyl, discs often placed in white cardboard envelopes with just a title and a photocopied image for the cover. They contained what seemed to me to be the most beautiful music in the world, although the audio quality was not always great. Unlike Young, Dylan, Hendrix, the Rolling Stones and others, there weren't many CSN bootlegs and I realised I would have to satisfy that sonic bulimia in some other way.

I began to respond to ads from collectors trading concert recordings on audio cassette and got in touch with a network of enthusiasts scattered in every corner of the world. I remember how exciting it was to receive a package all the way from the United States, containing the recording of some concerts on chrome C90 cassettes (always chrome cassette tapes – us traders insisted on getting our recordings on cassette tape of the highest quality). If the tape I received was from a show that had only been performed a couple of weeks before, the thrill of it all was just incredible! That innocent pleasure makes me smile to this day, as we now take live streaming of shows for granted.

1983 was the turning point for me. In the early Eighties, the music press didn't have much time for CSN anymore. During that summer, in London I found some issues of *Broken Arrow*, a fanzine dedicated to Neil Young. Finally, something with lots of news, stories, interviews. And, above all, a meeting point for fans and collectors of all nationalities.

One gap still remained to be filled: in *Broken Arrow*, CSN was only a marginal topic. In a moment of total madness, I thought somebody had to fill that gap and decided I should carry the torch for Crosby, Stills & Nash. *Wooden Nickel*, the fanzine of CSNY, was born: about 20 copies in Italian were printed in December 1983. When the last issue came out, about 10 years later, the print run was about 1,000 copies, half printed in Italian, the others in English.

Wooden Nickel was a fantastic experience, a dream realised together with Marco, Mauro and Stefano, supported by the contribution of many fans who sent us news, concert calendars, reviews, newspaper clippings, photocopies, tickets and posters. The fanzine was the wonderful tool that, 25 years before Facebook allowed us to meet thousands of people who loved the same music and the same artists we loved.

Wooden Nickel also had another incredible merit: it was the business card which allowed us to personally get to know CSNY and many folks who worked and played with them.

In the spring of 1987, myself and the *Wooden Nickel* guys (or the 'Crazy Italians', as CSN later labelled us) were touring Rome with Neil Young's Crazy Horse, and in August of the following year we were in Manhattan with CSN. Since then, I've had the privilege to experience many adventures that still seem incredible. To highlight just a few, Graham Nash sang on one of my records, I spent a week in a California garage jamming with Billy Talbot and Ralph Molina, and I sang backing vocals on 'Teach Your Children' for five memorable minutes on stage with Crosby, Stills & Nash during a concert in Rome back in 1992.

Beyond all this, there is an even greater value. It is the one brought by the many wonderful people I met during the years spent chasing dreams along the human highway. Bonds that have lasted for more than 30 years without being affected by time or distances. A mutual passion which gave me energy even when I was running out of juice. What can be said about Crosby, Stills & Nash that hasn't already been written? Do we need another book? What else should we know about these three extraordinary artists?

Music Is Love collects stories you've never heard before. These are the stories of photographers, luthiers, musicians, painters, DJs, journalists, and also ordinary people, fans and collectors, all of whom experienced their own unique moment thanks to CSN. These tales cover five decades and span five continents, testifying that – more than 50 years after that first record - the music of Crosby, Stills & Nash is not just a long road paved with extraordinary albums, but a river of emotions still touching the soul of millions of people.

Francesco Lucarelli

"To Graham, David and Stephen, who taught me how to dance to the rhythm of life"

ROCK AND ROLL HALL OF FAME INDUCTION

"I'm deeply honored and very happy to be here and to have been asked to induct Crosby, Stills & Nash into the Rock and Roll Hall of Fame.

"I heard about this supergroup before I actually heard the music, and I couldn't wait to hear it. I've been so profoundly influenced and impacted by The Hollies and by The Byrds, and especially by Buffalo Springfield that I couldn't wait to hear what they were going to come up with, and I was amazed, I was blown away. I think that personally they helped me to identify myself as a singer and a songwriter and a performer. I've always thought of them as having invented themselves, really, not particularly coming out of any mould, but just basically winging it.

"I think they helped an entire generation to define itself too. And I think of myself as being part of that same batch that they came out of. So, this is especially meaningful for me and it's a wonderful thing for me to be able to install them here tonight in the Hall of Fame.

"CSN is a working band. They worked the night before last and they will probably be working tomorrow night but, for our purposes, it's probably best for us to think of them sort of historically, and what they meant to us when they first sort of came out of the box.

"The content of their music was very socially relevant and very in-tune with the times, and very helpful to a nation and a generation that were trying to navigate themselves through a very confusing time. Fundamentally, it was about the music, and they took what had been started in those three individual groups that they came from and took it to another place. They took it forward.

"They were the quintessential vocal group. They were so complex and so sophisticated and yet so soulful. If I could have been a fly on the wall that night in 1968 when Graham Nash sat down in Laurel Canyon with Stephen and David and they sang together for the first time, that must have been an amazing thing. I'm sure they blew their own minds.

"With a nod towards Graham Nash, this is a great American group and it's really entirely fitting that they be inducted into the Rock and Roll Hall of Fame.

"Ladies and gentlemen, Crosby, Stills & Nash!"

James Taylor -
May 6th, 1997

Rock & Roll Hall of Fame 12th annual induction ceremony, Renaissance Cleveland Hotel, Cleveland, Ohio, USA.

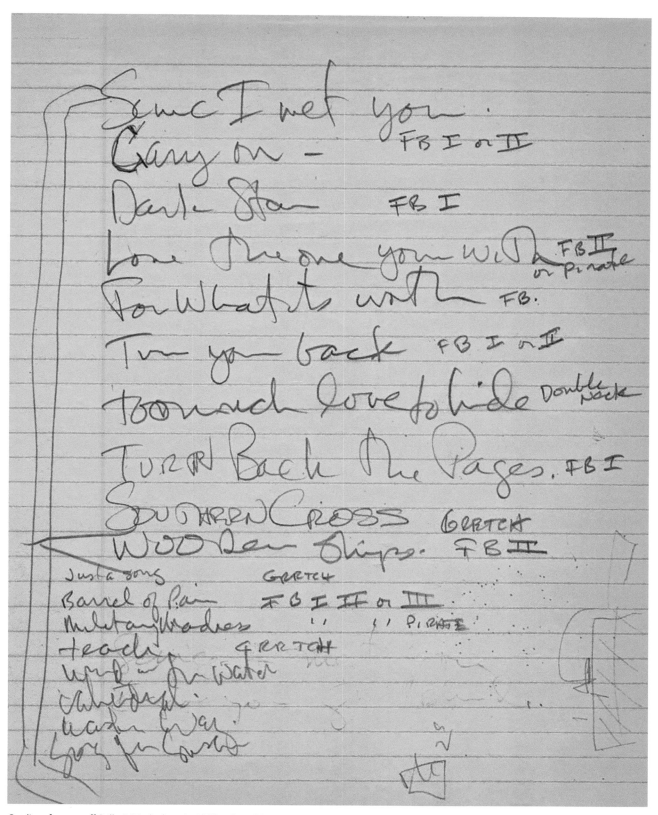

Set-list of a one-off Stills & Nash show in 1982, when CSN were on tour promoting Daylight Again. From R. Mac Holbert private collection

Oct. 4, 2015: Crosby, Stills & Nash concert at Sala Santa Cecilia, Auditorium Parco della Musica - Stephen's guitars. Photo courtesy of the Wooden Nickel archives

INTRODUCTION

Songs accompany us. I listened to the ones of Crosby, Stills & Nash - and of Neil Young, of course - with my friend Francesco, when we were learning to play guitar together, at the age of 14, an age in which music is still a lens through which to discover the world.

In my 20s, and I'm being honest with you here, I switched to listening to English new wave, then classical music, forgetting all about the Sixties and the West Coast. About 10 years ago, a little by chance, perhaps out of nostalgia, I bought the new version of 4 Way Street, just re-released with four extra tracks. The original 4 Way Street was the first CSNY record I ever bought. Little by little, as I began to listen again to the music of my youth, I took the guitar out of the cupboard and started to find the chords of 'Right Between the Eyes' and 'Love the One You're With'. In amazement, I realised I remembered those songs as if I had only recently stopped playing them. They were still capable of creating the same emotion that had stirred in me in the past and incredibly there was no sense of nostalgia about any of this. Maybe, even after all this time, I hadn't changed that much since childhood. In those melodies and in those words, I still found myself there. Without the naivety of being 14, but here I was in a familiar landscape.

Of course, it's difficult now to believe we can 'change the world', or that 'the darkest hour is always the one before the dawn' and, like everyone, today I know that no song can change the course of history. But I'm glad I believed it, and I'm grateful to CSNY for making me believe it might have been possible. That hope has not been lost and it is by no means certain that we cannot return to that hope one day. As we gardeners say, as certain seeds go 'into dormancy', all they're doing is waiting for the right conditions to germinate once again. And it didn't surprise me too much, a few years ago, to see Crosby and Nash singing 'Teach Your Children' on TV among the kids on Occupy Wall Street in New York.

Those musicians, along with a few others, like Bob Dylan or Jackson Browne, were my school, the real one. I learned a lot from them, and not just by playing their songs. I learned more from them than from my teachers in high school or from the ideologies of those times. A song cannot change the world, but it can change the life of a person. This happens when music is made of the same ingredients as life, hopes or dreams, outside of all the predefined cultural schemes of an era or of preconceived knowledge, but it seems to me that this was precisely the strength of the music of those years, the passing of which some of us regret a little (but we do so in a low voice, for fear of appearing as old hippies!).

When I've been to a CSN or Neil Young concert in recent years, I've noticed that there have always been several guys in the audience who were born many years after Déjà Vu was released. It means new generations learn to look at their lives through this music. The world doesn't seem to be getting much better since Chicago, but CSNY's songs accompany us, continue to feed our minds, teach hope, explain to us, just as David Crosby revealed to me when I first heard 'If I Could Only Remember My Name', that music is love. Otherwise, it's just not worth it.

Marco Martella

Bio: *A writer and gardener, Marco Martella, lives and works in Paris, where he edits the magazine, Jardins. From the days of his first Eko guitar to today, he has never stopped rehearsing 'The Lee Shore' without getting it right - but without giving up hope - and wondering what his life would have been like without music.*

Songs: *'The Lee Shore' (C), '4 + 20' (S), 'Our House' (N).*

60's

They are three together

SOUTHERN ACCENT

by Tom Gundelfinger O'Neal

It all started in June 1967 at Monterey Pop. A week before the festival, I was able to get a press pass and was talking to a friend, telling her I was quite excited about it. She said, "David Crosby and The Byrds will be playing and if you can get any pictures of David I will make sure that his manager sees these photos." I said "OK. I'll do that." So when the festival started, I focused on David in particular but took pictures of the whole band. Nothing more than stage shots and some candid shots backstage, but I wasn't really able to approach them.

Then, when it was all over, I sent my pictures down to LA and got a phone-call from David's manager, Larry Spector, who managed The Byrds, and he said, "I really like these pictures. Would you like to come down and we can meet?" I did, we hit it off and he gave me a couple of photo assignments. The next thing I knew, I met David in Beverly Hills and he and I hit it off. It was late June / early July 1967 and we started to build a kind of a relationship then, and it is still going on.

When I was introduced to David, I met a guy named Gary Burden who was working on an album cover for The Byrds. Within a couple of months of Monterey Pop, I was taking pictures of The Byrds for this album cover but there was a lot of turmoil going on within the group and David dropped out, but that kind of started the ball rolling. I remember being in a car with him and Gary, just cruising down through LA late at night, and I was fascinated by his conversation. He was extremely talented. All those guys are very bright, but David would be the most articulated, without a doubt. He is absolutely brilliant, a genius. They are all musical geniuses and that is probably the reason they weren't able to maintain the relationship: they are too powerful. Four powerful egos, extremely talented in so many ways.

In 1969, my good friend Henry Diltz took the photo for the first CSN album cover, but when they started working on the *Déjà Vu* album, what they really wanted to do was a bit more complicated than maybe Henry could do. I've always been a little bit more technical than him. So they got in touch with me to do this antique process that goes back to the Civil War.

Stereo-Mono
ATL 70.445

I attempted to do a ferrotype, the nickname was tintype, which is basically a photo on a very thin sheet of metal. They are very flat and have very little contrast.

I researched for a few months and rented a Civil War camera. I really never knew exactly why Stephen Stills was so animated about using this technique from that era.

A few years ago at a concert in Santa Cruz, I asked him, "Why the Civil War? I mean, you had a band called Manassas, which was at the battle of Bull Run. You're wearing a Confederate uniform on the album cover for *Déjà Vu*. Did you have an obsession about the South?" And he said, "No, not really. I loved the rebellious spirit of the Confederacy and what they stood up for in their own principles."

That's why he identified with it more than anything else. He chose that era because it was basically also an era of defiance of the rebellion, and that's really what he was kind of coming from. I was fascinated.

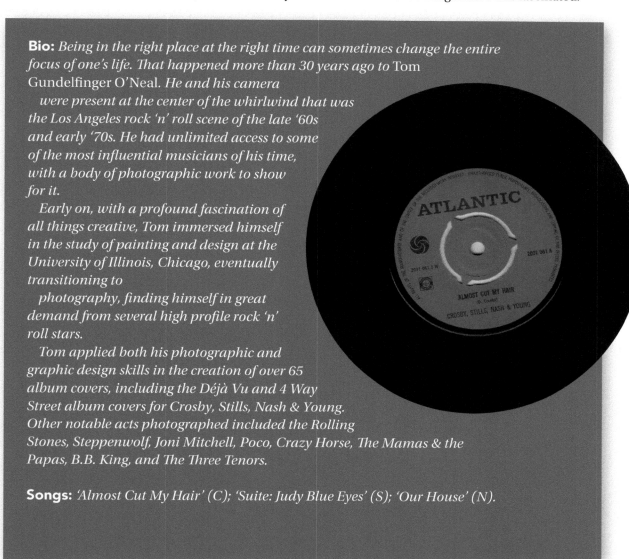

Bio: *Being in the right place at the right time can sometimes change the entire focus of one's life. That happened more than 30 years ago to* Tom Gundelfinger O'Neal. *He and his camera were present at the center of the whirlwind that was the Los Angeles rock 'n' roll scene of the late '60s and early '70s. He had unlimited access to some of the most influential musicians of his time, with a body of photographic work to show for it.*

Early on, with a profound fascination of all things creative, Tom immersed himself in the study of painting and design at the University of Illinois, Chicago, eventually transitioning to photography, finding himself in great demand from several high profile rock 'n' roll stars.

Tom applied both his photographic and graphic design skills in the creation of over 65 album covers, including the Déjà Vu and 4 Way Street album covers for Crosby, Stills, Nash & Young. Other notable acts photographed included the Rolling Stones, Steppenwolf, Joni Mitchell, Poco, Crazy Horse, The Mamas & the Papas, B.B. King, and The Three Tenors.

Songs: *'Almost Cut My Hair' (C); 'Suite: Judy Blue Eyes' (S); 'Our House' (N).*

BIG SUR FOLK FESTIVAL

by Richard Dowdy

I went to the 1968 and 1969 music festivals at Esalen Institute in Big Sur, held at a location right on the edge of the Pacific Ocean. At the time I lived in Santa Barbara with my girlfriend. I was working for Capitol Records as a writer, and a co-worker - also a writer - came along with a girl who worked at Capitol.

We drove up in my VW bug, camped in Big Sur that Saturday night, saw the two-day concert, and returned home Sunday evening. It was a great event, very low-key and everyone was friendly. I had a Pentax camera, a medium lens and several rolls of film, both color and black and white. My primary camera use was to shoot racing, surfing and girlfriends, sometimes with their clothes off. The photos I shot were okay, but that was 50 years ago, and the negatives and slides have lost some of their quality in the years since the concerts.

In 1968, on the Sunday, Ken Kesey and the 'Magic Bus' showed up on the way to the Democratic Convention in Chicago. I was foolish not to take photos of the bus and the occupants. I was focused on the musicians on stage. Our first festival featured Arlo Guthrie, Joan Baez, Judy Collins, Charles River Valley Boys, and Mimi Farina, Joan's sister.

Sept. 13, 1969: Joni Mitchell and Graham Nash at Big Sur Folk Festival, Esalen Institute, Big Sur, CA. Photo Richard Dowdy

The following year was much bigger; Joan, Joni, CSNY, John Sebastian, Dorothy Morrison & the Edwin Hawkins Singers, Chris Ethridge, Flying Burrito Brothers, and a couple of other acts I forgot. The odd thing I remember is that for both years, we didn't seem to have anything to eat the whole time the concerts were playing.

The highlight of the second year for me was CSNY playing 'Wooden Ships' in the late afternoon, with the beautiful Pacific Ocean way down below as the sun began to set. It was a very special moment. It was a magic time back then.

Bio: Richard Dowdy's *first camera, a Brownie Hawkeye, was given to him for Christmas when he was eight. After high school he began photographing surfing in Southern California and Hawaii. Eventually he became a writer at Capitol Records in Hollywood, and following that was editor/art director at Surfing Magazine in San Clemente. From there he worked as a writer on The X-Files. In addition to photographing performers, he was a staff photographer for the Indianapolis Motor Speedway and annual 500-mile race. He lives in Carlsbad, California with his wife, a dog and two cats.*

Songs: *Wooden Ships (C), Suite: Judy Blue Eyes (S), Helplessly Hoping (S).*

BIG SUR FOLK F[

The crowd at the 1969 Big Sur Folk Festival and CS&N on stage at Big Sur. Photos Richard Dowdy

THREE VOICES AND ONE MICROPHONE

by Bill Halverson

I remember the first time I worked with Crosby, Stills & Nash in the studio. I had no idea what they were going to do, so I kept asking Atlantic Records, but they didn't have a clue, except that they had booked some studio time. They showed up in David Crosby's Volkswagen van, just the three of them, a couple of guitars and a bass. Dallas Taylor was in New York finishing another project. They were impatient to cut a track but before recording we hung out for a while. Graham Nash was the only one who had any money, so he was the one who ordered a sort of fun dinner for us all at a take-out place called Chicken Delight.

When we started that session, I thought I'd record a little guitar first, let Stephen Stills take a listen, see if he liked it and what we could do to improve it. As I was fairly new at it all, I was always willing to try things he wanted to try, so I was a good match for him, I never said no. Back then, Stephen was my favorite. He was the real musician among the three of them and he was very inventive. If he wanted to put a microphone across the room, I did it. If he wanted to stand on his head, we did it. And we always kept on recording. I had a lot of energy back then and if he wanted to stay the night, we did it. That was part of why we worked so well together.

That night, when he sat down and started to play his acoustic guitar, the settings were still the ones from a previous session but I couldn't stop the take. Seven and a half minutes later Stephen took off his headphones, and we had just recorded the basic track to 'Suite: Judy Blue Eyes' in just one take. Stephen loved it and the boys were ready to sing

I had been doing a lot of jingle stuff and a lot of radio ideas with really the best background singers in Hollywood, and they always just got on one microphone and sang around that, blending themselves.

March 1969: Stephen Stills and Bill Halverson mixing the first CSN album. Wally Heider's Studio 3, Hollywood, California, USA. Photo by Rowland Scherman

Presenting

Crosby, Stills & Nash

on Atlantic Records

March 1969: Stephen Stills playing piano in Judy Collins' New York apartment, New York, USA.
Photo by Rowland Scherman

Usually they had only one headphone, so people could hear the room and hear what was coming up on tape. That's how I knew how to record voices. So, when it came to recording CSN, I was ready. I never thought to put up three microphones, only one. I just took the Neuman U67, put it up and opened it all the way around.

At the end of that first CSN session, we had recorded two songs: 'Suite: Judy Blue Eyes' and 'You Don't Have to Cry', with just an acoustic guitar and vocals

Stephen Stills had a lot of ideas and most of the music direction on the first CSN album was a result of him. David Crosby was a great rhythm guitar player, and Graham Nash was a great singer and arranger. That's why they match together so well.

We did work very well on the first album. They were very rehearsed when they got to the studio. They had been rehearsing for months and knew the parts, so they were comfortable getting around one mic. It was a combination of all our experiences, too, and it all seemed to fit. The chemistry was fantastic, and they were really motivated to do it. Just the sound of their voices was so unique. All the harmonies were wonderful. I don't think you can pick one out: without any one of the three, it wouldn't have been what it became. They had only one rule: whoever wrote the song would have the final say. None of them was the star of it, that's the beauty of their first album.

Bio: *Legendary record producer, recording engineer and arranger* Bill Halverson *engineered the debut album by Crosby, Stills & Nash in early 1969. His methods for recording vocals and guitars contributed to the album's massive success and became highly influential. He continued to work with Crosby, Stills & Nash (& Young) in various combinations, engineering and/or co-producing Déjà Vu, 4 Way Street, Stephen Stills I and II, and for Graham Nash and David Crosby in 1970-72. He resumed working with Crosby, Stills, Nash & Young on their 1999 album, Looking Forward.*

THE FIRST CONCERT AND A BOUQUET OF ROSES

by Elizabeth Bavor

The first time I saw CSN was the first time they performed for a large audience. In the summer of 1969, I was 16 and we were all in Chicago at the Auditorium and Joni Mitchell backed them. It was August 16, the night before the Woodstock performance. CSNY were originally scheduled to play at the Festival on the 17th, but actually took the stage at 4am the following morning, as previous performances had overrun.

I had heard of them and knew about Joni for sure, and loved all of them and their times in Laurel Canyon. They were young as well and awfully nervous about performing. Of course, there was a lot of smoke in the air and people high on things. I sat, second-row center, front right by the stage. Lots of people didn't know who Joni was yet and were making lots of noise during her set, and I could see the CSN guys by the side of the stage, worried for her. Joni looked so sweet and innocent. After one song, David Crosby came out on the stage and said that Joni was one of their friends, really good and wanted people to quieten down so she could sing and others could hear her. The amplifiers and sound systems weren't like they are these days, huge and loud, but when people quietened down and Joni continued to sing, I could see the boys smiling and singing along with some of the songs they knew of hers. They all adored her, as we know, and when she was done with her set, she had gained the respect and admiration of the crowd and the boys hugged her as she left the stage and went right to them, smiling as well but shaky. Graham Nash had a huge bouquet of red roses for her. They all bowed to her as he presented them, and she went out to take a bow quickly then disappeared with them, following further backstage where no one could see them.

After a 20-minute break, CS&N came out with Neil Young. The crowd was cheering, and the guys started singing: they were amazing, playing guitars and with their harmonies spot on. There were a lot of good vibes in the place that night, although at the time we were all concerned about the war in Vietnam and people did march in Washington to protest, but CS&N and Joni had no comments about it that night. We all just enjoyed the music and the good time we had.

About half-way through the concert, they stopped and started to talk between themselves and to the audience, telling a few stories about how they met and how excited they were to be playing for their first big audience

I vividly remember them announcing the fact that there was going to be a little gathering at a place called Woodstock on some guy's farmland and they were going to try to get there and play, announcing some of the other performers and inviting us all to go too.

There had been bad weather coming towards Illinois and they were wondering about airplane flights and being able to leave. They were thinking about driving but knew they'd never make it, since it began the next day, a Friday, and wondered if anyone in the audience had a private jet they could use, saying they'd pay what they could to fly, since they already had to pay for commercial tickets all the way from LA. They didn't know how they were going to get back there but would figure it out somehow. None of them had much money. Of course, we all laughed, but sure enough, one guy raced up from the audience and said he'd take them, saying he was a pilot and would do it for free. With that, David Crosby, the most outspoken, repeated that if anyone wanted to come join them, we were all invited to get out east and see them perform again.

Little did they know how many would be there at Woodstock.

BY THE TIME WE GOT TO WOODSTOCK WE WERE HALF A MILLION STRONG.

by John Bowan

My friend Bob and I got psyched up for the music festival in New York state long before 15 August 1969. We dreamed of seeing Jimi Hendrix in person, so we mailed away for tickets to Three Days of Peace & Music at An Aquarian Festival. Besides Hendrix, I wanted to hear many of the bands scheduled to appear — especially a newly-gathered trio billed as Crosby, Stills & Nash. As a fan of The Byrds, Buffalo Springfield, and The Hollies, I already loved the hits made separately by David Crosby, Stephen Stills, and Graham Nash. Now I was eager to hear the new music they would create together.

Bob and I drove through mobs of traffic on Friday to park within a few miles of the festival grounds. We trekked in by foot. By the time we got there, the fences were down, our tickets were unnecessary, and

the music was on. But what stopped us in our tracks was the unprecedented size of the crowd, with all its incendiary energy and makeshift madness. Through thirst, hunger, rain and songs, the massive throng bonded as one huge organism. Three days later, after Jimi delivered a rousing finale to those of us who remained until the end, we drove home to lives that would never be the same. The cultural phenomenon that became known as Woodstock had changed us and indelibly marked our entire generation with stellar music at the very core of our collective consciousness.

On the second day of the festival, deep into the dark of night, onto the stage sauntered Crosby, Stills & Nash. They were google-eyed at the crowd. And we in the audience were about to be blown away by the unique harmonies and essential brilliance of this 'super-group.' When they launched into their first song, 'Suite: Judy Blue Eyes', I was mesmerized by their music. Not just a song, this was a musical journey, a tour de force of talents, lyrics, rhythms, and melodies, woven together with love and magic. Their acoustic set continued, with the guys bathed in bright light against the darkest skies.

To our surprise, after several songs, Neil Young suddenly sat in, amping up our delight even further. The trio was now a quartet, driving the depth and complexity of musicality still higher. Later adding electric amplification on 'Pre-Road Downs', we were all on our feet, throbbing and grooving to the beat. By their last song, '49 Bye-Byes', I knew we had witnessed musical history being made at Woodstock.

It would be decades before I saw CSN in person again. It happened in 2009 at Theater at Foxwoods,

Mashantucket, Connecticut. With an oriental rug on the stage, in strode three much older men, to the enthusiastic roar of generations of fans who gathered to hear them. Grey locks were on display, belt notches long since let out, yet the musical mastery of the trio was matured by many years of experience, mostly apart from each other. But, oh, when they joined together again, the singular sonority was still there. Though Stephen Stills' voice was but a shadow of his youthful growl, his peerless guitar virtuosity was better than ever. Graham Nash's high tenor (and barefoot dances) moved us. David Crosby's white halo of hair, glowing in the spotlight, framed his delirious expression while he harmonized. Their hits were awesome. We also thrilled to a bevy of cover songs from their contemporary artists' classic hits — songs like 'You Can Close Your Eyes', 'Ruby Tuesday', and 'Uncle John's Band'. What a treat!

Twice more this decade, my wife and I saw CSN, once in Providence, Rhode Island, and for our final time in New Brunswick, New Jersey. The audiences again were multigenerational, all bound together by love for this music, these men, and their mastery. And all of us could sing along to every word of their songs.

Sadly, the band members are once again estranged from each other, torn apart by volcanic quarrels never evident on stage. Crosby, Stills & Nash are once again solo artists, each making memorable new music. But I dream of one more reunion tour. Can lightning strike twice (as it struck first at Woodstock)? As David Crosby penned long ago, 'Everybody's saying that music is love.' Let love reign in your hearts, gentlemen, overcoming any differences between you, for there are fewer years ahead of us than behind. With bated breath, we await in hope the return of CSN.

Dec. 22, 1969: CSN&Y live at H.I.C. Arena, Honolulu, Hawaii, USA. Photo by Paul Wultz (courtesy of Wooden Nickel Archives)

Bio: *John Bowan was born in New York City and lives in Westerly, Rhode Island. During a long career, he worked in advertising. These days he is a marketing consultant.*

Songs: '*Wooden Ships' (C) – 'This Fanta-Sci-Fi wonder is amazing in every way, musically and tonally immersive; marvelous storytelling; voice weaving.'*
'Suite: Judy Blue Eyes' (S) – 'This is the song that made me a fan forever. Beyond folk. Beyond rock. Beyond marvelous. Many moods and tunes in one journey.'
'Marrakesh Express' (N) – 'I always loved the Brit Pop creativity of Graham Nash; this takes those roots - and listeners - for an exotic, fabulous, toe-tapping ride.'

THE PHILOSOPHER

by Bani Kinnison

Crosby Stills & Nash to me are more than just a band. They are all geniuses on their own but together they make something truly magical. The songs are not just good, they are thoughtful, poetic, heartbreaking, triumphant and exciting, filled with exquisite harmonies, beautiful melody and soaring guitars.

David's Beautiful Imagination by Bani Kinnison Aug. 2015

They write songs that take you to strange and exotic places, songs that break your heart, songs that make you want to take action, songs that make you want to be a better person. David Crosby, Graham Nash and Stephen Stills work together to make the music better than it ever could have been if they all had not touched it with their own special magic.

David, 'The Philosopher' who writes music and lyrics with passion full of unusual ideas and images. Graham, 'The Poet' whose songs come from his life's quiet triumphs and crushing tragedies; the words seem to be ripped from his diary or straight out of his heart. Stephen, 'The Cowboy' whose songs are energetic adventures of words and remarkable escapades of sailing, riding, flying and action.

Working together they form a special musical bond that not only highlights the best characteristics and abilities of each individual but amplifies them as well. I love them. I love their music. It makes me happy when I'm sad and when I'm happy it can make me cry. I've been listening almost daily for more than a decade and I always want more. It comforts me, sometimes it crushes me, but it always inspires me.

David's Imagination is the first of the CSN themed pieces I created. It started as a pencil on paper sketch and ended as a mostly digital image. It was inspired by his words and lyrics overall. His lyrics are so much about his thoughts and visions that it seemed reasonable to me to try and portray that.

I used a renaissance style perspective to signify the vastness of time and space and of ideas reaching forward and backward. I used objects from nature to represent his gentle spirit. The light beams radiate from his head like early religious painting portrayals of saints. This is a portrait of a philosopher and thinker. It is painted in shades of blue, the color of dreams and of night, giving a nod to his darker past but also the wonders hidden that have not yet been explored in the light.

Bio: Bani Kinnison *is an Iowa girl who grew up living all over the United States. She moved around a lot but now all she wants is to stay in one happy little place with the person she loves. She spends her days painting, baking and keeping an eye on the forest creatures in her backyard and has never been happier. She studied art and art history but has always been a painter. Her earliest memories were with brush in hand. 'It is a very lucky thing to be about to do when you love. I try never to take that for granted and knowing that other people out in the great big world also like what I do makes it even better.'*

Songs: *'Guinnevere' (C), 'Southern Cross' (S), 'Our House' (N).*

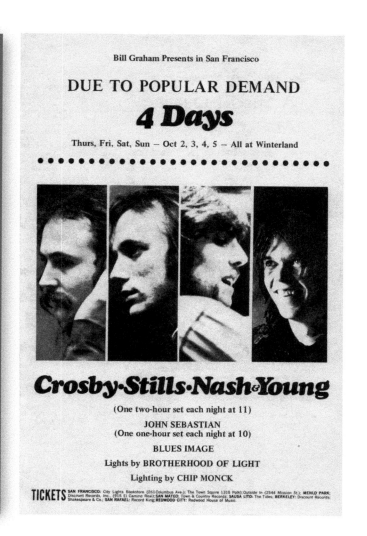

Bill Graham Presents in San Francisco

DUE TO POPULAR DEMAND

4 Days

Thurs, Fri, Sat, Sun — Oct 2, 3, 4, 5 — All at Winterland

Crosby·Stills·Nash&Young

(One two-hour set each night at 11)

JOHN SEBASTIAN
(One one-hour set each night at 10)

BLUES IMAGE

Lights by BROTHERHOOD OF LIGHT

Lighting by CHIP MONCK

TICKETS SAN FRANCISCO: City Lights Bookstore (261 Columbus Ave.); The Town Squire 1318 Polk); Outside In (2544 Mission St.); MENLO PARK: Discount Records, Inc. (915 El Camino Real); SAN MATEO: Town & Country Records; SAUSALITO: The Tides; BERKELEY: Discount Records; Shakespeare & Co.; SAN RAFAEL: Record King; REDWOOD CITY: Redwood House of Music

70's

Everybody's saying music is love

Painting by Simon David Smith - simonsmithart.com

WAVING A FREAK FLAG

by Ernesto Assante

I was 12 and already listening to rock music and buying records, my bedroom wall covered in posters. When the *Woodstock* movie was screened at Quattro Fontane cinema in Rome, obviously I went. When I walked in, the movie had already started and on the screen was the beginning of the performance of Crosby, Stills, Nash & Young (even though Neil Young doesn't feature in the film). From that moment the three - or two, or four, or singles, as the case may be - have become, together with The Beatles and The Who, my favorite band.

I love all their music; I own all their records in every possible combination. I've had the good fortune to interview Graham Nash several times, and Neil Young and David Crosby a couple of times, too. Alas, I never had the opportunity to talk to Stephen Stills.

Talking with them has always been beautiful and exciting, there are so many stories and tales they can tell. And their music, especially the ones composed at the turn of the Sixties and Seventies, tells in a unique and perfect way the dreams and desperations of at least a couple of generations, generations who have lived the hope of changing the world and have lost it - but never, however, completely abandoning the battle.

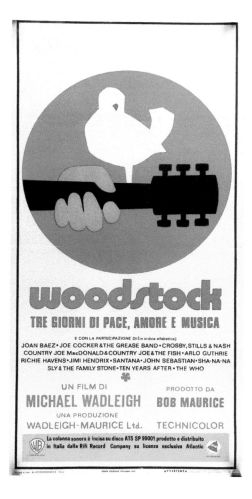

April 1972: Three separate promo posters commissioned by Atlantic Records to artist Stanislaw Zagorski

If today there are artists who are just as magnificently and coherently engaged with their audience and society, it is due to CSN, to their way of writing songs and living life, including all the excesses and the quarrels, the bullshit and the mistakes they committed often and willingly. But the freak flag they waved we have hoisted in many of our own wooden ships, which we are still trying to sail the sea of life with.

Bio: Ernesto Assante *is in his 60s and happy to have reached that venerable age. He is a music journalist at La Repubblica, works on radio and TV, writes books and teaches. He loves music, but loves talking and writing about music more, and he likes the idea of having contributed in his long career from the Seventies to today to persuading people to listen to the music he loves. He lives in Rome, is married, has two daughters, a dog, four or five guitars he cannot play, many computers, and an incredible number of records and books.*

Songs: *'Almost Cut My Hair' (C), 'Suite: Judy Blue Eyes' (S), 'Simple Man' (N).*

BEHIND THE IRON CURTAIN

by Frank Busjahn

I can't exactly say which year I first listened to CSN. My interest in music started around 1971 when I turned 14. I got my first turntable that year and maybe one year later the first cassette radio. Living in East Berlin meant that records from the West were hard to get, but you could listen to radio stations from West Berlin, including AFN and BBC. So, there's a good chance I listened to CSN not much later than 1971/72.

And I still remember two highlights from the first half of the Seventies. The first being the Czech pressing of *Déjà Vu* (Supraphon label) I got in 1974. I listened to this album again and again and fell in love with their music. This period also included listening to Neil Young a lot, especially *Harvest* and *Everybody Knows This Is Nowhere*.

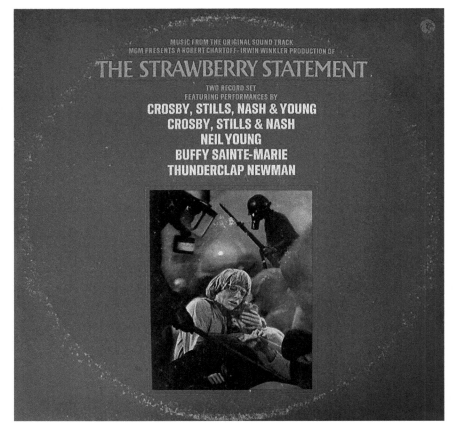

The second highlight was watching the movie *The Strawberry Statement*, which came to East German cinemas in spring 1973. I probably saw it four or five times and it was one of the strongest influences on me at that time. And it was the message of the film as well as the music. Some of those songs, along with the film content, became all-time favorites: 'Circle Game', 'Our House', 'Down by the River', 'Something in the Air', 'Helpless', and 'Give Peace a Chance'. I will never forget what I felt when I watched the movie and listened to those songs for the first time.

I got most of The Beatles' albums and a few more in the first half of the Seventies. This period of intensive listening to music lasted till I left school in 1975. Then there was a long break: the army, family, house, university, the 1989 events, and the Nineties. I really started listening to music again and buying CDs in the late Nineties. Neil Young became my favorite artist but CSN were right there with him.

The first Crosby & Nash concert I attended was in 2005 and then again in 2011. For a long time, there was no CSN concert in Berlin but, when they came back in 2013, I was there. How did I feel? Of course, it had been a long-time dream to see CSN (or maybe even CSNY) live. I was still a bit sad for having missed the opportunity to see CSN in Bonn in 2009. Crosby & Nash shows had been very good concerts and I was glad to listen to their beautiful songs and hear them talking. But surely, I was longing to see Stephen Stills, at least once in my lifetime!

After 40 years, I knew I could not expect to hear the songs the same way they sounded on *Déjà Vu*. From a few more recent recordings, I knew Stephen's voice had changed a lot; in my opinion, much more than the voices of David and Graham. Consequently, I was excited to attend the CSN concert but without having exceedingly high expectations. What I really wanted to see was how good was Stephen on guitar. Apparently, that night he did not really feel very comfortable and stood a few metres away from his companions. It was more Crosby & Nash and sometimes Stills. Not really a unity. Maybe only a detail, but so was the concert. His voice apart, Stephen lacked *the fire*. Anyway, I enjoyed the show and I am glad I didn't miss it.

In 2015, Crosby, Stills & Nash came to Berlin again. This time Stephen was in excellent form and in a good mood, smiling and clearly enjoying himself. The audience could feel it and encouraged him. His songs and guitar playing were outstanding and the crowd kept pushing him. That night Stephen Stills was on fire and he turned a great concert into an unforgettable experience.

At last, after so many years, I was able to fulfill my wish.

Bio: *Born in East Berlin in 1957 (and still there),* Frank Busjahn *finished university as a historian specialising in South Asian history, and has worked in the department for Asian and African Studies since 1983. For the last 16 years his main role has been as an IT manager at the institute, but he still teaches Indian history.*
His main interest and hobby is live music, and he loves to go to concerts, especially those where there's a chance to talk to musicians about their music, not least Neil Young, CSN, Nick Cave, Wilco, Patti Smith, Lucinda Williams.
Besides music, he loves to take photos, especially landscapes, and of cities and villages. And he loves meeting friends from near and far. 'I met many of them on the internet and later also in person. Life is good!'

Songs: *'The Lee-Shore' (C); 'Bluebird' (S); 'Wasted on The Way' (N).*

January 18 - 19, 1972: Crosby & Nash recording at Wally Heider's, Los Angeles, California, USA. Photos by Henry Diltz

Oct. - Dec. 1970: Stephen Stills at Brookfield House in Elstead, Sussex, England. Photo by Henry Diltz

THE STRENGTH OF CROSBY, STILLS & NASH

by Carlo Verdone

I love music, all good music, even classical music. Like everyone in my generation, this love blossomed when I discovered The Beatles' 'Please, Please Me' and 'Twist and Shout', then my musical culture gradually blossomed. I followed every genre and continue to follow the music, even if it is no longer the same. Today you have to go and look for artists. There is no longer a music industry: LPs are finished, and the CD is also gone.

In the second half of the Sixties there was an important step: we had left Elvis Presley behind and thanks to The Beatles a new musical wave was coming. Parallel to the British pop and beat culture, there was this new American pop, rock and folk culture, with Bob Dylan of course a huge turning point. His songs combined poetry and music, ballads the like of which we had never heard before. A proletarian, protesting voice - even a little intellectual, if you like - that did not seem suitable for bel canto. But that was Dylan's strength.

When bands such as Crosby, Stills, Nash & Young were born in the late Sixites, America began to give musical body to its voice. In those days, I saw Jethro Tull at Teatro Brancaccio and The Who at Piper Club, both in Rome. I saw them all, and also travelled to England to see Cream. But only with Woodstock did I realise this new music was getting serious. Woodstock wasn't just a one-time concert, Woodstock was more. A large fresco that testifies to a very well defined historical, social and musical moment. There were some performances we will never see again for their genuineness, for their power, for what they meant.

Joe Cocker's interpretation of 'With a Little Help From My Friends' *is* Woodstock. There is everything: this great pagan prayer of 500,000 people and a man singing, giving his soul, completely stoned, with that psychedelic shirt on. It was a very specific moment and Woodstock gave us back that historical-cultural passage in full: the hippie movement, drugs, the ideals of peace and freedom, total freedom.

What did we have in Italy? Nothing. Only this small Festival of Poets in Castel Porziano.

The first time I heard Crosby, Stills & Nash was when I saw the *Woodstock* movie. It was a beautiful performance and I immediately knew this unknown group was going to be a great success. Their strength was the perfect harmony of those voices and, of course, 'Suite: Judy Blue Eyes' impressed me tremendously. They were wonderful.

After Woodstock, I bought CSN's first album, where there was a song I loved, David Crosby's 'Guinnevere'. I realised that, of all three, David was the one who fascinated me the most. I liked his warm voice. I liked the chords he was using.

David's first solo album is huge, one of those records to listen to all the time. Along with the first Crosby & Nash album, this is an extraordinary

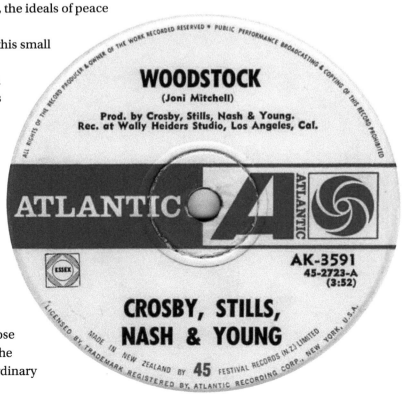

March 20, 1973: David Crosby's guest appearance at Neil Young's concert - Winterland, San Francisco, CA. Photo Donald Leary

LP, containing very intelligent and original songs, such as 'Games, Whole Cloth', 'The Wall Song'. It was probably the album I listened to most frequently during the early Seventies.

Then Stephen Stills' first solo record, a great album including that wonderful composition 'Church'. Stephen is a fantastic guitarist and it is no coincidence that Eric Clapton and Jimi Hendrix were on that album.

I was often in London in the Seventies, and remember in clubs you danced to songs like 'Carry On'. Disco music hadn't even been thought of.

I continued to follow CSN both as a group and as soloists, but always with a fondness for David Crosby. Crosby and 'If I Could Only Remember My Name' remind me of my youth. At the time when we went out with the girls, we went by car. We were students and we didn't have our own home. I always carried a tape recorder with a cassette and invariably would play David's music. With his poetry he immediately created the ideal atmosphere to kiss, to make out, to be together. It made everything very peaceful, soft, very intimate. It was the perfect soundtrack for being with a girl.

When I made my first experimental Super8 short films, which have nothing to do with the comedies I made later on in my life, I was very influenced by Kenneth Anger, Jonas Mekas, Yoko Ono, and even Alberto Grifi's American underground cinema. I made some very particular visual poems and I used 'Traction In The Rain' as the soundtrack of *Elegia Notturna*. They were images that went from dusk to night and ended at dawn. It was details, macro zoom, blurry images. There were fade-outs, incredibly difficult to achieve with the Super8, using slow motion by hand. Roberto Rossellini saw it and selected me to attend the Experimental Center of Cinematography, on the Directors course.

This music deeply affected me and energised my personal and artistic journey. But most of all, these three musicians - four if we add Neil Young - made my youth more beautiful. Even today, when I listen to one of their songs, I instinctively go back in time and relive those moments with great serenity and a sense of fullness.

> **Bio:** *Born in Rome,* Carlo Verdone *is an actor, director and screenwriter. Between 1970 and 1975 he made experimental Super 8 short films and documentaries. In 1978 he made his television debut on the Non Stop show. A meeting with director Sergio Leone marked the beginning of his own directing career. From his debut behind the camera with* Un Sacco Bello (1980) *to* Si Vive Una Volta Sola (2021), *Carlo has directed 27 films, his passion for rock music often emerging.*
>
> **Songs:** *'Guinnevere' (C), 'Carry On' (S), 'Suite: Judy Blue Eyes' (S).*

LOVE THE ONE YOU'RE WITH

by Gerri Winchell Findley

I sketch and post to Instagram daily ~ pop culture people, music and more – and everyone's smiling. I aim for delight.

Some days an art prompt is the inspiration, and a few days before Valentine's Day, 'Love the One You're With' popped into my head. Sketching that first Stephen Stills album, which I played the grooves out of, was a perfect fit - combining art prompts 'memory that makes you smile and love.'

In 1970, my family lived in the Catskills, near where Woodstock happened. As a matter of fact, our milk was from Yasgur's Farm. Listening to and

Image by Gerri Winchell Findley, www.gerrifindley.com

sketching this album brought back great memories. Posting and sharing the sketch creates community, and reconnects us with the music.

> **Bio:** *A graphic designer ~ editorial design, Nashville, travel and history publications, signage – in his spare time (and not so spare time)* Gerri Winchell Findley *sketches. 'Mostly I quick-sketch daily events, musings, people on award shows and Shark Tank and lots of music, entertainers and pop culture. When I sketch live events, I wear a belt with 40-50 coloured markers, stroll around and sketch people, and they all get a smile.'*
>
> **Songs:** *'Long Time Gone' (C); 'Love the One You're With' (S); 'Wounded Bird' (N). 'Just a Song Before I Go' (N).*

FROM THE JUNGLE OF VIETNAM TO THE STADIUMS OF THE UNITED STATES

by Glenn Goodwin

While stationed with the US Army's 1st Infantry Division in Vietnam, I was fortunate to have not been sent to the front line and was assigned to a support unit within the division. Though I did see a small amount of action, I was certainly blessed to have spent most of my time in our base camp in Dian, South Vietnam. While there, a few of my friends sent me audio cassette tapes of hours of FM radio broadcasts in California. It was so great, I played those tapes in my hooch, which held around 25 to 30 soldiers. We all enjoyed listening to the many incredible songs from the hottest musicians in the world, including Santana, The Grateful Dead, Creedence Clearwater Revival, The Animals, and Jimi Hendrix. But the one group that knocked me out was Crosby, Stills, Nash & Young. My stateside friends sent me their cassettes, and I couldn't stop playing their music. Everyone in our hooch loved them as well.

I was so disappointed I couldn't attend Woodstock, since it took place while I was in Vietnam. I read about it in US Army newspaper, *Stars and Stripes*. Guaranteed, if I wasn't drafted, I

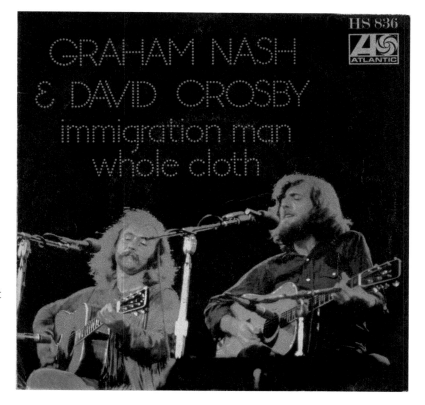

would have definitely attended, and could have met Crosby, Stills, Nash & Young sooner than I did.

The moon landing also took place that summer. I watched Neil Armstrong set foot on the moon with dozens of soldiers, on a black and white television in the middle of a war.

Throughout my tour in Vietnam, I often wondered what I would do when - or candidly if - I came home. Before I was drafted in May 1968, I played in a couple of bands and worked at an awesome record store. I knew music was going to be a part of my future, but with the Vietnam war looming and the likelihood I would be drafted, I wasn't sure what my career would become. Once I got home, I made the decision to become a disc jockey and to meet CSNY. With perseverance and an undying commitment to realizing my dream, I became a disc jockey in Carmel, California on a progressive rock station, meeting Graham Nash and David Crosby within two years of my return from Vietnam.

In the summer of 1973, Crosby & Nash were on tour, with David Blue as opening act. At the time, I was living in San Francisco. They were coming through town, playing the Civic Center. I felt I would do what

I could to show them I was very interested, deciding to hang out as they set up, see if I could help in any way. I basically volunteered my services to work on the show. This was a Bill Graham Presents production and his crew handled the basic needs of the show, including box office management, radio and print promotion, union labor, general logistics, backstage and green room management. That's where I spotted an opportunity. Apparently, the promoter's representative had forgotten a basic need all bands request: to have plenty of towels on hand, so when they come off stage after performing, they can wipe the sweat off. So, I took charge!

I asked each member of the crew where they were staying. It was the Miyako Hotel (now the Hotel Kabuki), Japantown, a short drive from the Civic Center. I requested each crew

member's hotel keys, then drove over to the Miyako and took all the towels from each room, loaded them in my car and drove back to the gig. Voilà! Towels for everyone!

I accomplished my objective: both Crosby & Nash lighting director, Steven Cohen, and road manager, Leo Makota proved hot to hire me. As luck would have it, David Lindley, one of the musicians in the Crosby & Nash band, had gotten very sick earlier in the tour and was not getting better. They decided to do the remaining few dates left on the tour but were not going to extend after the break. Bummer for me in the short run. They promised the next gig that came up would be mine and lived up to that promise. After a few small gigs and studio work, the legendary 1974 Crosby, Stills, Nash & Young tour was put together and I was hired to be stage and equipment manager for David, Graham and Tim Drummond, the bass player on the tour. This began an exciting and memorable life of touring, working on albums in recording studios and many other projects with them through to 1982.

Bio: *Born in Hollywood, Glenn Goodwin began his career playing drums in garage bands and selling records at music stores. After a tour of duty in Vietnam, in 1970 he moved to Santa Cruz and in 1973 was hired by Crosby & Nash, beginning a steady career as a stage/equipment manager and later as road and production manager with CSN, Carole King, Jackson Browne, Phoebe Snow, and many others. From 1981 and into the early 1990's, he worked as a video promo producer, winning awards with 'Lucky Star' by Madonna, 'Dancing on the Ceiling' by Lionel Richie, 'Just A Gigolo' by David Lee Roth, and Rod Stewart's 'Some Guys Have All the Luck.'*

In early 1992, his career path led to job opportunities in the corporate marketing and communications industry. He is now working on a feature film with old friend Michael Stergis, a former guitar player and vocalist with Crosby, Stills & Nash, the latter an executive producer on the film project. Glenn and his family reside in Plano, Texas.

Songs: *'Teach Your Children' (N) – 'One of my all-time favourites.'*

'Wind on the Water' (N) – 'This had a special place for me, since the video we played live in concert had incredible footage from the Cousteau Society. We had a wonderful lunch meeting in Hollywood in the mid-Seventies with Graham, David, Mac Holbert, Leslie Morris, Jacques-Yves Cousteau, Philippe Cousteau and his wife, one of my most amazing memories working with David and Graham. Our meeting went on at least two hours, and to be in the same room with Jacques Cousteau, along with the rest of our group, was a joy. The meeting was to discuss how we could access awesome whale footage from their organization that we could use on tour in conjunction with 'Wind on the Water' and how we could reciprocate and help them further their membership development. Jacques and Philippe agreed to provide footage, and help edit it for use on tour. What we did was bring a representative and membership booth from the Cousteau Society on the road with Crosby & Nash, set up in the lobby area of each show to enlist more members. It worked out perfect.'

'Wasted On the Way' (N) – 'My brother Wayne played the violin solo on this song. He passed away in December 2008. It's still emotional to hear and remember my brother, even after all these years.'

R.P.M

4058
o., Putzy
zy Music,
ASCAP
82 Atlan
Recording Cor

VOCAL
Time: 2:52
ST-A-42918-AR
STEREO

WASTED ON THE WAY
(Words and Music by Graham Nash)
CROSBY, STILLS & NASH
Produced by Crosby, Stills & Nash with
Stanley Johnston and Steve Gursky
From Atlantic LP 19360 -
"DAYLIGHT AGAIN"

MFG. BY ATLANTIC RECORDING CORP 75

A WARNER COMMUNICATIONS COMPANY

45

Oct. 4, 1973: Crosby, Nash & Young's guest appearance at Manassas concert - Winterland, San Francisco, California, USA. Photos by Bob Sheridan

ANGELS AND BODYGUARDS

by Kenny Passarelli

Between February and April 1969, Stephen Stills was visiting a couple of friends in Gold Hill, above Boulder in the mountains of Colorado. I believe the picture of Stephen taken by Henry Diltz, depicting Stills with guitar and a giraffe in the snow for his first solo record, is the spot: 8,000ft high in the Rocky Mountains. Anyway, a local music store owner in Boulder, where I was living, told me Steve Stills, as he was called then, was up in Gold Hill. He said Stephen had just finished a new record and was looking for a bass player. I was told the location of the house and I think I was given the telephone number.

Stephen invited me up to the house. I had a reputation for being a solid bass player and felt confident that I could play with anyone, I was 19. Stephen looked and dressed just like on the cover of the CSN record, in hiking boots and flannel shirt. He was really nice and excited to play me an acetate of his new group, CSN.

I couldn't believe what I was hearing: the music was unbelievable, the harmonies and vocal blend, a new sound. After hearing the record, he showed me the 1966 Fender bass he played on the record and suggested I play a Fender. I was playing a Gibson at the time. It began a teacher-student relationship that exists to this day.

I never saw Stephen till either late 1972 or early 1973. I was working with Joe Walsh at the Caribou Ranch recording studio from 1972 and I believe Stephen had just moved back to Colorado. I think he came up to the ranch to start on or finish the last Manassas record. I had not seen him since the Gold Hill meeting back in 1969. What a surprise to see him again! I remember driving with him, after just seeing him, to this great cabin he had with this concert grand piano in this tiny place way up in the mountains.

He moved into a big house in Rollinsville, Colorado, close to Caribou and Boulder. He had a lot of jam sessions there. At the time we were on the road a lot, and so was Manassas, but when we were in town we hung out and jammed. I believe at one of these jam sessions, Stephen asked if I would like to join Manassas. I told him I couldn't leave Joe. He came

"Stills"
a Brilliant
New Album
on Columbia
Records and
Tapes

up with the idea of Barnstorm, opening shows and me playing both gigs. Wow! That summer of 1973 was great. Musically, the tour with Manassas and Joe Walsh was a high point for me.

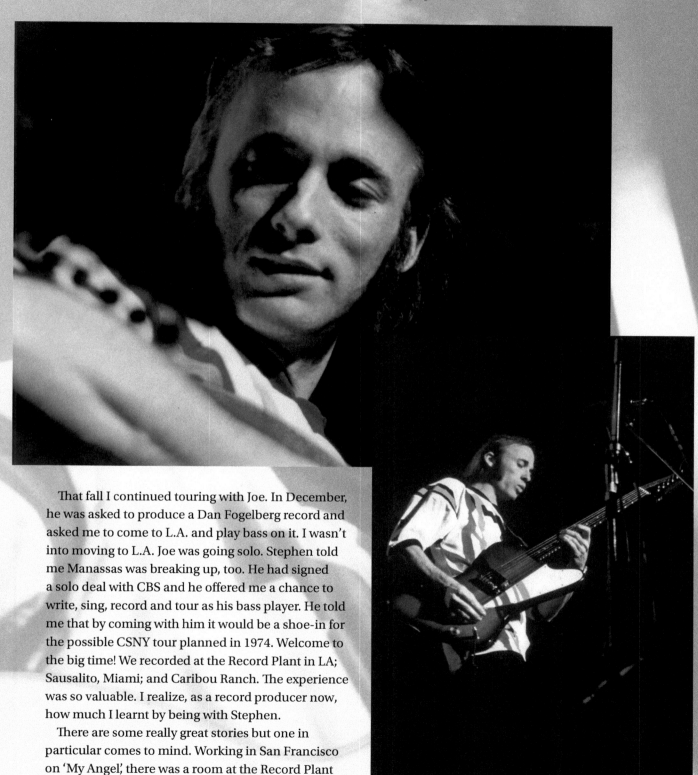

That fall I continued touring with Joe. In December, he was asked to produce a Dan Fogelberg record and asked me to come to L.A. and play bass on it. I wasn't into moving to L.A. Joe was going solo. Stephen told me Manassas was breaking up, too. He had signed a solo deal with CBS and he offered me a chance to write, sing, record and tour as his bass player. He told me that by coming with him it would be a shoe-in for the possible CSNY tour planned in 1974. Welcome to the big time! We recorded at the Record Plant in LA; Sausalito, Miami; and Caribou Ranch. The experience was so valuable. I realize, as a record producer now, how much I learnt by being with Stephen.

There are some really great stories but one in particular comes to mind. Working in San Francisco on 'My Angel', there was a room at the Record Plant

May 13, 1972: Manassas live at William and Mary Hall, College of William and Mary, Williamsburg, Virginia, USA. Photos by Charlie Wine (courtesy of Shari Avenius)

that you could only get to by walking through our recording session. Unexpectedly, Sly Stone walked in with a Chinese bodyguard and a couple of other guys, and they walked right in on our session. We happened to be in the control room and, while listening, looked out the glass and there was Sly with his creepy henchmen. It looked like they were making some kind of business deal, extremely suspicious. Stephen was speechless.

The King Biscuit Flower Hour presents: Stephen Stills and Maria Muldaur, Sunday, July 14, 1974.

Stephen Stills   Maria Muldaur

On July 14, the King Biscuit Power Hour will present a taped live radio show featuring Stephen Stills and Maria Muldaur. The show hosted by Richard Robinson (on FM only) is in Quadraphonic sound. So you can hear it the way you'd be seeing it.

In the future, shows will be on the second Sunday and the last Sunday of every month. Check the listing below for times and stations.

For further information, stay tuned to Rolling Stone. Or, better yet, contact Bob Meyrowitz or Alan Steinberg at DIR Broadcasting, 527 Madison Ave., N.Y. 10022. Or call 212-371-6850.

This was 1974 and it looked like a drug deal to me. It didn't look like a real estate deal. Sly was clearly familiar with the studio and felt he could do whatever he wanted to do. Stephen looked at me, I looked at him, and we said: "What are we going to do here?" It looked kind of scary. People were armed. We said, "How are we going to get him out?"

Then Stephen figured out the song we were doing. He coaxed Sly to come into the control room to listen to what we were doing and give us some kind of advice. You know, it was really kind of bullshit. We did it to get him out of there. The other guys came along into the studio. We played this track, Sly gave some pointers, vocally, and Stephen sang it like Sly would have sung it, with that deep low voice. A different kind of vocal than Stephen did. I think Stephen gave him some credit on the album. He just thought, 'Let's get him involved, see what happens, and come out with some ideas for the song.'

That's how he got him out of there. It was incredible. Stephen was pretty hot-tempered, but these guys with Sly were scary. Believe me, you could not throw these guys out. Stephen used the situation for the best.

Bio: *Born in Denver, Colorado,* Kenny Passarelli *studied classical trumpet from the ages of seven to 18, entering the University of Denver as a trumpet performance major. He started playing bass at 16. Dropping out of college to become a professional musician, his first big break was with Joe Walsh and forming Barnstorm. He co-wrote the classic 'Rocky Mountain Way' with Joe, then went on to tour and recorded with Stephen Stills, Elton John, Hall and Oates, and Dan Fogelberg, finally touring with CSN in the summer of 1983. He stopped touring in 1984 to write, getting a deal in 1987 with CBS International. He started producing in 1995, notably Otis Taylor, Eddie Turner, and David Jacob-Strain. Back on the road with Stephen Stills in 2007, 2008 and 2011, he also in 2009 recorded The Roadsinger with Yusuf Islam (Cat Stevens). Still performing, he was inducted into the Colorado Rock and Roll Hall of Fame with Joe Walsh and Barnstorm on 13 August 2017.*

Songs: *'Guinnevere' (C); 'Suite: Judy Blue Eyes' (S); 'Lady of the Island' (N).*

SALT, OIL AND TOMATO SAUCE

by Russ Kunkel

Stephen Stills is great. In order to understand him, you have to spend time with him. I play golf with Graham Nash. He got me into playing golf. Graham is very grounded, a real down-to-earth guy. And David Crosby is…well, David is David! He's been up and down the rollercoaster all his life. He can be way up there or way down there, but he's always got that sparkle in his eye and *that* smile. He's one of my dearest friends.

July 14, 1974: CSN&Y live at Day on the Green show produced by Bill Graham at Oakland Stadium, Oakland, California, USA. Photo by Bob Sheridan

Actually, I can't compare them: you can separate them, you can do anything you want but you *can't* make any sense of 'what's this one like without the other one?' It's not about that, it's about what they are together, and when it's really working it's one of the most magical things in the world. It doesn't matter how they are separately.

It's like olive oil, salt and tomato sauce. Separately, salt is bad, tomato sauce is okay, but there's nothing else in it. But put them together with some olive oil and it tastes good.

Bio: *Born in Pittsburgh, Pennsylvania,* Russ Kunkel *has played drums for many well-known artists, including CSNY, James Taylor, Dan Fogelberg, Linda Ronstadt, Bob Dylan, Stevie Nicks, Carole King, Jackson Browne, Carly Simon, Joe Walsh, and Glenn Frey. In the Seventies, Russ worked so frequently with bassist Leland Sklar, keyboardist Craig Doerge and guitarist Danny Kortchmar that they eventually became known as The Section, recording three albums under that name.*

TIN SOLDIERS AND NIXON COMING

by Steve Paul

In the summer of 1974, I had just graduated high school and was taking to the road to follow The Grateful Dead - my second summer on the road. It just so happened that if you plot out the Dead tour and the CSNY tour that July and August, you find them weaving in and out of the same stadiums, including the Capitol Center in Landover, and the Jersey City shows.

The Watergate scandal was coming to a head and CSNY were the big band that had stayed political after the Jefferson Airplane disbanded. CSNY were the cheerleaders at that point of the counterculture, along with the Dead (the Dead weren't political but everything they stood for involved a change of society).

We really wanted Nixon impeached and brought down hard. Very hard! I was a hippie, so to speak, and a veteran of many concerts by this point. And the girl Neil Young sings about in 'Ohio' was my next-door neighbor growing up in Maryland. So many of my schoolmates were really into CSNY, as I was, and the Kent State University killing really hit home, us knowing the college student from 'what if you knew her and found her dead on the ground?' Her name was Allison Krause and she babysat my younger sisters before the family moved to Ohio around 1969. Allison's sister Laurel Krause was a close friend of my sister and came to visit us the summer after the killing. She knocked on my door and I answered, not knowing what to say to a girl whose sister was shot by the National Guard a few months earlier.

As Watergate rolled to a head, it was obvious Nixon was going down, so the CSNY shows of that period were like rallying shows, rallying the troops to be more and more active politically.

August 8 was a very hot night down by the docks of the city across the river from Manhattan. Whoever had a ticket for CSNY at the Roosevelt Stadium in Jersey City, New Jersey, had not bought a ticket for a protest evening, but it totally turned into that, when it was announced Nixon was going to give his resignation speech.

The original schedule of the show changed, the concert delayed till 9pm, until the announcement was made. America tuned into television, waiting. I'm guessing CSNY were backstage watching too, as they came out right after the announcement. The audience was poised to go crazy when it happened.

As soon as CSNY appeared on stage, they went to the microphones saying, "President Nixon has just resigned!" Graham proudly and defiantly added, "Today, I am proud to be an American citizen!" Then they broke into 'Love the One You're With', which proved a really joyous romp.

We thank our fans in the New York area for their warm response to our recent appearances. Watch for our Special Finale, in this area, to be announced soon. Some of our best friends will be joining us.

CHEERS!

DAVID CROSBY, STEPHEN STILLS, GRAHAM NASH and NEIL YOUNG

Aug. 18, 1974: ad published by CSN&Y in the New York Times

Bio: Steve Paul *was born in Philadelphia, Pennsylvania, moving at 10 years old to Maryland, a close suburb of Washington, DC. He graduated from high school in June 1974, taking the summer off to follow The Grateful Dead and CSNY, criss-crossing the US Northeast coast, mostly hitchhiking between venues, sometimes recording the shows. He still lives about 45 minutes from the White House in Maryland, and for 35 years has managed a high-end jewellery store.*

Songs: *'Almost Cut My Hair' (C); 'Suite: Judy Blue Eyes' (S); 'Military Madness' (N) – 'This song hit America when it was really gripped by the Vietnam War. It is very stirring live and the singalong at the end gets me really juiced. Great melody and great rock 'n' roll.'*

53

July 14, 1974: CSN&Y live at Day on the Green show produced by Bill Graham at Oakland Stadium, Oakland, California, USA. Photo by Bob Sheridan

HELLO, I AM GRAHAM NASH!

by Giancarlo Susanna

I have a long career as a music journalist behind me and, strange as it may seem, there are characters that for one reason or another I have not been able to interview. With CSN, however, I made more than one attempt.

Once, my friend Paolo Correani and I drove to a nice beach-town south of Rome, where Crosby, Stills & Nash were recharging their batteries for a concert in Rome in 1983, which was later cancelled due to a storm. No luck, once again.

Years later I had the chance to talk to Graham Nash and Stephen Stills but not with David Crosby, who I had seen at Wembley in 1974 (with the other three) and in 1976 in London (with Graham Nash). No meetings, only phone interviews. Good fun though. Stephen was recovering from quite a serious illness and Graham was busy promoting a solo album. I expected a secretary to call me but instead one day the phone rang, and a voice called out, "Hello, I'm Graham Nash!" I've never got used to meeting in person or on the phone with the musicians I love. I jumped up in my chair, but then everything about the interview went fine.

Perhaps CSN have not always lived up to their standards - the 1974 Wembley concert is the perfect example - but there is no doubt that they have marked a fundamental turning point in the history of rock music. On that particular occasion, the event was represented by their presence in Europe and the pure magic of their voices. We didn't really care about imperfections. When CSN (Y) are around, a miracle is always possible.

Two years after the CSNY Wembley show, Crosby & Nash were at Hammersmith Odeon in London with David Lindley, and I remember David Crosby wearing a wristwatch that was bothering him. He took it off and tossed it to the stage technician, who clumsily missed it.

Of the other live appearances, I oddly remember little. Perhaps only the immaculate beauty of a bunch of songs which at times seemed almost miraculous.

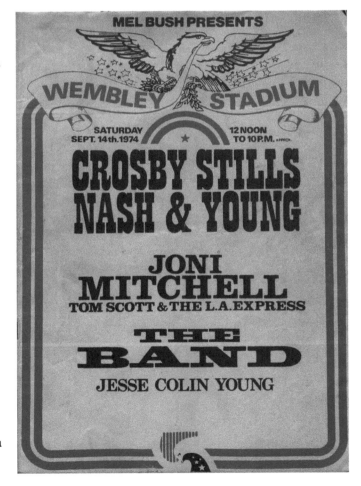

I do however perfectly remember an article about them published in Italian music magazine *Ciao 2001* from 1969. In those days, we didn't even know who CSN were. Our sources were relatively few. Fortunately, the newsstand in Piazza Vescovio in Rome sold *Melody Maker* and *Rolling Stone*. It was like we were in the province of the Empire, but our passion and thirst for the music nevertheless remained unquenchable.

Those were the days! Even finding records was a challenge but, no matter what, I would definitely do it all over again.

July 14, 1974: David Crosby live with CSN&Y at Oakland Stadium, Oakland, California, USA. Photo by Talitha 'Tai' Stills (courtesy of Fred Arellano)

Bio: *Shocked by The Tokens' 'The Lion Sleeps Tonight,' Giancarlo Susanna lived on music since the early 1960s. He collaborated with specialist magazines, newspapers and Italian radio broadcasts. Considered one of the historical voices of Rai Stereonotte, he published books on Neil Young, REM, Tim and Jeff Buckley.*

Songs: *'Guinnevere' (C), 'Suite: Judy Blue Eyes' (S), 'Teach Your Children' (N).*

ONCE A FAN, ALWAYS A FAN.

by Carolyne Mas

When I was 19, I was a huge Buffalo Springfield and CSNY fan. I am not sure how it began, but I remember that I was living in Hollywood, and have a very vivid memory of buying a couple of bootleg albums, one of Buffalo Springfield, and a double album called *Young Man's Fancy*, a bootleg recording of a solo, acoustic Neil Young concert. It quickly became a favorite of mine, not only because the music was great, but also because he was very funny.

THE HOWARD ROSE AGENCY, LTD.
9720 Wilshire Blvd.
Beverly Hills, California 90212

June 6, 1975

Mr. David Crosby
Mr. Graham Nash
c/o Gregory E. Fischbach
1888 Century Park East
Los Angeles, California 90067

Gentlemen:

1. This will confirm our agreement whereby the Howard Rose Agency, Ltd., is hereby engaged to render its efforts to arrange, negotiate ,contracts for and to book a concert tour for DAVID CROSBY and GRAHAM NASH from July 15, 1975 through September 15, 1975. For this purpose, we are engaged as the sole and exclusive agent and representative in the personal appearance field (concerts, television) for the United States for the period commencing on the date May 21, 1975 and ending September 15, 1975.

2. For our services you agree to pay the Howard Rose Agency, Ltd., or cause the Howard Rose Agency, Ltd., to be paid, a sum equal to Ten (10%) Percent of the gross monies or other considerations paid and received pursuant or pertaining to contracts for said tour, including any and all modifications, extensions, renewals, replacements, supplements or substitutes for such contracts.

3. The term "contracts" as used herein includes contracts or agreements entered into by you or on your behalf or by any other person, firm or corporation in which you have or shall have any interest of any kind or otherwise.

4. The term, "gross monies or other considerations" means total payments and income,without any deductions,received directly or indirectly pursuant to contracts entered into hereunder in connection with the aforesaid tour, other than deductions for costs incurred by you in connection with the employment of accompanying acts, and the rental of lighting and sound equipment used in conjunction with the concerts.

5. This contract shall be interpreted in accordance with the laws of the State of California, applicable to agreements wholly to be performed therein.

6. If the aforementioned confirms your understanding please so indicate by signing in the space provided below and this shall constitute our agreement.

THE HOWARD ROSE AGENCY, LTD.

BY: _____

AGREED & ACCEPTED:

_____
DAVID CROSBY

_____
GRAHAM NASH

Courtesy of Mark Kelly

While I never did get to see Crosby, Stills, Nash & Young together, I did manage to see them broken up into pairs. I saw Crosby & Nash on 14 September 1975 at a beautiful amphitheater, Santa Barbara Bowl. Being the mid-Seventies, people were very casual, and I actually went to the concert with a guy I met while standing in line for tickets. The concert was part of the tour to support new album, *Wind on the Water*. The concert was pure magic, with soaring, lush vocals. Helium balloons of all colors were passed around the audience, the majority of whom were high, myself included. Well, it was the Seventies!

By contrast, when I saw Stills & Young perform together on 2 July 1976, the focus was on loud, shredding guitar work. There was a hint of pre-punk in the music. I was back on Long Island, living at my parents' house, and bought a ticket to see them at Nassau Coliseum in Uniondale, New York. My parents drove me there and back. My seat was at the end of a row, up against a metal railing. I could feel it vibrate every time Neil Young took a solo.

That fall, I remember persecuting my parents into buying me a fringe jacket for my birthday. By this time, I had a huge crush on Neil Young, but I also wanted to emulate him in some way because he was my idol that particular year. I had already learned how to play harmonica because of my crush on Bob Dylan back when he was my idol in ninth grade, when I made a harmonica holder from a coat hanger and rubber bands, so it was easy for me to learn every single Neil Young songs on piano and guitar. I needed the jacket to complete the look. Fringe jackets were not as popular in 1976 as they had been in the late Sixties and early Seventies, so were hard to come by, but we finally located one at a tiny shop in Massapequa, Long Island.

I have that jacket to this day, nothing short of a miracle since I can no longer count all the moves I have made and places where I have lived. Some objects in our lives are like that - we cannot seem to lose them. And so it is with the idols of our youth: once a fan, always a fan.

Although I rarely listen to the music of Crosby, Stills, Nash & Young anymore, separately or together, their music is still deeply woven into my musical identity, and hearing one of their songs can easily transport me back in time to a place where everything seemed possible and the world was brand new. I know that many of you can relate to this feeling. It was characteristic of the music back then. I am not sure if it was our perception as a generation, or if it was something in the notes themselves, but the music we listened to was a vehicle for hope. I am so happy that people are still interested in this message.

Bio: Carolyne Mas *was born in New York in October 1955 to parents who passed on their love of music. Like many musicians her age, she was greatly influenced by The Beatles, the reason she picked up a guitar at 11, having played piano since she was six. She eventually made for Greenwich Village, New York City in the mid-Seventies amid a 'sort of music renaissance going on at the time, which yielded many great singer-songwriters as well as punk bands, all of whom made an impression on me musically'. She found touring the best part of being a musician, leading her to many places all over the world, including performing on television in Moscow in August 1990, before the dissolution of the Soviet Union. 'This show was broadcast to 40 million people, which I guess I can say is my largest audience to date. I am not shy at all to admit a great deal of my music that is out there today in digital form has been bootlegged by me, in an effort to make sure the public has a chance to hear all of it.'*

Songs: *'Games' (C); 'Suite: Judy Blue Eyes' (S); 'Our House' (N).*

THE FIRST TIME

by Ezio Guaitamacchi

My first memories of Crosby, Stills & Nash go back to Woodstock, probably more to the triple-record than the film, since the latter arrived on Italian screens at least a year later than in the United States.

Before them, my idol was Jimi Hendrix, but those acoustic guitars and those voices impressed me greatly. I was captivated by 'Suite: Judy Blue Eyes'. Their performance in the movie confirmed my fascination with their vocal harmonies and acoustic guitars, so much so that, captivated by their music,

David Crosby and Grham Nash. WN archive ... *ul Wultz*

Dec. 12, 1975: Crosby & Nash at Waikiki Shell, Honolulu, Hawaii, USA. Photo by Paul Wultz

I sold a beautiful semi-acoustic Gibson 335 stereo to buy an acoustic guitar. Not only did I make one of the many bullshit errors of my career by selling that Gibson, I also got the acoustic guitar all wrong and bought an Ovation, like the one featured on the cover of *My Goal's Beyond* by John McLaughlin, who had replaced - in my heart and in my eyes - Jimi Hendrix. Naively, I thought that with that guitar I would be able to reach the dizzying speeds of McLaughlin in his acrobatic pentatonic scales.

None of this happened, just as nothing happened when I tried to imitate Hendrix, but with that Ovation I started playing the music of Crosby, Stills, Nash & Young.

Within a couple of years, I formed a high school band with two other friends and, at a time when the term tribute or cover band had not yet been coined, we were a CSNY tribute band or rather a Crosby, Stills & Nash one, as there were only three of us. That was until the day when one of the three - the one who in our imagination personified David Crosby - said he had a friend who could join us: he said he sang well and could play a little guitar and percussion. This friend turned out to be a certain Fabrizio, a handsome boy with a semi-intellectual look. Fabrizio joined the group, albeit in a somewhat reduced role, because in reality his percussion sounded awful, and he didn't sing well at all.

However, our group began to have great success. The audience was drawn to that very strange music, unknown to most. We are talking about the mid-Seventies and the records of Crosby, Stills & Nash (& Young) were difficult to find in Italian stores. We listened to those records hundreds of times to learn the different vocal parts and arrangements. We didn't even realise guitars were not always in standard tuning. That very intense period saw us immersed in this Milanese version of Crosby, Stills, Nash & Young with the same structure as their shows: our favorite record was *4 Way Street*, so we decided to have, in addition to acoustic guitars, bass and drums. We played an acoustic set and then the electric one.

At that stage, another guy joined the band. He had a beautiful PA system and wonderful guitars, so Fabrizio was kindly invited to quit. Subsequently he attended the acting school of the Piccolo Teatro in Milan and would become known as actor Fabrizio Bentivoglio.

Foolishly we thought the female audience followed us because we were so cool and because we played music that nobody was playing locally at the time. As a matter of fact, Fabrizio's departure drastically slashed our female audience, which triggered countless meetings among us in which the repertoire was discussed, probably according to the same dynamics experienced by our four heroes in the past and even in more recent times.

My infatuation with the quartet's music continued and a short time later, in 1976, I made my first trip to the United States. With my older brother and some friends, we left for California and landed in San Francisco.

I remember we had a huge station wagon we all got into, seven or eight people. I couldn't drive that vehicle. I was only 19 at the time and should have been 25 according to American law for that type of car. On the first day, I by chance saw a poster in a record shop advertising a Crosby & Nash concert at Stanford University's Frost Amphitheater. I forced my brother to persuade everyone that we couldn't miss that show. The others were totally unaware of who those two musicians were but, in the end, they were convinced because I persuaded them this concert would be the event of the century.

We arrived hours early. I remember very well the closed gates and all the other guys cursing me. Stanford University is huge and beautiful to visit but not in the summer, because there is no one there. However, I didn't care about seeing the university. I just wanted to go to the concert. I managed

ON
AT CHAPEL HILL
ORIUM

9:00 P.M.
THIS DATE —
—$4.00

P803
4854C
DULT
01
OH68E
W
2AUG7

BASS
231676

NO REFUND
NO EXCHANGE

Montag, 20. Sept. 1976 · 20,00 Uhr
MÜNCHEN · CIRCUS KRONE
MAMA CONCERTS PRESENTS

CROSBY·NASH
in Concert

Einheitspreis: 18,00 DM
zzgl. Vorverkaufsgebühr

Keine Haftung für Sach- und Körperschäden.
In keinem Falle Rückerstattungsanspruch
auf den Kaufpreis. · Vor Mißbrauch wird gewarnt.

Das Mitnehmen von Tonbandgeräten, Filmkameras
und Flaschen in die Halle ist grundsätzlich verboten!

№   1974

№   26836

ARSITY STADIUM

Retain Stub — Good Only

MON.   SEPT. 2
00 P.M.

Davis Printing Limited

ROSBY · STILLS
NASH · YOUNG

THE BAND

THSH
www.thsh.co.uk

Symphony Hall, Birmingham
Thu 6 Oct 2011 8.00PM
£55.00

3A Entertainment presents
CROSBY & NASH
no support

Level 3 Door 2(b)
Front Stalls
Row E Seat 11

Order Number 1051527
Standard Price

Full terms and conditions of purchase are available on our website at www.thsh.co.uk

PIA "Votre Music-Hall"

obre 1972, 21 h
re de la Bastille
HEN STILLS

5 Octobre 1972, 21 h
Gare de la Bastille
STEPHEN STILLS

AL FESTIVAL HALL
ECTOR: JOHN DENISON, C.B.E.

AN EVENING WITH
CROSBY AND NASH
WITH JUDEE SILLS

., 4 DECEMBER, 1971
8.30 p.m.
Management: Peter Bowyer

GANGWAY 5
ROW   SEAT

RED
SIDE

Please enter the
auditorium by
DOOR
4
LEVEL

ABC Printers, Manchester

FREE TRADE HALL, Peter St., Manchester

JOHN REID PRESENTATIONS present-

An Evening with
CROSBY and NASH

Friday, 17th September 1976
at 8.00 p.m.

No Tickets Exchanged. No Money Refunded.
Official Programme Sold Only in the Hall.

STALLS   27   £3.50
                      including VAT

to enter something like five hours before showtime and ran to the front of the stage. I stood mesmerised, admiring all their instruments and guitars.

At the time, Crosby & Nash had an amazing band - Russ Kunkel, David Lindley, Danny Kortchmar, Tim Drummond and Craig Doerge. It was a long concert, something like three hours of music, maybe even a bit too long, but it was my dream come true.

That passion never faded, rather it changed and evolved once music became my profession. And that Crosby & Nash concert came back to me in 2004 when I went to Boston to interview them on tour, promoting their latest album as a duo.

Shortly before leaving for Boston, I found the box in which I had kept some enlargements of pictures taken during the concert at Stanford by one of my brother's friends. I thought of taking one of those pictures with me to have it autographed. At the end of the interview, I told David and Graham I had a memory with me that tied me to the two of them and I told them the story of that concert. A little controversy arose, because David Crosby insisted the photos were from the Greek Theater in Berkeley. Graham, always very lucid, intervened, saying, "Do you not think he would remember the first time he saw us in concert?"

Bio: *Journalist, music critic, author and radio/TV presenter, writer, musician, teacher and performer, Ezio Guaitamacchi does a lot of fun things in his life. When he's not running JAM TV, broadcasting on the waves of LifeGate, teaching at CPM, writing an essay on rock, or on stage with his guitars telling Rock Files stories, he plays tennis, supports AC Milan and travels the world, often 'on the streets of rock'. In 2011, his Crimes Rock became a successful programme on Italian TV channel Rai 2. The day after landing for the first time on Californian soil, he attended his first Crosby & Nash concert at Stanford University's Frost Amphitheater in August 1976.*

Songs:
1) The politically correct choice – 'Long Time Gone' (C), 'Suite: Judy Blue Eyes' (S), 'Our House' (N)
2) The slightly sophisticated selection - 'The Lee Shore' (C), 'You Don't Have to Cry' (S), 'Wasted on the Way' (N)
3) The solo tunes – 'Triad' (C), '4+20' (S), 'Chicago' (N).

EVOLUTION OF A COVER

by Gerard Huerta

In early 1976, CBS Creative Director John Berg presented me with his rough sketch and idea: to put a beautiful label on a Mason jar and photograph it. He also did the copywriting. I proceeded to create a tight sketch which was approved with minor revisions, it was then inked and printed in two colors: gold and brown. It was cut out and pasted onto a jar and photographed by staff photographer Don Hunstein. I assembled the back label with credits and a photostat was cut out and also pasted on the jar and photographed.

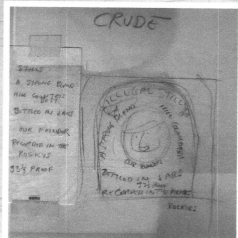

1. John Berg's rough idea (sketch)

3. Final inking

4. Final printed label

5. Final back cover

6. Final front cover

2. Final sketch for inking

65

Bio: Gerard Huerta *is a designer of letter forms. Born and raised in southern California he graduated from Art Center College of Design and began his career at CBS Records in New York creating artwork and iconic logos for Boston, Blue Oyster Cult, and later Foreigner, ACDC and many others.*

He left CBS to expand his work beyond the recording and movie industry to design logos for HBO, CBS Records Masterworks, Spelling Entertainment, Nabisco, Calvin Klein's Eternity, The National Guitar Museum, Monterey Peninsula Country Club, the mastheads of Time, Money, People, Architectural Digest and many others. He designed watch dials for the Original Swiss Army Watch and their complete line for fourteen years and also created original product illustrations.

Gerard also designed the multi-necked fully-playable stringed instrument known as The Rock Ock for the National Guitar Museum, which is on tour along with his Vintage Guitar Art. His work is in the permanent collection of The Museum of Modern Art.

Songs: *Long Time Gone (C); Helplessly Hoping (S); Teach Your Children (N).*

CSN: 'THE BOAT ALBUM' AND THE STORY OF A LOGO

by John Hartmann

I first met David Crosby and Graham Nash when I joined the Geffen-Roberts Company in 1971. I had known Stephen Stills since I signed Buffalo Springfield to the William Morris Agency in 1966. As general manager of GR I was responsible for booking and servicing the careers of Neil Young, Joni Mitchell, Laura Nyro, and Crosby, Stills & Nash, among others. Others included the fledgling Eagles, America, Jackson Browne, and all the early artists on Asylum Records.

In late 1972, Harlan Goodman and I left Geffen-Roberts and formed Hartmann & Goodman to manage Poco, who had just lost their lead singer, Richie Furay to Geffen's dream band Souther, Hillman & Furay. A year later, we had Poco well on their way to their first platinum album, *Legend.* Shortly thereafter we signed America and managed them on a string of six George Martin-produced platinum LPs, scoring half a dozen top-10 singles in the process.

In the summer of 1976, David Crosby called me and said, "Get on a plane and meet us in Albany, New York at the

CSN logo: original sketch by Phil Hartmann
(courtesy of John Hartmann)

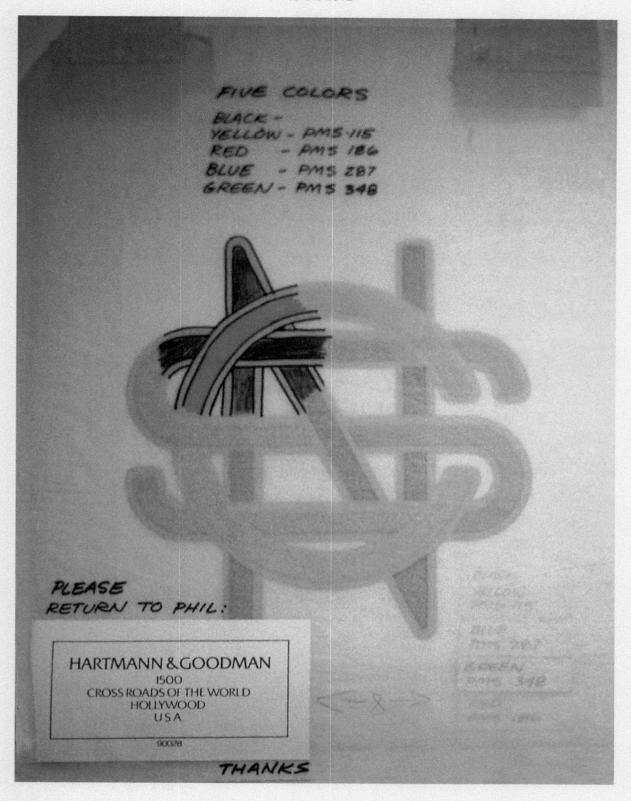

Holiday Inn tomorrow afternoon." "What are we doing here?" I queried. "We're on our way to Hyannis Port for a gig," was the response. "There are no gigs in Hyannis, where are you playing?" I asked. "We're playing the hockey rink," Graham added sheepishly. "Why?" was my one-word reply. "We're doing a benefit for Teddy Kennedy's senate bid," Dave confessed.

"Okay, let me get this straight. You're doing a benefit for one of the richest guys in the world, who is running for a job he couldn't lose if he tried, is that it?" "That's why we need new management," Graham affirmed. "Okay, 15 per cent of the gross, including publishing, and we're in," I promised. "We don't pay on publishing," was David Crosby's immediate retort. "Then we can't manage you," I informed them. "America and Poco pay on publishing and we share the same business managers. I can't give you a better deal than I gave them, and America sells way more records than Crosby & Nash ever has. So it's a pass," I said. They thought I was joking.

We did the Teddy benefit and met his mother Rose and his sister Caroline, but Teddy never showed. Then it was off to New York for two sold-out dates at Wollman Rink in Central Park. Although CSN were signed to Atlantic Records, Stephen Stills was a Columbia Records artist for his solo career. At the time, Crosby & Nash were not signed to a label as a duo. Walter Yetnikoff, the president of Columbia Records, and his right-hand man, Bruce Lundvall showed up backstage. It was immediately obvious to me that they coveted Crosby, Stills & Nash. After denying that I was their manager through several introductions, David and Graham capitulated on the publishing commission and suddenly Harlan and I were the personal managers of one of the greatest bands of all time.

We were all crashing from 'God Coke' (cocaine analysed at the USC drug lab, which came back with a gold ribbon and a star accompanied by a declaration that it was the purest they had ever seen) when we arrived in London for a European tour that would terminate with dates in London, Manchester and Edinburgh two weeks later. It was a good thing I was there. Upon arrival I immediately called our long-time British agent Barry Dickens. "I'm in London," I informed him. "What for?" he asked. "The Crosby & Nash tour," he was surprised to hear. It turned out that the American agent had assigned the tour to Elton John's manager John Reed, who forgot to promote the UK dates. Fortunately, they had given the European gigs to the right promoters. I fired John Reed and, by the time we got back from the Continent, Barry had sold out all three British shows.

As soon as we got back to LA, my first call was to Michael John Bowen, an ex-green beret who was Stephen Stills' manager. Stephen had been estranged from David Geffen and this had kept CSN separated for several years. "Guess what we've got," I asked Bowen. "What?" he said. "Crosby, Stills & Nash," I informed him. "You've got the guys?" he begged. "Yep, are you coming to LA?" His response was affirmative and the Crosby, Stills & Nash reunion was in play.

I immediately ordered up the CSN recording agreement with Atlantic Records. It turned out there were two. The original, and the one David Geffen had renegotiated. They were both bad deals for the artist and good for Geffen and Atlantic. I called up Ahmet Ertegun, the chairman of Atlantic, and demanded a renegotiation, which he refused. I literally threatened Ahmet with blackmail, declaring that the only improvements in the second agreement were that Atlantic got more product, and Geffen got Geffen-Roberts' commission written in, so they got their 15 percent paid directly. This clause had to be removed, or Hartmann, Goodman and Bowen wouldn't be able to commission any new albums. After I threatened to expose this to the entire music business, at the top of my lungs, Ahmet was unmoved. "They'll never deliver the albums they already owe me. Why would I renegotiate?" he said.

The band was excited to be back together, and we immediately booked studio time at Criteria Studios in Miami, with the Albert Brothers producing. We leaked it to Atlantic that we were in the studio and when they called to see if Criteria needed purchase orders, they were informed that it wasn't necessary as we were making the album on our own dime. A few weeks later, when the *CSN* album was finished, I called Walter Yetnikoff and asked if Columbia wanted the record. We all flew down to Miami on the CBS jet and played the LP for him. I told Walter all he had to do was indemnify us against Atlantic's inevitable lawsuit and it was his. We flew back to New York at three in the morning. Everyone but me fell asleep, so, I lit up a joint and enjoyed the ride in William S. Paley's seat.

This too was leaked to Ahmet and I got a call inviting us to come to New York and talk a new deal. In three days of negotiations, we made the most artist-friendly agreement ever negotiated with a major label. And, we got the Geffen commission removed from the contract. After the meeting Ahmet said we should have our commission written in, but I refused, feeling that the manager of record for any given album should be the one who gets paid.

My brother Phil worked on a logo idea and he did the CSN design on his own without a consignment. The band was delighted and used it on the album *CSN* and a myriad of merch items. Phil said the C was red for David Crosby's passion, the N was green for Graham Nash's earthy nature, and the S was blue for Stephen Stills' love of the Blues. Graham gave Phil a beautiful Martin guitar in appreciation. It now hangs on my office wall.

"The original is not what you think," remembers my other brother Paul. "It was done long before Photoshop and you did something with a material called Amber, less where you actually had to cut out the mass for each layer that was what made this piece so brilliant. It was a piece of engineering and art. Each layer had to be cut out individually by hand and Phil did all this. I have those individual layers in the description on how it's supposed to be printed and I would have to have somebody read rot for you to be able to use it digitally."

The *CSN* album was released in 1977 and contained hit single "'Just A Song Before I Go', which streaked to the top of the charts, driving the LP well past platinum status, with over a million copies sold. The cherry on top was that the new terms were applicable to the entire CSN catalogue, improving the band's earnings on all their previous records to the new level. Then we went on the 'Triplet tour', with three days on and one day off. Every date sold out, and it was a wild and crazy ride.

Bio: *Author, educator and music industry expert* John Hartmann *began his professional career in the mailroom of the William Morris Agency. He later served as the Morris office liaison to Colonel Tom Parker, legendary manager of Elvis Presley. A veteran music agent, personal manager and record executive, Hartmann has provided career direction for such luminaries, among others, as Chad & Jeremy, Sonny & Cher, Buffalo Springfield, Neil Young, Joni Mitchell, The Eagles, Jackson Browne, Peter, Paul & Mary, Crosby, Stills & Nash, America, Poco, and Ringo Starr.*
John also founded the Holodigm Corporation, an internet company engaged in the creation and execution of a new music industry paradigm, its mission to ensure the next generation of music belongs to those who create it.

Songs: *'Shadow Captain' (C); 'Suite: Judy Blue Eyes' (S); 'Teach Your Children' (N)*
NB: comedian Phil Hartmann - *famed for roles in The Simpsons, NewsRadio and Saturday Night Live - was also a solid graphic designer. In 1974 he graduated from California State University, Northridge, with a degree in graphic arts. In the decade that followed, he designed over 40 record covers for the likes of Steely Dan (Aja), America (History), and Poco (Legend).*

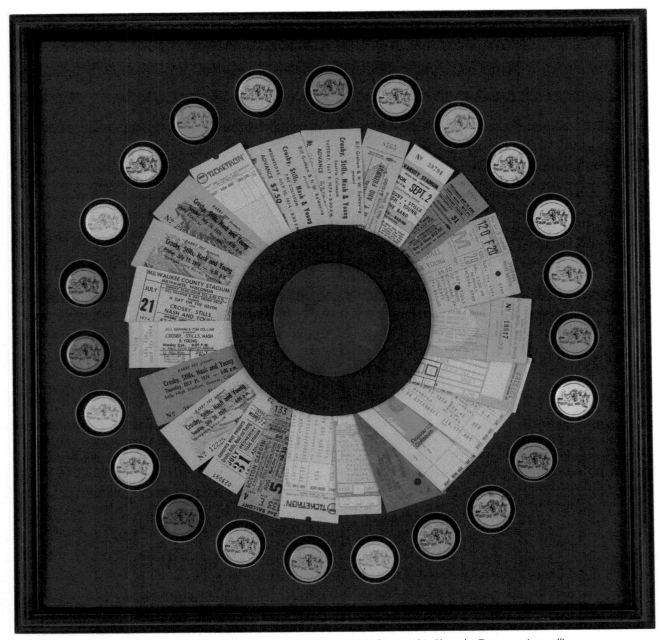

Framed tickets of CSN&Y 1974 tour. Lookout Management, Santa Monica, California, USA. Photo by Francesco Lucarelli

September 28, 1976. David Crosby and Graham Nash with Craig Doerge on stage at Hammersmith Odeon, London, England. Photos by David Prockter courtesy of Pete Long

Aug.12, 1977: Neil Young & Graham Nash guest with David Crosby at United Farm Workers Benefit, Santa Cruz Civic Auditorium, Santa Cruz, California, USA. Photo by Tom Hambleton

SHADOW CAPTAIN AND CAPTAIN MANYHANDS

by Craig Doerge

Oct. 22, 1977: Oakland-Alameda County Coliseum, Oakland, California USA. Photo by Tom Hambleton

After I and most of The Section helped Crosby & Nash record their third hit album as a duo, *Whistling Down the Wire*, David Crosby invited me for a cruise on his great sailboat. We sailed for hours in San Francisco Bay and under the Golden Gate Bridge. Not ever having been on a boat such as his, I was knocked out. Also on this sail were his friends, Carole King and her man.

My best memory of this day is how happy David looked at the helm of his fine boat.

For me, the great chance to play with Stephen Stills was something I really wanted to do. I had already made records with David Crosby and Graham Nash but had not had a chance to play with Stephen. So, when they got back together for the second CS&N album, that offered a huge opportunity for me.

The first night I got to play with Stephen I was so scared, having heard what a great musician Stephen was. After a short session, somebody told me, "Stephen did not like what you played." He came over and showed me what to play. He is very gifted and can tell people what to play on the basis of being able to play various different instruments.

Within the first half-hour in the studio with him, I sat down at the piano and must have played a blizzard of notes. I played everything I ever learned in my life and Stephen left me alone. He did not come over to tell me to do anything. We slowed down and started jamming together. I just loved playing with Stephen, and I think he enjoyed playing with me. That was the night we cut 'Shadow Captain'. I was very pleased, as a writer, being able to work on 'Shadow Captain'. David Crosby had given me those lyrics on a single piece of paper and said, "Craig, can you do something with this?" There was no real form to it. I really had to experiment where to take it, and that comes out in the music.

Stephen and I stayed the whole night in the studio and cut that track. We were the last ones in the room at 6am, David and Graham having already gone home. Stephen and I did a lot of jamming and playing to work up to the cutting of 'Shadow Captain'. If you listen to Stephen's guitar on that, it's burning. He played the greatest guitar on that song. As a matter of fact, that night Stephen had more energy than any of us, so much energy that he told us he was going to go back home running. I bet him $10 that he could not run from Criteria back to the house, but he did. Stephen actually jogged back; he actually took a work-out, ran back. He probably didn't get up until three in the afternoon but, by God, Stephen could go all night when he knew the track you are cutting is really smoking.

That night it really got to what I consider one of those magic times in the studio. Obviously, the tune turned out great and CS&N wound up opening with it on their album.

Bio: *One of LA's top studio players, songwriters and producers,* Craig Doerge*'s keyboard skills have been enjoyed on countless albums, for such diverse artists as Linda Ronstadt, Phoebe Snow, The Temptations, Barbara Streisand, and Frank Zappa & the GTOs. As a performer, he's best known for keyboard work with Crosby, Stills & Nash, James Taylor, and Jackson Browne. He is also a founding member of rock/jazz fusion band The Section.*
Craig won a Grammy for his music for the song 'Life Goes On' (lyrics by Paul Williams), sung by Lena Horne. He continues to write songs, play sessions and perform, often with legendary singer and lyricist, Judy Henske. He remains active, helping raise money and awareness for causes through concerts. On a personal note, Craig, traditionally a dog guy, now has a cat named Raymundo ... 'but you can call me Ray.'

Songs: *'Carry Me' (C); 'Dark Star' (S); 'Cold Rain' (N).*

December 12, 1977 ▪ 60¢

People
weekly

Patty Hearst told the truth, says a lie detector expert

Eric Sevareid signs off, talking

Erica Wilson's crewel world

Crosby, Stills & Nash

Brawling and bad vibes over, they're making great music again

THE BOAT ALBUM

by Paolo Vites

In the 1970s, music magazine reviews influenced decisions on whether to buy a record or not. We were kids, there was no internet, there was little news and we trusted what we read. We devoured those newspapers to find out more. Today, everyone is a music critic, everyone knows everything. It was an adventure then.

Expectations of a record were high however, and reviews were not kind. The comparison was between the first CSN album, released in 1969 – the one for us who loved the Californian dream and who kept it in our hearts - and the second one, recorded after a hiatus of eight years. It was 1977, the summer of punk, and since the 'Couch album' there had been CSNY tours and records, solo and duet albums. Now the three guys, instead of being portrayed on the cover with long, messy and probably dirty hair, shabby jeans and sitting on a rumpled sofa in front of an abandoned house, were on a yacht, smiling peacefully, probably satisfied with their bank account.

This is what the press wrote at the time, which was not a good introduction to the new album. We bought the record anyway. And it was a beautiful album, even if difficult to understand at first. The 'We can change the world' era seemed to be truly over.

Not only that: the furious electric guitars we had become used to had been replaced by languid piano and Latin or even jazzy percussion. We were puzzled.

But - *CSN* remains the perfect, classic record 45 years after its release, still offering new discoveries, new dimensions, new emotions. The sound quality is extraordinary, something which in 1977 not everyone could afford. *Crosby, Stills & Nash*, in comparison, sounded quite poorly recorded, with its fuzzy and often muddied sound. Here everything sparkled. And their voices: they had never been so distinct, never so clear and exciting, never so perfect. On the back cover there is perhaps the most beautiful photo of the three, a chiaroscuro of them singing in front of a single microphone. All the magic of this trio. Mystery and darkness, light and visions.

There is also a verse from one of the songs on this record that summarises everything this album is:

'Ten years singing right out loud I never looked, was anybody listening? Then I fell out of a cloud I hit the ground and noticed something missing.'

Taken from 'See the Changes', the second track on the record, written by Stephen Stills, those words encapsulate everything *CSN* represents.

Although still just in their mid-30s, this was a record of maturity and disillusionment. They had ridden success for 10 years: women, drugs, money. With this album, while facing marital and musical crises, and the shattering of the hippie dream, the trio reflect upon and look at reality. Time is running by fast, and it's time to come to terms with it. That's why, apart from rare moments, the whole record sounds so elegantly melancholy, without those angry electric guitar riffs, when the idea was to proudly fly your own freak flag and change the world.

On this album, Graham Nash, often unfairly considered as the weak link of the trio (or quartet), the most commercial, the least committed, offers some of the most beautiful songs of his career in terms of intensity and ability. Piano tunes, suffused, full of sadness: 'Carried Away', where perhaps we can still feel the regret for the breakup with Joni Mitchell; 'Cold Rain', a sketch so realistic that the listener feels the rain on the face and the anxiety and loneliness of the rush hour of any city in the world. We can almost feel that frozen rain on our bones:

June 1977 & July 1978:
CSN live at Pine Knob
Music Theatre, Clarkston,
Michigan, USA. Photos by
Michael Curcuru

'Cold rain down on my face, Buses hurry on. Works out here comes the race, People heading home.
  Wait a second, don't I know you? Haven't I seen you somewhere before? You seem to be like someone I knew. Yes, he lived here but he left When he thought that there was more.'

'Just A Song Before I Go', a reflection on the role of the star and our little miseries. And, above all, the majestic, epic and disturbing 'Cathedral', a song about visiting the cathedral at Winchester under the influence of LSD. For the first time, a string orchestration accompanies CSN's sublime vocal performance and leaves us breathless in front of such expressive power.

On the album, David Crosby seems to be on the sidelines, beginning his long fall into the darkness of hard drugs and loss of creativity, but he sings like never before. On 'Shadow Captain', which he only wrote the lyrics of, the eternal question about the meaning of life keeps haunting him: is there a God who plays hide and seek with us? Who are we and where are we going? Who guides us on our path? A number of questions that are rarely found so clearly expressed on a rock album, asking the mysterious captain to finally show himself:

Who guides this ship Dreaming through the seas, Turning and searching Whichever way you please?
  Speak to me. I need to see your face, Shadowy captain, In a darkened space.
  If I were to spy a city Floating just above the sea, Could we stop and look for me Among those playing on the pier?

As for the marijuana-scented irony of 'Anything at All', an elegantly jazzy piece, I think it is one of his best vocal performances, including his barely audible giggle.

Stephen Stills, although a bit predictable with the Latin groove of 'Fair Game', delivers a masterly Latin-rock hit with 'Dark Star', dives deep into his blues soul in 'Run from Tears', and closes the album with the bombastic 'I Give You Give Blind', an orchestral rock song where he and his electric guitar scream out man's inability to build lasting relationships.

Over the years I have seen CSN in concert solo and in all possible combinations. Like all Italian fans, at least those who had not been able to afford a trip abroad previously, I saw them for the first time in Milan in 1983. It was one of those classic moments when you find yourself in front of your favourite artist after a lifetime of waiting and you almost don't think about the music, the overwhelming emotion making you say in disbelief, "They really exist!"

Alas, from a musical point of view, the concert was not great, as David Crosby was deep in his 'dark period'.

In 1992, they announced an acoustic tour with a show in Milan. Somehow, I managed to sneak backstage in the afternoon when the sound-check was over. David was the only one still there. I took courage and approached him. He looked at me, annoyed, and dismissed me, kind of curtly, with, "For interviews, you have to talk to my manager." I'd arrived with a fanzine dedicated to Bob Dylan that I had been curating for some time. I had obviously brought the right issue, as it had a picture of David and Bob on the cover, singing into the same microphone. As soon as he saw it, he melted into his sly Siamese cat smile under his moustache and, amazed, asked me, "Where did you find this photo?", happy to see himself portrayed together with the man who had given him a career with his songs at the time of The Byrds. I asked if I could take a photo with the fanzine in his hands, and he kindly accepted. What a beautiful person, I thought. The concert was memorable. CSN played mostly acoustic guitars and piano throughout the evening. Stephen Stills also played some electric guitar and Graham Nash sang a beautiful cover of Bob Dylan's 'Every Grain of Sand'. Who could be happier than me?

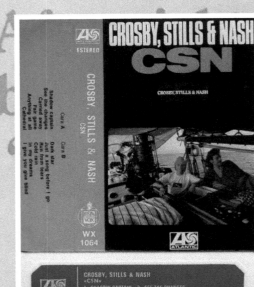

April 2, 1992: David Crosby, PalaTrussardi, Milan, Italy. Photo by Paolo Vites

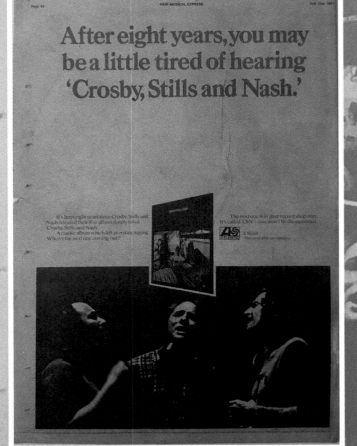

Bio: *Born in Lavagna (Genoa) in 1962, Paolo Vites is a journalist, editing the newspaper ilsussidiario.net, where he plays the wild card: politics, crime news, gossip, sometimes even music. His only interest outside work is listening to music (Fifties, Sixties, and Seventies) - the only time there's a possibility of not having anyone around (he even keeps himself to himself at concerts). He has written monographs on Bob Dylan and Patti Smith, among others. The moment he remembers with the most emotion, in addition to the birth of his daughters, was his 15-minute interview with Paul McCartney, in preparation for which he did not sleep for 48 hours due to a mixture of anxiety and excitement.*

Songs: *'Laughing' (C); 'Carry On' (S); 'Cold Rain' (N).*

A LARGE FAMILY

by Kim Bullard

In the mid-Seventies, I was working with Stephen Stills' then wife, Veronique Sanson, living in Paris, being her band leader. Stephen would come and visit, and sit in, plugging direct into my keyboard amp, right next to my head. The sound was so expressive! It was permanently engraved on my brain from that point on. He and I would hang after the shows because Vero had to meet the mayor, or whatever. We were both southern boys, so had some common ground.

In 1977, I came back to the States, trying to figure out what to do next. One day I got a call from Stephen, which went something like this: "Hey, it's Stills...David and Graham and I are going out on the road. You want to come down and play with us?" I was dumbfounded. Like, Crosby, Stills & Nash?! So, from my guest house in North Hollywood without plumbing, I put my keyboards in my beat-up Volvo station wagon, showed up at a huge soundstage in Hollywood, and went on the road with one of the biggest bands in the world at the time. I was 22.

A fascinating thing for me was that they seemed to be intentionally under-rehearsed. I did my fair share of top-40 gigs, so I was ready with charts and knew all their material before I went down there, but by the time we did our first show, on 18 October in Portland, I had never played about half of the set.

In front of 20,000 people, I was playing these songs for the first time. And some were in different keys from the record. It was crazy, but that's the way they rolled. What we did at rehearsal was just jam together, getting our footing as a band. And that's kind of what Stephen wanted. All three CSN guys seemed to thrive on that feeling that anything could happen. They wanted something cool to happen; they liked being on a tightrope.

Music meant something back then. It was attached to a cultural revolution, and Stephen Stills was right in the middle of it, in Greenwich Village with Dylan and Baez and the folk protest music revolution, then on the West Coast with the electric folk sound, all underpinned by the hope that this tribe, reflected in this music, could change the world. The people who came to the CSN shows in the Seventies were still all part of the tribe. It was our tribe. It was a great time for music.

March 14, 1979: Stephen Stills live at Center Stage, Canton, Michigan, USA. Photo by Michael Curcuru

Bio: *Born in Atlanta, Kim Bullard studied classical music and later moved to Los Angeles, continuing his musical education at UCLA. A keyboardist, singer, producer, arranger and programmer, in the mid-Seventies he moved to France, working as musical director for Véronique Sanson. Through her, he met Stephen Stills and subsequently toured with Crosby, Stills & Nash. Through extensive session work in LA, Kim developed friendships with people within the Elton John music community. When Guy Babylon passed away, Kim was asked to become the keyboardist for Elton's band. He remains in LA, living in the house where hit Sixties TV show Mr Ed was filmed.*

Songs: *'Bittersweet' (C); 'Suite: Judy Blue Eyes' (S); 'Cathedral' (N).*

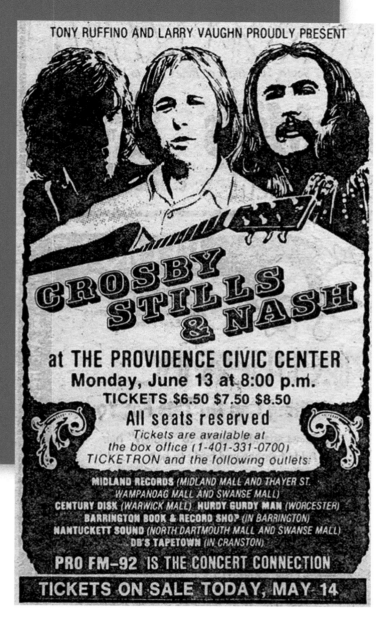

TONY RUFFINO AND LARRY VAUGHN PROUDLY PRESENT

CROSBY STILLS & NASH

at THE PROVIDENCE CIVIC CENTER
Monday, June 13 at 8:00 p.m.
TICKETS $6.50 $7.50 $8.50
All seats reserved
Tickets are available at
the box office (1-401-331-0700)
TICKETRON and the following outlets:
MIDLAND RECORDS (MIDLAND MALL AND THAYER ST. WAMPANOAG MALL AND SWANSE MALL)
CENTURY DISK (WARWICK MALL) HURDY GURDY MAN (WORCESTER)
BARRINGTON BOOK & RECORD SHOP (IN BARRINGTON)
NANTUCKETT SOUND (NORTH DARTMOUTH MALL AND SWANSE MALL)
DB'S TAPETOWN (IN CRANSTON)

PRO FM-92 IS THE CONCERT CONNECTION
TICKETS ON SALE TODAY, MAY 14

FOUR AND TWENTY YEARS AGO

by Mark Arnquist

My dealings with Crosby, Stills & Nash are not really on a personal level. Except for one. One day Stephen Stills sat with me and showed me how to correctly play a couple of songs.

In 1978 I was working for Dave Mason. Our tour ended and I returned to my home in the San Francisco area. I got a call from the road manager that Dave was to be a guest at a Stephen Stills show and I agreed to take care of Dave's gear. At the venue, I sat with Stephen's guitar tech and swapped stories. There were to be several guests. As I tuned guitars, I played '4+20' in double-drop D tuning. All of a sudden, from behind me a familiar voice said, 'That's working too hard! I don't play it that way.'

Stills proceeded to give me a guitar lesson in D-A-D-D-A-D tuning. He showed me the fingerings for '4+20', 'Carry On' and 'Singing Call'. I had heard about the Bruce Palmer tuning, the infamous E-E-E-E-B-E one. But here was *the* guy showing me the other. I must assume in hindsight he had edited his tuning.

In 1982, I met Stephen again after a CSN gig in Seattle. I had a 1961 Fender Esquire and he was looking for a pre-CBS Esquire of no particular year. At that time, we discussed tunings and guitars, and he took me into the guitar room and had me look at a Stauffer/Martin guitar in a rosewood coffin case. That evening we talked again about '4+20', and it was the D-A-D-D-A-D version once more. I've had several internet acquaintances try to correct my info but - sorry - I learned it from Stills himself, who might have lowered a step during the 1977 tour.

March 14, 1979: Stephen Stills live at Center Stage, Canton, Michigan, USA. Photo by Michael Curcuru

Bio: *Mark Arnquist was born in Minneapolis, Minnesota, and now lives in the Seattle area. He has repaired and built guitars since 1972.*

Songs: *- As CSN: 'Wooden Ships' (C); 'See the Changes' (S); 'Taken at All' (N). Solo: 'Laughing' (C); 'So Begins the Task' ('with the 'illusion' extra verse he only sang live') (S); 'Simple Man' (N).*

THE MESSAGE

by George 'Chocolate' Perry

I think Stephen is a 'songaholic'. I don't know if there is such a word, but if you looked up the word musician, there should be a picture of Stephen Stills there. When I met him, I found him to be driven with the desire to tell stories through his songs, songs that had something to say about the world. And as a young African American, songs had a big influence in my life.

I found Stephen to be head-strong about music and dedicated to the art of making songs. His songs seem to capture moments in time, and with the combination of all three, there is a blend of time, message and feelings. This is how I have always seen them.

I have always liked all types of music, but I found CSN's music soothing and fun to create cool bass parts for. Their songs always bring a beautiful message. It doesn't matter if they are talking about unity for the world or love. What matters is the message behind their whole output.

I would say definitely one of the highest points in my life was to play with Stephen Stills, CSN and the Stills-Young Band. Great musicians, all of them. And having a chance to be a part of a group that sent a message like that into the world, I think it was a blessing to me as well.

Thanks CSNY for the opportunity!

Bio: *Born and raised in Carvers Ranches, Florida, George Wesly Perry, known as 'Chocolate' Perry is a bassist, songwriter and producer. He has worked with the Bee Gees, John Cougar, Crosby, Stills, Nash & Young, Al Kooper, Joe Walsh and many more. Perry still lives in South Florida and stays active writing, recording, and producing tracks that can be heard on his self-titled YouTube channel.*

FIRST TIME AROUND: CROSBY, STILLS, NASH, AND ME

by Dave Zimmer

It's been said that you should never meet your heroes and that music journalists should never become friends with the musicians they write about. Well, I ignored both of those bits of advice, as I met, became friends with, and ended up writing the authorized biography of Crosby, Stills & Nash.

Stephen Stills was my way into CSN. How he infused his songs with muscular, melodic and sensitive touches reached my heart at the outset and led me to David Crosby, Graham Nash and, of course, Neil Young, too.

The first time I saw any of them in concert was on 5 October 1973. I was in the second row for Stephen Stills & Manassas' concert at the Sacramento Civic Auditorium. They were powerful, moving and explosive that night.

On 20 February 1979, ten years to the month after CSN recorded *The Couch Album,* on assignment from *BAM: The California Music Magazine*, I interviewed Stephen Stills for the first time at his old bricks and mortar estate in Bel Air, California. There was a large 'S' on the gate guarding his driveway. I pressed a buzzer and the gate swung open for me. When I knocked on the front door, actress Susan St James answered, then Stephen, wearing a Lance Allworth #19 San Diego Chargers NFL football jersey, appeared right behind her, extending a hand in greeting, while telling Susan, 'Time for work', and then gave her a quick kiss. Over the course of the next two hours, armed with a binder full of questions, I interviewed Stephen in his den, dining room and The Pub (stocked with guitars, amps and recording gear) in his basement.

Evidence of Stills' musical dedication was everywhere. A small silver platter bearing in bold blue letters, 'Buffalo Springfield', leaned against a bookcase; the interlocking Crosby, Stills & Nash logo was pressed into a varnished block of wood on a low shelf; framed Stills and CSN concert posters hung in a main hallway, with several gold and platinum records adorning another wall.

Stephen was in constant motion that day as we talked. His words were honest and direct. One of my favorite Stills comments was when I asked about writing and recording the songs 'Run from Tears' and 'I Give You Give Blind' that featured on the 1977 *CSN* album. Stephen told me, 'All I can remember is the broken heart and the futility of the situation. I can't remember how the songs evolved, just that they did. There's a point where you just... you suck it in and say, 'I'm gonna take the hill'. If there is something to the mythology of a 'star', I'd like to think I set some example with that kind of courage, because it took everything that I had. But I'll be damned if I'm gonna let something stop me.' At the end of the afternoon, when our conversation was over and Stills walked me to the front door, he said, 'Thanks. You did your homework. I like that.'

Nine months later, *BAM* sent me to Hollywood to interview Graham Nash at Crossroads of the World. Graham and I connected immediately. We talked for more than two hours straight. No break. Again, I came prepared with a binder filled with questions. Here is a favorite CSN story Graham told me, his eyes alive and voice excited like it happened yesterday: 'I remember me, David and Stephen rehearsing our entire first album and being able to play it on two acoustic guitars. We would sit people down and say, 'Listen'. Then we would sit down and play 'Suite: Judy Blue Eyes' right in front of them, great. And we would follow it with 'Helplessly Hoping', 'You Don't Have to Cry', 'Marrakesh Express', 'Right Between the Eyes', 'Guinnevere', 'Long Time Gone'. By the time they'd sat down and listened to this hour of music, they were on the floor! We used to play deliberately to blow people away.'

Nash blew *me* away that day with his many stories. Before I left Crossroads of the World to go back to my Sunset Boulevard motel room, Graham gave me a gift: a copy of *The Graham Nash*

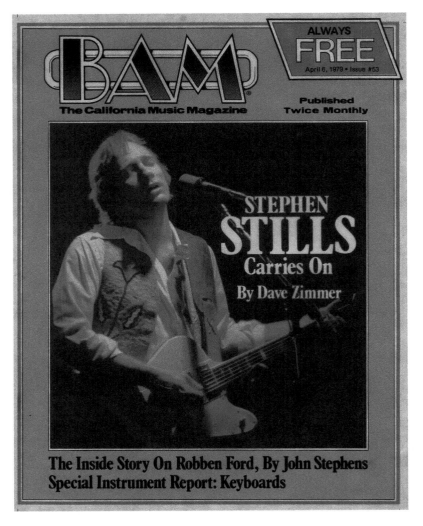

Collection, his first photography exhibition catalogue, which he inscribed, in pencil, 'To David, with respect, Graham Nash 10/11/1979.' It is a personal memento I treasure to this day. My Graham Nash interview is contained in a book I compiled and edited, *4 Way Street: The Crosby, Stills, Nash & Young Reader*, 24 years after our first conversation was published as a two-part interview in *BAM* in March 1980.

A week after the first part of the Nash interview hit the streets, the phone rang at my old Mountain View, California studio apartment. The *BAM* front desk reception said, 'Dave? I have a call for you on the other line. He says he is David Crosby and wants to talk to you. Can I put him through?' Of course, I said, 'Yes.' Seconds later, there was that unmistakable voice, 'Hello! David? This is David Crosby. I just wanted to call and let you know how much I liked your interview with my friend, Graham Nash. You did a really fine job. And he told you some stories even I have not heard.' We talked a bit more, then David said, 'If you ever want to interview me, I would be happy to talk with you. Here's my phone number. Call me anytime.'

Two weeks went by and one early afternoon I called David and asked when he might be free to talk. He said, 'How about today?' Crosby gave me directions to his house and off I drove, heading north on the 101 Freeway, along the Peninsula, through San Francisco, across the Golden Gate Bridge, then into Mill Valley. I managed to wend my way to his secluded home, surrounded by high trees, ferns and bushes. When I first met David, he did not look in the best of shape, nor did his then-girlfriend and future wife, Jan Dance. But they were both as warm as could be and very gracious hosts.

When David and I walked down into his living room, he had laid out, as if he didn't believe I was already aware of his musical brilliance, a collection of Crosby musical treasures: the original master tapes of Joni Mitchell's first album (which David produced) and Crosby & Nash's *Wind on the Water* album; a glossy color print of CSN&Y standing on the beach in Hawaii – the prospective cover shot for the never completed *Human Highway* album; and a customized Martin 12-string (which he referred to as 'The Mothership'). Other guitars, electric and acoustic, were scattered about on the floor, forming a crooked path to a grand piano across the room. While talking, Crosby would usually be fingering some sort of open-tuned progression on his 12-string, and he would periodically break into a scat vocal when a certain melody struck his ear.

He told me that afternoon, 'I can get off playing by myself in an empty room ... heavily. But when I get to play with someone else in that empty room, the feelings get multiplied by four, ten sometimes. Because you can catch another cat's lick and interlock with 'em in some exquisite way and make the hair on both your arms stand up, his and yours. Well, that's just heaven. It makes drugs look like kid stuff, sex even. And that takes some beatin'.'

'So I didn't want to stop workin' with Graham. I didn't want to stop workin' with Crosby, Stills & Nash. That was the best music I made in my whole life. And because it's not happening, it's hurting me so bad, man. But I gotta keep goin', I gotta keep making music, even if it's by myself, because it's still the main thing in my life. Whenever I ask myself, 'What am I supposed to do in this world?' I keep saying, 'Play and sing.'"

Crosby did continue to play and sing in 1980 and throughout 1981, mostly on his own and with a solo band that he pulled together. In December 1981, I was at Rudy Records and witnessed the recording studio reunion of Crosby and Nash (Stills was on the road at the time), as David overdubbed a harmony line on the chorus of Nash's 'Song for Susan': 'Fooling myself about how to exist/ All by myself there was much I had missed/ You came and showed me what happiness is.' Words that hit home and a performance that raised warm goosebumps.

In the spring of 1982, photographer Henry Diltz and I approached Crosby, Stills & Nash about doing their biography. They agreed to authorize – Henry having known each guy since 1966 and my positive interactions with each of them opening the door to the project of a lifetime. I talked to CSN as a trio for this first time in July 1982, when they were rehearsing at Zoetrope Studios in Hollywood for the first leg of the *Daylight Again* tour. Henry captured this magical moment on film.

Being a friend of CSN did not prevent me from reporting honestly about their lives and careers, as they afforded me open access into their homes, the studio and backstage on tour. CSN and Henry also connected me with many of their long-time friends, such as Joni Mitchell, John Sebastian, Grace Slick and Paul Kantner, as well as bandmates such as Neil Young, Richie Furay, Chris Hillman, Dallas Taylor and Gene Clark, to name a few.

It's been said that you should never meet your heroes ... Rather than diminishing my appreciation for CSN, getting to know them better as I delved deeper into their lives only enriched the experience and my respect for them as musicians and people, the first time around and to this day.

Bio: *Dave Zimmer was born in San Jose, California, but his musical heart started beating in Laurel Canyon. He has been CSN's biographer since the early Eighties – with three editions of his authorized CSN book, featuring photographs by Henry Diltz, (1984, 2000 & 2008). Dave was the editor of 4-Way Street: The CSN&Y Reader anthology book, (2004), with long tenures at BAM and Universal Studios. Now living in New Jersey, Dave was a member of the teams that published David Crosby's Since Then autobiography and Neil Young's two memoirs, Waging Heavy Peace and Special Deluxe.*

Songs: *'Déjà Vu' (C); 'Bluebird' (S); 'I Used to Be a King' (N).*

FROM THE MARROW OF MY BONES

by Bonnie Bramlett

Playing at the Havana Jam festival was scary and wonderful. With that concert in Cuba, March 1979, we made history doing with music what the politicians could not do with their sabre- rattling, threats, and stupid embargoes.

For instance, I still remember we were able to reunite a mother with two sons who hadn't seen each other in the 20 years since the embargo. They were musicians in the Irakere band. The mother had come to NYC to visit her sister for a couple of weeks when the embargo went down and the borders were closed. She left babies behind, and we brought her grown men.

It was so sad because she was devastated and happy at the same time. It was a sad event to watch the mother look at two strange men and make it work in her head that these were her babies. So sad.

I think Stephen showed his classy, educated word merchant self to the Cubans by writing a special song for the event, 'Cuba al Fin', and we sang it to them in their own language. Phonetically on my part. That thoughtfulness was very appreciated by the Cubans.

During that tour, Stephen and I did 'Love the One You're With'. He let me sing lead on it, sang my chart on his big hit, and spotlighted it.

He is a very generous man. I love him from the marrow of my bones!

March 3, 1979: Stephen Stills and Bonnie Bramlett live with the California Blues Band at Teatro Karl Marx, La Habana, Cuba. Photo courtesy of Ernesto Juan Castellanos (from Havana Jam '79 archives)

Bio: *Bonnie Bramlett was born in Alton, Illinois. In 1967 she moved to Los Angeles and met Delaney Bramlett. Delaney and Bonnie shared the stage with Eric Clapton, George Harrison, Rita Coolidge, Gram Parsons and John Lennon, to name just a few. After touring with Stephen Stills, Dickey Betts and Gregg Allman invited her on the Allman Brothers tour, and she became known as the only 'Allman Sister.' Bonnie returned to LA in the 1980s. She had a role in the TV series Roseanne as Bonnie Watkins, with David Crosby appearing as her husband.*

March 3, 1979: Stephen Stills live at Teatro Karl Marx, La Habana, Cuba. Photo courtesy of Ernesto Juan Castellanos (from Havana Jam '79 archives)

CUBA AL FIN

by Carolyn Baker

In 1978, I was a crew member on a 42' ketch, the Solan Goose, sailing with a small fleet of sailboats, 'racing' to Havana from Key West, under the auspices of a Key West Yacht Club Regatta. We did try to sail there as fast as we could, but most of us were cruisers, not racers, happy to make it through the night in the Gulf Stream without a run-in with a freighter. Having no idea what to expect, it was a fine trip. We were warmly received by the authorities, the Cuban gunboats docked across from us in the marina. We were all happy to socialize at the marina, including the Cuban soldiers. We enjoyed trips into Havana, where we were free to walk anywhere and take photos and did that with great fascination, amazed that we had so much freedom in this Communist country. We rented bicycles, fresh out of their Czechoslovakian boxes, which we biked way into the countryside, led by two volunteer teenage local boys. We even spotted the infamous 'missiles', planted in the countryside; our guides nervously steering us away and back to town.

While there, I became acquainted with the name of CubaTur, the national tourism

March 22, 1979: Stephen Stills live at Roberts Center, Boston College, Boston, Massachusetts, USA. Photo by Mark Kelly

bureau. Little did I know that knowledge would take me on a most interesting journey. A few months later, I read a newspaper article in *The Key West Citizen* about CBS flying down some of our American top performers, sound equipment and personnel for a three-night music concert at the Karl Marx Auditorium in Havana in March 1979. After conferring with a few boat captains, and with little hope, I walked down to the Western Union Telegraph Company on Simonton Street in Key West, where I sent a telegram to CubaTur, asking permission for about six sailboats to sail down for the music festival. Much to my surprise, a prompt answer was received from CubaTur to the affirmative, requiring only the names of the boats and crew members.

So off we sailed, around six sailboats, leaving at sunset, arriving at sunrise at what was then Barlovento Marina, now named Marina Hemingway. Again, the Cubans were most thoughtful and receptive. A gunboat towed our smallest sailboat, which didn't have an engine, to its place on the dock. Buses were provided to take us to and from Karl Marx Auditorium and the Marina. We were issued 'credit cards' at the marina bar, a copy of which I have kept. Appearing in alternating acts were American/Cuban performers and bands; Billy Joel, Weather Report, Stephen Stills, Kris Kristofferson, Rita Coolidge, Stan Getz, John McLaughlin, and more than a dozen other talented Americans, along with equally-talented Cubans. We were spellbound, to say the least.

During his set Stills stepped off the stage and played among the crowd, his guitar equipped with one of the first wireless sound transmission systems. When Stephen sang 'Cuba al Fin', a song in support of the Cuban people he had written especially for the occasion, I remember being emotionally moved, as were the Cubans in their response by his performance in Spanish.

Suffice to say, this sweet trip was a once in a lifetime event, if not an 'historical event', especially considering it took place in a Communist country, only 20 years after the 'Revolution'. The Bay of Pigs had already taken place and the embargo employed. CBS had to fly quite a few planes into Havana with the equipment, performers, camera and sound crew and assorted support staff. No problema!

March 1979: Stephen Stills and Joe Lala, La Habana, Cuba. Photo courtesy of Joe Vitale

Thank goodness, CBS recorded the double album, *Havana Jam*, with colorful photos and relevant information on the covers; otherwise, I might think it was a wonderful dream.

Bio: *Born in Kansas City, Missouri. Carolyn Baker lives in Cortez, Florida, an authentic fishing village. In the Seventies, with her first husband, she built a 32' sailboat in Redondo Beach, California, and sailed it to Key West. Attending Havana Jam '79, sailing to Havana, is high on her list.*

Songs: *'Cuba al Fin' (S); 'Love the One You're With' (S); 'It Doesn't Matter' (S).*

The MUSE CONCERTS for A NON-NUCLEAR FUTURE

September 19-23, 1979

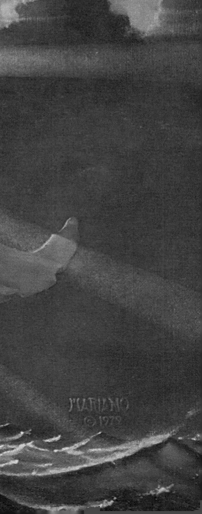

NO NUKES

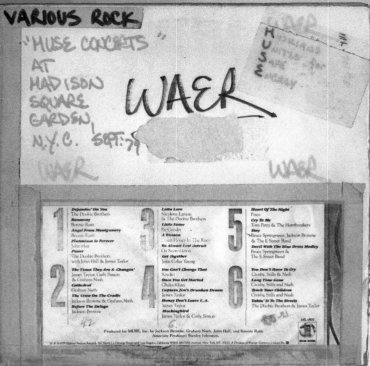

NO NUKES
EXPERIENCE THE MOVIE
**JACKSON BROWNE · CROSBY, STILLS AND NASH
DOOBIE BROTHERS · JOHN HALL · GRAHAM NASH
BONNIE RAITT · GIL SCOTT-HERON · CARLY SIMON**

93

ALBERT KOSKI présente
HIPPODROME D'AUTEUIL
SAMEDI 11 JUIN 1983 / 21 H.
Ouverture des portes : 18 H.

Nº 10269

imp snvt rouen

80's

Time we have wasted on the way

WEMBLEY

Crosby Stills & Nash

1983

HARVEY GOLDSMITH ENTERTAINMENTS PRESENTS

An Evening With

CROSBY STILLS & NASH

Monday, 11th July, 1983

at 8.00 p.m.

ENTER A
SOUTH DO

SOUT
AREN
SEA

ROW

SOUTH ARENA SEAT

£8.50

See conditions on back

BOOTLEG HUNTER

by Stas' Gawronski

July 23, 1980 - La Carovana del Mediterraneo tour: Stephen Stills and the California Blues Band, Stadio, Bolzano, Italy. Photo by Franco Paissan (courtesy of Paolo Carnevale)

In June 1980 I was a 16-year-old boy tracking his search for horizons and the meaning of life with music. Rock music was a phantasmagoric place of visions, images aroused by songs, record covers and stories that came to me through vinyl, tapes, nighttime FM radio (I often found myself sleeping on the school desk in class!) and music magazines. When I was 13, I bought *4 Way Street*. It was 1977 and I had read about the reunion of three members of a mythical supergroup in Italian magazine *Ciao 2001*. I was seduced by the imagery produced by the incredible harmonies and sonic digressions of CSNY: the four musicians were the focus of my affection, attention, and imagination.

School was almost out, the boundless space of summer opened up, and anything could happen, even the miracle announced by local newspaper, *Il Messaggero*: Stephen Stills was scheduled to play with his band at Castel Sant'Angelo in Rome at the end of June. Every morning, obsessively, I called the only concert ticket presale outlet in Rome to ask for news, but the Roman date of Stephen Stills' tour was unconfirmed. As days went by, that event seemed like a chimera: no one was able to give me any update. June flew by and when I learned that my hero had played at the San Siro stadium in Milan and at the San Paolo stadium in Napoli, where Graham Nash had also appeared, it was too late. I could not believe it!

In July, the streets of Rome were sun-drenched, the asphalt was melting, and loneliness thundered with the beautiful sounds coming from the vinyl spinning on my hi-fi stereo system. I asked my parents for permission to visit my brother in Milan, where he was attending university. They gave me just enough money to spend a few days with him and come back, no more. At the time, trains took almost eight hours to get you to Milan from Rome, but on the Express trains you could travel with the windows rolled down, the wind ruffling your hair, the deafening chirping of cicadas surprising you at every sudden stop in the countryside. I knew there was a shop that sold rare records in Milan, located a few steps from the Duomo, but I didn't visit it until the last day there. At that stage all my money was already gone. I didn't have a penny. I couldn't even afford a 45rpm single, but I couldn't resist, curiosity got the better of me and there I went. I was a bootleg hunter and when I walked in, I asked if they had any CSNY. Pirated records, unofficial live recordings were usually hidden in the back room, accessible only to trusted customers; I had to climb up a fireman's ladder. I leaned over the shelf, recognised the basic covers which, at best, consisted of pale monochrome images printed on a sheet glued to the blank cardboard of the cover. The proximity to those mysterious records caused me much excitement. Their physical presence confirmed, nourished and made palpable the myth of those unreachable divinities. And I will never forget the emotion I felt when I came across one of those records.

It looked like an official product, the color cover, a beautiful photograph of Crosby Stills Nash & Young with a title I'd never heard of before: *Nice to See You: The 1974 Excursion*. I picked it up and, from the weight and from the list of songs, I understood it was a double album. My breathing slowed down, but my heart was beating at a faster pace. I looked at it and looked again, knowing I only had the money I would need for the return train ticket with me, 40,000 lire - corresponding exactly to the price of that record.

I bought it and went back to my brother, hoping he would lend me the money for the train. He did not get upset but told me that if I wanted to go home, I would have to hitchhike. Next morning, he took me to Piazzale Corvetto and, in front of the junction for the ring road towards the Milan to Rome highway, he said goodbye and gave me a simple instruction: 'When any car stops at the stop sign, ask them to drop you off at the highway toll booth or at any service area'. I was carrying a denim jacket, tennis shoes, and a backpack over my shoulders, the CSNY bootleg record under my arm. I returned to Rome in five and a half hours (two less than the train). The trick was to be dropped off at rest areas on the highway until the next ride. It was my first hitchhiking trip between Rome and Milan. There were others, but that one is forever engraved in my memory because of that one record that I have listened to and loved the most in my life.

I have to admit, the sound quality was not good: the source was an audience tape recorded by one of the 60,000 fans who flocked to the CSNY concert at Nassau Coliseum, New York on 15 August 1974. The recording opens with a distant, indistinct din of percussion and bass (the guy who recorded the concert was not close to the stage), then a ramshackle electric guitar solo and the harsh, scratchy, barking voice of Stephen Stills singing 'Love the One You're With'. It was the first time I had heard an electric version of this song; I couldn't believe it.

For a long time, that initial roll of the band's rhythm section made me dizzy, and when 40 years later I heard the same song from the very same concert opening CSNY's 1974 tour official boxset, I still preferred the cumbersome, indistinct, and confused bootleg version. I don't know how many times that obscure recording has allowed me to experience the concert from the audience's point of view, as if you were there, far from the stage, among thousands of wild fans. When the crowd clapped their hands, as in the overwhelming version of Ohio, I felt like I was at Nassau Coliseum, with thousands of fellow fans, in the presence of Crosby Stills Nash & Young in a dream that my imagination made real each and every time.

Bio: *Born in Rome, Stas' Gawronski is the author and host of television programmes dedicated to literature, teaches creative writing, and believes that Stills (1975) is one of the most beautiful records in rock history.*

Songs: *'Song with No Words' (C), 'Johnny's Garden' (S); 'Teach Your Children' (N).*

STILLS, NASH AND ANGELO

by Angelo Branduardi

The idea came to promoter David Zard, who invited Stephen and Richie Havens to play dates in Europe with me in the summer of 1980. Stills didn't know me. He asked about my records, listened to my music, and immediately said yes. Graham Nash joined the tour, and we soon became Stills, Nash and Angelo.

During those extraordinary weeks, the person I got to know best - and who remained in my heart the most due to an unexplainable empathy - was Stephen Stills. And I'm glad to know this feeling is mutual. To the point that once, during a CSN concert in Milan, he even dedicated a song to me. Initially I blushed and wanted to hide under the chair, but I felt happy about our friendship and this mutual respect.

At that time, I knew Crosby, Stills, Nash & Young from having seen the *Woodstock* movie many a time. I was surprised by their harmony vocals, by that polyphony typical of the groups of the time. The record I had listened to the most was *Déjà Vu* but, honestly, I didn't know much else about them at the time. Years later, it was such a great honour when Stephen and Graham asked me to add my voice to the 'Teach Your Children' harmonies during concerts on that tour.

Before the tour started, we rehearsed a lot and I had the chance to spend many hours with Stephen, talking not necessarily about music, but about life. We both felt a mutual empathy, a great strength which made us feel very close.

Stephen had many beautiful guitars and one day started showing me how he played, even the things Jimi Hendrix had taught him about electric. I learned a lot from him about the American technique of playing the acoustic guitar. I am a classical violinist with a degree in music, but I learned the guitar on my own and over the years got to play with some great musicians. Stephen was sort of a teacher to me: during those days, for instance, he helped me discover open tunings. I had never used them before, but it was another interesting thing that helped me understand how some American guitarists were able to obtain effects that were impossible for me, and that were much simpler than one might think.

Stephen claimed that I had a good right hand, because I have a lot of articulation on my right hand, even though I am left-handed. This results in a much greater amount of sound than another guitarist with the same guitar. He didn't sound like I did, and of course we were intrigued by each other. Somehow, in the end he took something from my style, too. It happened spontaneously. Musicians are always open to new ideas, and he was very interested in my fingering and certain guitar setups, which seemed like open tunings to him but weren't at all. For my part, I've tried to use them, but don't like them. The most I do, and I almost always do, is lower the low E to D.

We spent beautiful evenings, in a hotel in Rome during those rehearsal days. We talked and talked about our lives. Stephen could be easily moved. At the same time, we had a lot of fun. There were many musicians there, including the guitarist, Roberto Puleo. We sat around in a trio and played things that I wouldn't even call a session, but jeux. In short, we played. Often even at soundchecks, when one 'interfered' with the soundcheck of the other.

I have this concept that not only concerns me, but also definitely concerns Stephen: musicians are luxury outcasts. It does not necessarily have a negative connotation: true artists bring so many things along with them that, psychically, their minds are somehow different. As attested by so many psychiatric studies, musicians' minds are shaped differently. They have other kinds of references; they behave differently from the mind of an ordinary person. This is the strength and, at the same time, the weakness of most artists. And Stephen is a typical example.

We spent almost a month in Rome rehearsing that tour. Thus, it was that the acquaintance turned into friendship. We rehearsed in the service shed we had at the time, called *La Sc*ossa, historic because it was built by Pink Floyd's engineers, located in Prima Porta. It was a very large studio. A beautiful set-up.

Stephen liked a song of mine that was far from the American style and that couldn't be more Renaissance: 'Ballo in F# Minor'. Very close to the early Baroque style. There have been many versions of it, especially in Germany where - incredible but true - I am considered as sort of one of the Founding Fathers of that acoustic genre by heavy metal musicians, because many times I write based on archaic.

The first time Stills listened to that song was by chance: he walked into the room while we were rehearsing and listened to us playing.

Eventually, he came to me and hugged me. He was crying, moved.

101

July 1980: Stephen Stills and the California Blues Band on the road with La Carovana del Mediterraneo (Italy, Germany, Switzerland). Photos by Geraldine Peters

Bio: *Born in 1950, Angelo Branduardi is an Italian folk/folk-rock singer-songwriter and composer. He experimented with piano and violin before settling on guitar. He scored a big success in Italy in the Seventies and has released about 30 albums. Angelo regularly tours in Italy and other European countries.*

July 15, 1980 - La Carovana del Mediterraneo tour: Richie Havens, Stephen Stills and Angelo Branduardi live at Stadio San Siro, Milano, Italy. Photo by Nicola Pietro de Rienzo

TEST, TEST, TEST

by Andy Clearfield

I grew up living around the block from Joel Bernstein, who became CSNY's guitar tuner, archivist and official photographer in 1970. Among many other iconic images, Joel took the cover photo of Neil's *After the Goldrush*. In 1973, Graham Nash visited Joel's home in suburban Philadelphia, while on his first solo tour, and that's where I met Graham for the first time.

The following year, CSN&Y played the Atlantic City Racetrack during their 1974 tour. Many of my friends attended the show, which took place in a driving thunderstorm with lots of lightning. One of them, who I will call 'BS' here, was a bit of a rebel back then. In fact, Cameron Crowe used his life story as part of the Jeff Spicoli character in popular film *Fast Times at Ridgemont High*. Cut to the chase, 'BS' talked his way onto CSNY's stage, telling uniformed stagehands he in fact was Joel Bernstein, the official CSN&Y photographer. There he was, center-stage, waving to us as he tapped the tall standing microphones - 'test, test, test'. Next thing we know, he is being escorted off stage and redeposited back into the drenched sea of fan madness.

Fast forward to 1980. Graham Nash was doing his first solo tour in many years, appearing at the Tower Theater in the Philly area. He was supporting the *Earth and Sky* LP, and I had arranged a pre-show interview with Graham and my friend Joel Bernstein, who was supporting Graham on guitar and piano. Sat on a couch, we smoked rock star weed during the interview. I got so lost I forgot to keep asking questions, just happy to keep hanging out with my heroes.

After 45 minutes, Graham politely asked me to wrap up, and I moved to the auditorium, where the soundcheck was amazing. The show, or what I recall of it, was a wonderful recap to date of a brilliant career.

Bio: *Andy Clearfield was born in Elkins Park, Philadelphia, and was family neighbors with CSN(Y) photographer Joel Bernstein in the Sixties. His first CSN-related show was the first Crosby/Nash tour in 1972, followed by Neil Young's Time Fades Away tour in 1973, with many more shows over the years since. Andy lives in Southern New Jersey, where he is retired following a career as an attorney. Today he spends his time with his family, travelling, and collecting music memorabilia.*

Songs: *'Song with No Words' (C), 'Four Days Gone' (S), 'Pre-Road Downs' (N).*

April 15, 1980: Graham Nash live at Music Theatre, Royal Oak, Michigan, USA. Photo by Michael Curcuru

THE BIRTH OF A CLASSIC

by Ken Weiss

During the period when I was both Stephen Stills' music publisher and his manager, there were many occasions where my duties and responsibilities served both objectives. Stephen is a very complex character. It took me ten years working close together with him to just to begin understanding him, but I've learned how to get through to him. Above all, he's a tremendous artist, surely the best acoustic guitar player I've ever seen. No one does what he can do on that instrument.

In 1980, we were preparing to do another solo record for CBS, one for which Stephen had written a number of songs. But we both felt something more was needed, that singular kind of song that has always defined Stephen's contribution to CSN and CSNY albums as well as his solo work. Think of 'Suite: Judy Blue Eyes' for the first record, 'Carry On' for the second, 'Love the One You're With' for his first solo record, 'Sit Yourself Down' for the second, and so on. Going all the way back to Buffalo Springfield, the most enduring song on all their records is clearly 'For What It's Worth'.

Understanding very well what he is capable of, I spent a lot of time combing through ideas, including existing songs in my song catalog. I always felt Stephen was as capable of contributing to another writer's piece, making it into a classic, as he was writing his own – although it was rare for him to co-write.

In the mid-1970s, working together with Malcolm Jones, we signed The Curtis Brothers Band's two principal songwriters, Michael and Richard Curtis, to a songwriting and publishing agreement. These are very gifted songwriters who recorded many works of their own on a couple of albums. But their success as songwriters - they also wrote 'Blue Letter', which Fleetwood Mac included on their 1975 eponymous album and which sold many millions of records - did not extend to their efforts as artists.

Believing in them as I did, I listened again to many of their songs and compiled a cassette with half a dozen of their best pieces, including 'Seven League Boots'. I believed this was the one we can work with, as its unique melody and style got my attention, while the chorus, in my view, was less exciting than it could have been - the perfect Stills scenario. And, quite candidly, I never liked the lyrics very much – another Stills strength. All the songs on this tape were what I believed to be candidates for the Stephen Stills treatment, none more so than 'Seven League Boots'.

I remember quite clearly the moment. We were in the living room of his Mulholland Drive house playing some music. As the tape played, he nodded along somewhat approvingly, but no dancing around the room type enthusiasm. Then came the song. His eyes brightened, his head turned, and I could tell this one had a different resonance for him. I have a vivid recollection of him saying the hairs on his arm was standing up while listening. That is a very good thing for a songwriter/artist to say. We talked about it a little and played it again and again, and his interest grew. Given the time of night, around midnight or later, I thought it the perfect time to leave 'songwriter Stephen' alone for the night and let him take it from there.

Over the next couple of days, I guessed he would either work on it and come up with little, abandon it altogether (entirely possible of course), come up with a new version of the song that is not all that much better, or come up with a much better, more polished and exciting song. To my delight, it was the latter. And that is how 'Southern Cross' was born.

When I heard what he did with the Curtis Brothers' song, I flipped out, knowing it was the typical Stephen Stills standout song on the album, something he has done so many times before. He reinvented 'Seven League Boots', keeping the spirit of what made that song work but changing the theme to that of sailing in the exotic south seas, where the Southern Cross can be seen in the sky. Its brilliant expression, its romance and its perfection gives the song its unique and special nature, things that always set Stephen apart as a writer. It's who he is. He can't help it.

Stephen was getting set to record the new album for CBS and 'Southern Cross' was included. A cool video of the song was made to support the record. But then, the unpredictable nature of the music business being what it is, suffice to say the album was not released, locked away somewhere, not to this day ever heard by the general public.

This was 1980 and we were preparing for a stadium tour of Europe with Stephen Stills and the California Blues Band, co-headlining in Italy, the great Angelo Branduardi and Richie Havens opening the shows. Of course, the song played very well to live audiences on the tour. We always knew it was special. And now, so did everyone who got to hear it.

While all this was going on, there was music afoot with Crosby, Stills & Nash. And in 1982, work began on the album that became *Daylight Again*. Making this record was an epic experience, worthy of a book, but in the end the enormous effort paid off. Wonderful songs were being tossed around, written by each of the three guys. David Crosby came with the brilliant (and totally underrated) 'Delta', and Graham Nash contributed a wonderful and, as always, perfect top-10 hit song of which he is so capable, 'Wasted on the Way' the song that really launched the album. And Stephen, the great song craftsman he is, contributed six songs, fully half the album, including the beautiful and radio-friendly 'Southern Cross', its arrangement little different than that on the CBS solo record, the one few people ever heard. But the group's contribution to this version made it sparkle with their inimitable sound. And with the hit single 'Wasted on the Way' having paved the way, it was the second single released, and also a hit.

Daylight Again went platinum, double platinum, and a national sold-out Crosby, Stills & Nash tour, with a lot of new material, ensued. The tour was a smash success and the show at the Universal Amphitheatre in LA was recorded for a *Showtime* television special, a home video Laser Disc and, later, a DVD.

*Malcolm Jones, Stephen Stills, Ken Weiss
- Los Angeles, CA 1973 (from Ken Weiss
private collection)*

This photo (below) was taken in Hawaii on the north shore of Oahu at a house we rented for vocals on what became the Daylight Again album. Crosby was in California and was unreachable at that time. The house was Elvis Presley's. I don't know the guy on the left – I think he worked at the studio. The next guy is Steve Gursky who co-produced the record with Stanley Johnston. Next is Bob Russell, a friend of ours we met at the White House in 1977 during a trip to D.C. Bob worked for Jimmy Carter who was the president at that time – and who we met at the White House. After Reagan was elected in 1980, Bob retired from politics and hung out with us for some years. The next guy is Stephen's guitar tech, Doug Breidenbach. Then it's Stanley Johnston, me, Nash, Finnigan and Stills." Ken Weiss. Photo from his private collection

Poster for the Barcelona 1983 cancelled show. Poster from Daniel Ruiz

To this day, 'Southern Cross' remains a crowd favorite, included on every Crosby, Stills & Nash set-list for the last 30-plus years, a mainstay on radio and a few cover recordings as well. Even Jimmy Buffet cut it. A classic song was born and is now the property of tens of millions of people. It was an effort, but an entirely gratifying one. And now, the world can peek inside how a great classic was born and raised.

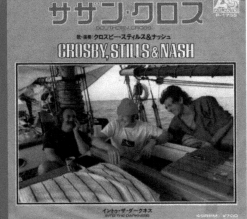

Bio: *Ken Weiss was born and raised in New York City. He began his formal music career during a three-year stint at Warner Chappell Music during which his associations with diverse songwriters such as Bob Dylan, Van Morrison and Stephen Stills led to his venturing out as an independent. With Gold Hill Music he led one of the industry's most successful independent music publishing companies, garnering multi-gold and platinum albums with Crosby, Stills & Nash (& Young), Firefall, Stephen Stills, Fleetwood Mac, and numerous others.*
He teaches the Artistic track in the Entrepreneurship Minor at the University of North Carolina at Chapel Hill, the town in which he has lived since 2007, in addition to managing his music publishing catalogue through Bronx Flash Music, Inc.

Songs: *'Déjà Vu' (C) – 'the musical arrangement, rhythmic changes and haunting vocals carry the song. A transformative piece'; 'Helplessly Hoping' (S) – 'brilliant poetry, breath-taking harmonies, a great artist at the top of his game.' 'Just a Song Before I Go' (N), 'a perfectly written song about touring and its overall madness and perils that lends itself so well to the CSN harmonies - typical Nash, a short song with a message and a brilliant performance. I've stuck to CSN songs only. I might have different opinions if solo stuff is included.'*

PEACE SUNDAY

by Lisa Law

In 1981 Stevie Wonder arrived in Santa Fe, New Mexico with his recording crew, lawyer, personal assistant and brother. Stevie took up residence in the fifth-floor suite of the La Fonda Hotel, the same hotel the Los Alamos scientists used for a meeting place during the making of the atomic bomb. Stevie and his gang basically took over the hotel, especially the Casa Blanca nightclub on the bottom floor. His mixing truck was parked in the back parking lot, cords running into the back door to the main room, where Stevie added tracks to his newest album, *Stevie Wonder's Original Musiquarium I.*

Being a connoisseur of music and having worked for many bands either as an assistant to Frank Werber, the manager of the Kingston Trio, or a roadie or photographer for others, I was right there at his door asking to visit, and rapidly we became friends. My kids fell in love with him too, and he even hung out with them after school was out. Baba loved watching him play the piano, and Sunday Peaches was enthralled with it all.

During Christmas we were up in Stevie's room, sharing presents, when a call came in from Alan Myerson, the director of the Committee, a political satire group known for their great improvisational theatre both in San Francisco and Los Angeles.

Alan said Graham Nash was trying to get hold of Stevie, wanting him to be the lead act at the *Peace Sunday: We Have a Dream* Concert to take place at the Rose Bowl in Pasadena, California in the summer. Graham's main goal was to raise funds with all the church groups in the area to help the Nuclear Freeze. I told him I would be glad to help and to have him call. Stevie was in the middle of eating dinner and would call him back and not only would he do it, he'd

Early 80's: Stephen Stills live. Photo courtesy of Ernie Osborne

ask Paul McCartney to be there too, since he had just finished recording 'Ebony and Ivory' with him. We left it at that, me assuming Graham would get in touch with Stevie's manager, Abner.

On 29 April 1982, I flew to LA to document one of Wavy Gravy's fundraising events for the SEVA foundation. Graham Nash, Jackson Browne, Ramblin' Jack Elliot, Kate Wolfe, Holly Near, Odetta and Country Joe McDonald were all there for a wonderful, joyous concert at Santa Monica Civic Auditorium. While backstage photographing everyone, Graham told me that Abner had not returned his calls and without Stevie being on board, they could not secure the Rose Bowl. Was there anything I could do to move things along?

It just so happened that on that very night, Stevie was recording at his studio in LA on Western Avenue. I went to an after-party till late morning then drove to Stevie's studio, where I sat in the waiting room watching TV (*The Planet of the Apes* was playing, starring Severn Darden, a good friend of mine and Wavy's) until 6am, when Stevie shuffled through the hall towards me, wearing a soft brown outfit of pants and matching pullover, having just completed a night of recording. 'Where is my Sunday Peaches?' he said. He had fallen in love with my 10-year-old daughter when they hung out together at the La Fonda. 'I want my Sunday Peaches!' he exclaimed. I jumped right to the point, 'When the nuclear bombs drop, they will drop on white people, yellow people, brown people and black people, and if we don't do something about it we are all going to be hurt or contaminated, so we need for you to be part of this concert. In fact, without you it won't happen.' 'No problem,' he said, 'Just call my manager and he will set things up with you. I told you I would help.'

I met with Graham and the Reverend James Lawson that morning in the basement of a church in downtown LA, just after a march for nuclear disarmament, telling them the good news. Everyone was excited; a big group of volunteers from the church were already working on the logistics of the concert.

But that wasn't the end. I got a call from Graham the next week saying no one would return his calls at Motown.

Now I had to pull out all the stops and get serious about this adventure. I was still in LA and knew where Johanna Vigoda (Stevie's attorney) was staying - at the Hyatt House on Sunset - so I made my way over there and called his room. 'You are here, Lisa? Come on up and give me a massage like you did in Santa Fe.' I had been massaging a lot of them during their stay and must have been good at it because they always wanted more. We ended up on the roof of the Hyatt, me in a crushed red velvet Native American skirt and top, Johanna in his bathing suit. I was dripping wet within minutes, massaging away.

'Abner has never answered any of Graham's calls, and there is only one week before we lose the Rose Bowl, so you really need to help us get in touch with Abner. We need him to meet with us.' Within the hour, Graham had made the connection and our meeting was the next day at Motown.

Reverend James Lawson, Graham and I met Abner and his men, and I suggested to Graham that Motown co-produce the concert and we should make sure the concert was audio and videotaped for history's sake. Much to my chagrin, that never happened, but that day Abner and Motown agreed they would co-produce the concert, and we were on! It was to be the biggest concert since Woodstock, over 16 groups playing and 85,000 people attending.

Wavy Gravy was there in full regalia, loads of children sending notes of peace up to the skies in helium balloons. Three presidential children spoke, and the 80 Voices of Japan sang, John Trudell blessed the entire Rose Bowl with a sage smudge stick way up high in the bleachers behind the stage, and Yogi Bhajan was there with a large group of dressed Sikhs, all dressed in white. Taj Mahal flew in from Hawaii to play 'Mailbox Blues' and 'Stagger Lee' solo. He had been one of the first people to offer to play free for the concert.

Gil Scott Heron was the first to play, then Reverend Jesse Jackson spoke. Jesse Colin Young sang John Lennon's 'Imagine' then 'Get Together' by Dino Valenti. Graham sang 'Military Madness' and with Bonnie Raitt duetted on 'Love Has No Pride'. Donovan drove in from his home in the desert to sing 'Sunshine Superman', 'Season of the Witch' and 'Mellow Yellow', which blew everyone away because it was so Sixties, so out there, so psychedelic.

Timothy B. Schmit & Don Felder sang 'I Can't Tell You Why' and Crosby, Stills & Nash were dynamic on 'Long Time Gone', 'Chicago', 'Love the One You're With', 'For What It's Worth', and 'Dark Star'. Then Dave Mason joined them on 'Hoochie Coochie Man' and 'Rocky Mountain Way'. I was right up in the front of the stage to capture them. What a moment for Graham. I could see the excitement written all over his face. The concert was a success due to all his hard work.

I was running back and forth between backstage and the front of the stage and once captured Stevie Wonder with my camera, marching alongside the stage, his entire band flanking him as they sang their way to the main platform. After a speech and a poem he'd written, he played 'Front Line', 'Master Blaster', 'Do I Do' and his 'We Demand World Peace Today' chant. He was spectacular.

While backstage, a producer from Motown pulled me aside and told me he was so glad we had asked them to co-produce the concert. That was a great moment for me.

Joan Baez sang solo 'Do Right Woman', 'Warriors of the Sun', 'Imagine', and 'Diamonds and Rust', then Bob Dylan showed up in a van which was driven right down to the stage. He got out, sang with Joan then got back in the van and drove away. I was able to grab a few great shots of him and Joan harmonizing on 'With God on Our Side', 'A Pirate Looks At Forty', and 'Blowin' in the Wind'.

All sorts of people spoke - Jane Fonda, Thelma Adair, Professor Michio Kaku, Carrie Fisher, Patti Davis, Harrison Ford, Martin Sheen, Muhammad Ali, LeVar Burton, Caesar Chavez, Howard Hesseman, Ed Asner, and many more.

"RISE EVERYBODY"

Stevie Wonder (center), joins (left to right) musician Graham Nash; actress/singer/ anti-nuclear activist Patti Davis and Steve Sulkes, "Peace Sunday" Executive Committee member, in a call to end the nuclear arms race at a recent press conference held in Los Angeles.

Wonder, Nash and Davis are among the dozens of participants in "Peace Sunday, We Have A Dream", a June 6, 1982, Pasadena Rose Bowl celebration for universal peace.

80,000 people are expected at this unique event, bringing together organizations and coalitions from many religions, ethnic backgrounds, occupations and ages. All have the same goal in mind : to see that our world leaders take that important step back away from the threat of nuclear holocaust.

photo by Richard Aaron

Black Bull T.M.

Dan Fogelberg, Stevie Nicks, Linda Ronstadt, Bette Midler, Jackson Browne, Gary U.S. Bonds, and Tom Petty brought up the tail of the concert and everyone got on stage for Graham's 'Teach Your Children' then the finale, 'Give Peace a Chance'.

Graham made sure I had all the right wristbands during each set - if you didn't have the right one, you were out of luck, no matter who you were. He basically made me head photographer for the concert, shooting lots of rehearsals and the dress rehearsal the day before.

The show was able to raise over $350,000 for nuclear disarmament, and we experienced one of the greatest concerts in history, with the finest groups of the day. Since then, Graham and I have remained the best of friends. As the I Ching says, 'Perseverance furthers'.

Bio: *Lisa Law is an American photographer and filmmaker. Over the past five decades her still, movie and video images have chronicled the social and cultural changes in America, from Flashing on the Sixties, her film documentary of that vibrant decade to her moving contemporary still photographs of the indigenous people of North, South, and Central America as they struggle for sovereignty and survival.*

CSN, WOODEN NICKEL AND A DREAM

by Umberto Martuscelli

The best moment came when I locked myself in my room and sat in the armchair next to the stereo, under a lamp radiating a nice, soft yellow light, finally opening the nylon package, my fingers making direct contact with the cover of the album. From that moment, the journey into an emotion that really had no equal during those years in my life began. Girls? Sex? Yes, sure, but those were other emotions. I was leaning towards discovery but at the same time was held back by the desire not to let those moments - in which anything could happen, as nothing was formally declared yet - evaporate. I usually began searching for any little detail that could give me an idea of what awaited me once I put the record on, put the headphones on and closed my eyes, abandoning myself to the music.

-C.S.N. IN
ITALIA
-ALLIES
-LA RUGGINE
NON DORME
MAI!
-EVERYBODY'S
ROCKIN'

-TESTI
INEDITI
-J.ROGAN's
BOOK
-J. BROWNE
"LAWYERS
IN LOVE.

Dicembre 1983   n.1   £.2'500

Before listening to music, I wanted to experience the thrill of a slow and growing discovery. So, I would scan the cover, the front, the back, the inside, looking at every detail of the graphics and the images, certain I could discover something there already. The final step before listening was to read the liner notes and the info - when available - relating to each song, sometimes the lyrics, sometimes just who was playing what. And there each time I hoped I would be able find the first sign: 'Stephen Stills: acoustic guitar'. If these four words were there, I felt an awkward happiness spread through me. It didn't matter who the authors of that song were, or even the authors of the record: they could be CSN, or Stills alone, or Stills collaborating on some other musician's record. It did not matter. It was enough to find those four words: 'Stephen Stills: acoustic guitar', but best if inside a CSN record, of course. From that moment on, I could not wait to hear that sound, or rather, that set of sounds I heard the first time I put the acoustic part of the *Stephen Stills Live* album on the turntable. When I heard the version of 'Crossroads' / 'You Can't Catch Me', I no longer understood anything, I seemed to be listening to an unknown language, a set of sounds without logic and meaning, used as I was - at that time - to the small, simple, linear sound architectures of Cat Stevens or Paul Simon. But then that frightening force, that rhythmic violence, that kind of pagan rite, made up of a technique I didn't think possible on an acoustic guitar, became my greatest pleasure.

So, I began to inhale everything I could get my hands on that was published by Stills or CSN or CSNY, because I wanted to know more. Maybe inhaling is too strong an expression, because actually – in the late Seventies and early Eighties - there was not much to read about them. If there was anything to write about them, it was usually just to say they were dinosaurs. Nothing else. The years between the release of the sublime *CSN* in 1977 (the boat album) and *Daylight Again* were the ones when unwary music critics had decreed the death of a phenomenon - needless to say - still alive and kicking today. Therefore, in those days, even just a line, a paragraph, a quotation in brackets, a dot here and there, became fundamental elements for 'knowing' more, even if only of knowing about bad things. Nothing new was ever said about Crosby, Stills & Nash. No announcements of albums or tours. Nothing. Only useless comments of useless critics.

In the summer of 1982, I was in London. I worked in a stable. I only had one day off: Monday. And on one of those Mondays, I went for a long walk around the city. I happened to be in front of the Virgin store, I don't remember whether it was Oxford Street or Tottenham Court Road, entering the never-ending ground floor of that music paradise. I'd never seen such a large record store in my entire life. After just a few moments, my heart leapt into my throat: tied to very thin transparent nylon threads, dozens and dozens of blue covers hung from the ceiling that swayed slowly, moved by the movement of the air. A neon sign in red on each cover read Crosby Stills & Nash, and underneath, *Daylight Again*. I stood there looking dazed: was I really witnessing the launch of a new CSN record? For

me it was like a miracle. The appearance of a divine sign. I was seized by a tremendous emotion, and also a great sense of helplessness: I did not have a record player there in London and would not return to Italy for several weeks. I bought three copies of the record anyway - what if I had only got one and it was ruined during the trip back to Italy? Once home, in my London house, I opened a copy. I took out the inner sleeve containing the vinyl: there were the lyrics of the songs and everything else. There was also 'Stephen Stills: acoustic guitar'. I felt as if I was dreaming.

I stood there looking again and again, trying to imagine what kind of music each song's lyrics would be like. I did it practically every day for the time that separated me from my return to Italy. I tried to make sense of everything by putting all the elements I could take into consideration together. This was the most normal and frequent process I had of absorbing whatever information I was able to get about CSN: holding their records and studying every little detail.

At that moment I could not have known - nor would I have ever even surmised - that something would happen soon, that for me would prove to be as impressive a miracle as the one I had witnessed on the ground floor of Virgin that summer day: in December 1983 the first issue of *Wooden Nickel*, the Crosby Stills Nash & Young fanzine, was released.

The euphoria that the discovery of that treasure gave me is difficult to describe: suddenly out of nothingness there was news, previews, interviews, comments, explanations, analysis, reviews. All about them, about CSN then Young and everything connected to them in some way! It was like finding an oasis after walking in the desert. It was a crazy acceleration for my passion as a listener and as a reader. However, I did not understand how this was possible: who was behind *Wooden Nickel*? How did they get all that material? Who were these incredible characters who appeared to be so intimate with David Crosby, Graham Nash and Stephen Stills that they were almost suspected to be aliases? CSN themselves?

Those were great and pioneering times: *Wooden Nickel* was written on a typewriter, photocopied then stapled together, supported by the effort and passion and love of a group of young people who today - without emphasis and without rhetoric - can only be defined as heroes of the CSN world. There was no internet, there were no cell phones, there was no DVD, not everyone had a VHS player, or even a computer. Yet *Wooden Nickel* travelled unstoppable on a thrilling force of passion. Friendship often arises from passion, and today strong bonds have blossomed from it, the capacity for almost immediate understanding, almost fraternal proximity. Perhaps this is the treasure, the most important legacy of *Wooden Nickel*: everybody says 'music is love', after all.

Bio: *Umberto Martuscelli was born in Padua on 19 December 1961. A journalist by profession, he writes about men and horses, mainly in the monthly Cavallo magazine and for its website. He has published books about equestrian sports: the last two in chronological order a biographical novel and a photographic collection dedicated to brothers Piero and Raimondo d'Inzeo, icons of world showjumping. But he adds, 'I couldn't have done anything I do today if Stephen Stills and his music hadn't existed: everything else, musically speaking, comes after him.'*

Songs: *'Laughing' (C), 'Run from Tears' (S), 'Immigration Man' (N).*

THE HOLLIES AT TOWER RECORDS, NYC

by Roy Abrams

Working at the BBC in New York City during the summer of 1983, I received a phone call from my friend Ian, a drummer I had been working with since my teenage years. Ian informed me that Graham Nash was at Tower Records on West 4th Street, conducting an album signing session with his fellow Hollies. I immediately hung up, charged into my boss's office, and asked permission to leave a few minutes early. Receiving an affirmative reply, I hightailed it out of the office, down the elevator, and out into the impossibly warm, humid summer air of Manhattan, dressed in a three-piece suit, breaking into a run for the subway.

Reaching my destination a short time later, I eagerly entered Tower Records, went immediately to the giant promotional display case where *What Goes Around*, the new release from The Hollies, was packed to capacity. Grabbing a copy, I found my way to a line of a dozen or so people, each clutching a copy of the album, and waited my turn to approach the table where Graham Nash, Allan Clarke, Tony Hicks, and Bobby Elliott were sat side by side, patiently signing away while chatting with each and every individual.

Finally, it was my turn. I took a few steps toward Graham, who smiled, asked my name, signed my album along with a promotional poster, and remarked that I shared the same name as one of the band's assistants. I thanked him for being a musical inspiration, and stepped away from the table, watching the various conversations unfold as each new person met the group. Not long after, it was decided that the band needed a short break from the autograph session, upon which Graham invited those of us standing around to 'take a walk' through the store with him. Passing by a large promotional poster of Neil Young and the Shocking Pinks' *Everybody's Rockin'*, Nash stopped to gaze at it, smiled, shook his head, and said, 'Only Neil!'

I summoned the courage to inquire about David Crosby, who had recently been the cover feature of *People* magazine, revealing a man in the depths of drug addiction, drowning in despair, facing possible jail time. 'How's David doing?' I diffidently asked, to which Nash replied with his own question, 'How do you think he's doing? He's scared shitless!'

Bio: *A Long Island, New York-based educator, musician, and writer, Roy Abrams created and hosted the popular Island Zone radio show in the late '90s. He has written for several regional and national music publications and was a contributor to Crosby, Stills, Nash (and sometimes Young), the authorized biography (Gopher Publishers, 2002). His online column, Island Zone Update, features many conversations with CSN. The opportunity to maintain a 25-plus year dialogue with these three artists, whose music has been a foundational element of his life for 40-plus years, is one he deeply cherishes.*

Songs: *'Déjà Vu' (C), 'Black Queen' (S), 'Cathedral' (N).*

Aug. 30, 1983: Graham Nash and Allan Clarke, live with The Hollies at Pine Knob Music Theatre, Clarkston, Michigan, USA. Photo by Michael Curcuru

MR CROSBY, CAN I BOTHER YOU FOR A PHOTO?

by Christine Plumeri

Christine and Janine Plumeri with David Crosby. Photo by Randy Hylton

It was August 1984 and we had tickets for CSN at the Niagara Falls Convention Center in Niagara Falls, New York, my hometown. A good friend, Jen, worked the front desk at the Hilton across from the venue and couldn't contain herself, telling us the band was staying there. We all partied very heartily the night before, and she kept us updated regarding their arrival. We missed Stills' and Nash's buses, but she called us at 8am to tell us Crosby was coming any minute.

My sister, Janine, and I jumped out of bed, into pretty much the same clothes we wore the night before and bolted into the Hilton, leaving her Camaro double parked outside. We run in and Jen said, 'Any minute'. The bus pulled up shortly after, and in walked Crosby with then road manager, Randy Hilton. They walked right by us all, giggly, smiling, camera in hand, and Croz gave us a look like, 'Really? I just

September 3, 1984: CSN live at Pacific Amphitheatre, Costa Mesa, California, USA. Photos by Dan Birman

woke up …' then walked to the elevators. I was not going to miss this chance, so I said, 'Mr Crosby, you look like shit, but I can still take your picture, please?'

Well, he and Randy laughed, and Randy waved his arm, inviting Janine and I over, on to the elevator and up to Crosby's room. Needless to say, I almost peed myself, my sister punching my leg with excitement. We introduced ourselves and followed them into the room. I told David and Randy we only wanted a few pictures, that we already had tickets and were just true fans there for the music. We took a couple of pics and Randy left, saying he'd be back soon.

Croz kind of tested us, asking, 'So, what are some of your favorite songs?' My sister blurted out, 'Love the One You're With', 'Immigration Man' …, and changing clothes right in front of us, he threw his dirty shirt against the wall and barked, 'Those are Stills' and Nash's songs!' I went, 'Well, you haven't heard mine yet. I love 'Carry Me', 'Almost Cut My Hair' and …' He smiled, picked up the phone, and called Randy's room with this request, 'Hey, bring up my Martin.'

Randy came back with the most beautiful guitar I will ever hold in my life. We played, sang and talked. David indulged me with 'Carry Me', 'He Played Real Good for Free', other Joni songs, and so much more. We ended up getting four backstage passes and were invited to the soundcheck. We hanged on Crosby's bus before the soundcheck and dared to ask to edit the set-list. I chose 'Almost Cut My Hair' over 'Long Time Gone' and my friend chose 'Delta' over 'Guinnevere'.

After all these years, I'm still getting goosebumps typing this, remembering my special day-night-next-day dream come true.

FINDING CSN: HOW SNEAKING A CAMERA INTO A CONCERT CHANGED MY LIFE

by Dan Birman

I suppose writing about a moment in my life that's connected to Crosby, Stills, & Nash could come across as just a fan thing. But it isn't exactly. Oh, I'm a huge fan. But this story is about how music that rocketed in the 1960s inspired a generation to act, and how CSN's part in all that had an impact on my career.

Being born in the 1950s meant growing up in an era when everything was important, so much of it centering on a time of national uneasiness about politics and war, including an unpopular government that was driving all that. Perhaps the greatest outlet for young people back then, other than protests, was art – writing, painting, photography, and the greatest mass influencer, music.

A lot of music emerged that shot straight to the soul, and for me none was more relevant or important than the music of CSN. They just made sense. Between socially relevant lyrics, halting melodies, and meticulous harmonies, two things happened. I was inspired to learn their music (pretty sure playing guitar was a requisite for all youth in the 1960s) and do something to become a part of the discussion the band fuelled with their music.

The path I chose was driven in part by seeing CSN in concert, something I had the chance to do in the early 1980s. I was in my 20s when I saw them perform. Ideas that were already baking from music and lyrics playing on vinyl came to life when I saw the trio at a concert.

It was a very different experience seeing musicians perform live, their storytelling bigger on stage as they connect with the audience. This was a life changer for me because the issues they were singing about fed into my like-minded interests and inspired me to find my own brand of idealism.

Back then, I was studying documentary film in college, and I always had a Nikon camera attached to me, no matter where I went. Naturally I was going to bring my camera to the CSN concert, which meant sneaking it into the show. It was fairly easy to do that back then, despite the risk of being booted out of the venue.

Thankfully, everyone was on their feet during much of the performance. I was able to weave my way through the crowd to find good positions. I shot a roll or two until a guard found me and put a death grip on my shoulder. He promised to own my camera or wrap it around my head if I didn't put it away. He was a pretty big guy, so back into my camera bag it went. Later that night, I went to my dark room and processed the rolls of film, finding my best individual shots of David, Stephen and Graham, printing two sets of 11x14s, then going to bed around 3am.

It was pretty exciting having photos of my favorite band, the one that was causing me to think differently and about something other than self. I then decided it would be pretty cool to see if I could share my bootleg photos with them.

It wasn't so easy to find CSN to show them my photos. Google didn't exist, nor did the internet, or personal computers for that matter. I looked at the record albums to figure out how I might track them down. I started by making calls to the label. I reached an assistant to an assistant who aimed me in the right direction. She gave me a phone number to CSN's management offices.

This was becoming thrilling. I was starting to touch the music industry! One phone call to CSN's offices found me talking with a woman named Debbie Meister. My hope was to keep her from hanging up as I explained I had photos from last night's concert, which I had shot illegally.

She didn't hang up. Instead, Debbie listened to my story and was laughing when I told her what I went through to shoot the photos and end up with some prints. To my surprise she invited me to a place called Crossroads of the World in Hollywood, where CSN's management was housed at that time. Oh, and to bring my photos. I was scared to death. I'm pretty sure it was a combination of finding my way (Siri was not yet born) to their offices and being nervous that she might not like the photos. I thought they were good shots, but I was by no means a professional. I was a 20-something rookie, that's for sure.

Debbie took a look at the photos and proof sheets, then called Graham Nash. They agreed that I ought to be able to start shooting concerts for them. I think I was dizzy when she offered this up I didn't care that it wasn't for pay, this was an extraordinary offer.

So here was my opportunity – be at concerts not being shot by the classy, legendary rock photographer, Henry Diltz. Diltz was *the* guy. My greatest hope (in jest, of course) was that Henry would be on vacation, at a wedding, out of film, or something so I could shoot at the concerts he didn't attend. There I was roaming around before and during performances, being up close to the music – it didn't get any better than that.

I shot about a half-dozen concerts or more over the next few years. Graham was especially friendly. He made it his business to talk to me at each event. And later he invited me to meet him at a recording studio to show him proof sheets from various shoots. Graham is an accomplished photographer. I was thrilled when he asked for a bunch of my prints. Back to the dark room I went to create photographs that would become part of his collection.

Little did I know that any of this would come to the surface again. I was shocked to learn that my story might end up in a collection of many other such stories about the band. In preparing for this article, I went back to my disorganized boxes of slides and negatives and thought about how things might have been different had artists not bothered to be noisy about what was happening all around us. And I can't help but wonder who steps up next as we find ourselves in yet another volatile time when government and uneasiness is dominating the conversation.

Some of my greatest memories of these years are tied to their songs. I remember clicking away as David Crosby played 'Delta' during a soundcheck at the Concord Pavilion in Northern California. I was on stage, pulled up a chair and grabbed some shots as I sat right next to him. But the real imagery was that which I could see in my own mind from the lyrics and melody. It's a song that stops my heart to this day.

One of my more dramatic shots was of Stephen Stills. There was a moment at a concert at the Greek Theater in Los Angeles when he played 'Suite: Judy Blue Eyes'. I was backstage, and he sat on a monitor speaker and began to play the guitar solo. It was incredibly quiet in the audience, I suspect everyone was mesmerized and holding their breath as they listened to him play, almost as if there were two guitars and he was jamming with himself. It was an unbelievable moment.

The shot that somehow got away was of Graham Nash at the keyboard playing 'Cathedral'. The booming intro brought a reverent hush each time he played this. The group stopped to question everything about war, politics and love, but Graham took this a step farther as he wrestled with religion and morality in the face of war. I saw him perform this at several concerts. The intensity of the song and the harmonies with those lyrics caused a great stir for me and for the audience at a time when we were all looking for perspective.

Perspective through music remains their greatest legacy in my view. Decades later I remain nearly as idealistic as I was then. We who were fortunate to grow up with their music probably treated people a little nicer, cared a lot more about politics and ending war, worked harder to protect the environment because it mattered, did things to make our voices heard a little louder, and focused on hope, dreams, and the beauty of life. I miss this. Now, cynicism is eroding much of what their music and the music of so many other bands from that era stood for.

I have stopped trying to sneak cameras into concerts (mostly), but fight pretty hard to still grab images of things that matter. It is all part of being a storyteller that I set out to be after finding CSN.

Bio: *Dan Birman is a documentary producer in Los Angeles and a Professor of Professional Practice at the USC Annenberg School of Journalism, where he teaches documentary to budding journalists. Birman's company has produced for many networks but is perhaps best known for having made a documentary that exposed deep social issues surrounding a young girl who committed murder in Tennessee. They are now producing a follow-on feature documentary that they hope will help pressure America into rethinking many of its archaic laws centering on juvenile justice.*

Songs: *'Guinnevere' (C) – 'One of the greatest songs, a mastery of guitar playing, haunting melody, harmony, and lyrics. But then 'Long Time Gone' was the poignant side of Crosby, reminding us that the need for activism is enduring, and the cost if we do not stand up is freedom.'*
'Suite: Judy Blue Eyes' (S) – 'The recounting of the struggle of love and the merging of three different songs into one. The energy is on fire, the harmonies are classic. But it is a toss-up with 'For What It's Worth.' Stills managed to modify the ending of that song several times to meet the political now.'
'Chicago' (N) – 'This is one of those in-your-face activism songs that underscored the possibility that we can all make a difference if we choose to do so. 'Simple Man,' on the other hand, is a song that speaks about being humble about love and not taking relationships for granted. And 'Wind on the Water' was insanely relevant to me because I became interested in environmental issues as a child after reading a book about whales. Sorry - had to list three!'

September 3, 1984: CSN live at Pacific Amphitheatre, Costa Mesa, California, USA. Photos by Dan Birman

David Crosby scuba diving. Photo by Dana Africa

July 15, 1980: Richie Havens, Stephen Stills, Angelo Branduardi before "La Carovana del Mediterraneo" concert at Stadio San Siro, Milan, Italy. Photo by Guido Harari

January 17, 1982: Graham Nash during an interview at Rudy Records, Los Angeles, California, USA. Photo by Lisa Law

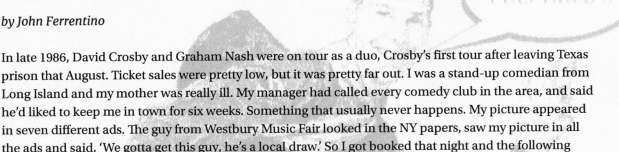

TWENTY-FOUR FIREBALLS

by John Ferrentino

In late 1986, David Crosby and Graham Nash were on tour as a duo, Crosby's first tour after leaving Texas prison that August. Ticket sales were pretty low, but it was pretty far out. I was a stand-up comedian from Long Island and my mother was really ill. My manager had called every comedy club in the area, and said he'd liked to keep me in town for six weeks. Something that usually never happens. My picture appeared in seven different ads. The guy from Westbury Music Fair looked in the NY papers, saw my picture in all the ads and said, 'We gotta get this guy, he's a local draw.' So I got booked that night and the following night in Valley Forge Music Fair, Philadelphia. My manager said, 'This is a win-win for you. Crosby & Nash will sell out and he will think it's you.'

The night after the gig at Westbury, I rented this car with a buddy to go down to Philadelphia and on the way down the car broke down, over-heated. There were no cell phones in those days, and I was trying to get to the theatre. I didn't know how to get there. It was just a mess. A police car pulled over and I offered them $500 to take me there, which they wouldn't do but one of the police guys said, 'I can make a call for you, Sir', so I was waiting for assistance.

At last, I was able to make it there and showed up to the theatre around eight o'clock. The show was supposed to start then, and I was promptly told by the manager of the theatre I wasn't able to go on. David Crosby said, 'Why can't he go on?' They replied, 'Well, you can't go on union rules. Shows have to be done by a certain time.' David suggested, 'So what if we just don't take an intermission? Let the funny fuckin' guy go on,' and adding, 'Let me talk to Graham.' So, he came out going, 'Graham says it's fine. Let him go on and he can introduce us.' A guy from the theatre picked up a walkie-talkie, saying: 'Comedian going on' and from the middle of nowhere I heard my name in a big announcement. All my equipment, everything from my act, was still in the car. Luckily a buddy of mine said, 'Just go. I'll get the stuff out on stage.'

So I go out there and just kind of talk to the crowd, tell them how I broke down and all of this. I had not even seen the room. I didn't have any idea what the room looked like, because it was dark when I walked out, but it was exactly like Westbury Music Fair where I worked the night before, except there was no apron around the stage.

I got to the point where I did a trick when I pushed a sword through a woman's neck. And this woman comes up on stage in a floppy hat and sits on a barstool and I give her like a little stick in the back of the neck, and with that she pees in her pants on stage. She's sitting on the barstool just peeing. Now I'm horrified. I don't know what to do. But everyone sees it and everyone's laughing. I'm making jokes about it, rolling up my pant legs, and of course she wet breakage isle number three.

I'm just figuring, 'This is going to be the worst experience of my life. There's no way they want me to work with them anymore.' I say goodnight and I walk off stage. When I got backstage, David was laying on a couch, crying laughing, and just looked at me and stood up and said, 'Anyone that can make a woman pee in her pants after the day you had, I want as my opening act.' And that's how I worked with them for years after that.

They asked me to open some CSN dates in January 1987 and asked me to meet them at Atlantic City, and then they went to Daytona Beach and from there to Ruth Eckerd Hall, Clearwater, Florida. I was kind of driving there by myself. By the third day, Graham Nash said, 'How you get around?' I said, 'Well, I rented a car and I'm driving.' He said, 'Why don't you just ride the bus with me and David?' You know, I got to Woodstock to see them, so I was blown away!

I started riding in the bus with them. It was me, David, Graham and Mac Holbert. It was lotta fun. We were just making fun of everybody. I had *Spinal Tap* on DVD with me, and we ended up watching it every single night. They had never seen the movie and never heard of it. I was having really good shows.

We got to Philadelphia and it was a 1,500-seat theatre. I invited everybody I knew to Philadelphia from Long Island to see me opening for a big rock band and when I get there it's a small old movie theater, 1,500-seat rock'n'roll Hell hole, a local DJ coming out and going, 'You like Crosby, Stills & Nash?' People screamed. 'All right. Here's a comedian!' I walked out on stage and it's just death. The entire time I'm doing my act, they are pounding on the floor, 'C – S – N! C – S – N!'. So I go, 'Look I was supposed to do 20 minutes, but you keep up this noise and I can do 30.'

They booed, and it was horrible. So now I know what to get. I must be fired. And I walk off stage and really, I thought like I got hit with a 2x4. My ex-wife was in the audience, going, 'Oh my God, I hope he doesn't think he did well tonight.'

I walked off stage and David walked out to me and just gave me this big bear hug, looks me in the eyes and goes, 'Man, they fuckin' hated you! Really, they fuckin' hated you.' And he started laughing and walked away towards the stage. And I'm thinking, 'I'm fired' or whatever. I got into my dressing room and Graham came in and said, 'I hurt for you as an artist. At this point in your career, you should never have to go through this. From now on I'm gonna come out every night to introduce you.' So after that he would come out every night. We'd be in Washington DC, and he'd say 'Hey! We're here in Washington, DC. We love Washington, DC. Every time we start a tour we say, 'Make sure Washington, DC is on the list.' And while he's talking, the audience is filling up time-lapse photography and all of a sudden, he goes, 'We're not quite ready to come out but right before we come out, we're gonna bring out a good buddy of ours, a guy we thought was so innovative we figured he will be in the first part of our show. So, let's have a big round of applause for John Ferrentino!'. And I walked out and the audience would just look at me and say, 'This guy actually knows them!'. The shows were always great after that.

There were so many fun things on the tour. There was the time David brought his motorcycle, this new Harley, in the back of the truck with the equipment. He went to stop and the brakes didn't stop. We had to lay his bike down through an intersection. He had screwed up his elbow pretty bad. They built a wooden box, and the roadies would lift his foot up onto the box and prep his arm onto his knees, so he

could still play. A week before the accident, I went to a magic store to pick up some supplies and Crosby came with me. There were these four-barrel match-paper shooters with a flash paper in it and a little trigger shot like a fireball out. David said, 'That's the coolest thing I've ever seen. How many do you have?' The guy goes, 'I have six.' So he goes, 'I'll buy all six!'. We bought all the flash-papers he had. Two nights later, Graham is on stage, getting ready to sing and I can see all the roadies laughing and knew something was up. I just watched

February 6th, 1987: Greenpeace Benefit - CSNY live at Arlington Theatre, Santa Barbara, California, USA. Photo by John Ferrentino

and Graham sat up at the piano and started singing 'Our House' and goes, 'I'll light the fire', and like 24 fireballs whizz over his head and Crosby just laughed his ass off.

About three nights after David's bike accident, when they brought the wooden box out, Graham had covered the top of the box with superglue and glued his foot to the box. So, he had his boat shoes that we stuck on the box and at the end of his set he went to lift off and it was glued to the box, and he just turned from stage and said, 'Fuck you, Ferrentino!' I had nothing to do with it but got blamed for everything. Their manager at the time, Bill Siddons, told me basically the reason I was on tour with them was to keep them laughing in the bus.

There were a lot of good times. I worked with a lot of groups, but they were the nicest people I ever worked with.

Bio: *There is a great deal of magic involved with comedy and there is a lot of good comedy involved in magic. In the case of John Ferrentino, that statement can be taken literally. The New York born and bred comedian has long been one of the most innovative forces on both the comedy and magic scenes. He has performed on over 80 television shows, on HBO, Showtime, A&E, and Fox, working with Jay Leno, Eddie Murphy, and Crosby, Stills, Nash & Young.*

May 1987: David Crosby and Jan Dance at their wedding. Photo by John Ferrentino

128

Atlantic Records promo poster courtesy of CSN&Y Archives and Scott V. Oxman, Director

SUMMER TOUR 1988

David Crosby
Christopher
Cross
VALLE

CROSBY STILLS
NASH
TOUR 1987

7

CROSBY·S
NASH
Chicago
WORKING
PROMOTE

ALL ACCESS PASS

An Evening of Acoustic Music with
David Crosby
Graham Nash

VIP 9/19

CROSBY
GN
9/10

MOTHER
International
Documentary

CRO
STIL
NA

CROSBY STILLS NASH & YOUNG
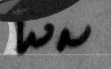
GUEST
AFTER SHOW

RECE

WN 15

Stil
Collin

STAFF

CROSBY, STILLS & NASH

An Evening of Acoustic Music with
David Crosby
Graham Nash

VIP
STG

Crosby Stills Nash
SPECIAL GUEST

ACOUSTIC
TOUR

AS

UNPLUGGED

MTV
MUSIC TELEVISION

CSN

FRIENDS OF THE
DREAM FOUNDATION
AN EVENING OF MUSIC
HONORING
JAN & DAVID CROSBY

September 28
Santa Monica
Civic

ALL ACCESS

CROSBY
STILLS
& NASH

2014
ALL ACCESS

ONES
and for
ography

BY
S
LS
SH

ION

CROSBY · STILLS

BEACON
THEATRE
OCT. 16TH-22ND 2012

NASH

CENTERSTAGE

PRESENTS

Stephen Stills

PREMIER EVENT
NOVEMBER 15, 2001

CREW

Belterra
CASINO & RESORT

GUEST
4/3

VIP

THE FILLMORE

STEPHEN STILLS

3-18

Crosby Stills & Nash

UNION CREW

CROSBY, STILLS & NASH
ER SHOW
MER TOUR 1988

Pierced Arrow Tour
VIP

Stephen Stills · Barry Goldberg
Kenny Wayne Shepherd

IN CONCERTO
David Crosby

VIP

Stills &
Collins

THE CSN&Y ARCHIVES PROUDLY PRESENTS

by Scott V. Oxman

Over the past 50 years, I have had the privilege to collect artwork and other memorabilia exclusive to Crosby, Stills, Nash & Young, and Buffalo Springfield - individually and collectively. I have had more than my share of fun, enjoying a musical journey with great friends and unforgettable experiences, while enjoying their acoustic songs, soaring harmonies, unmistakable guitar prowess and tone, beautiful

May 1987: Chris Hillman, Gerry Tolman, Ken Weiss, David Crosby at David's bachelor party. Photo by Henry Diltz, courtesy of Ken Weiss from his personal collection

artwork and stories. Here's one memory I will never forget...

In July 1987, CSN's business manager Gerry Tolman - aware of my CSN&Y Archives through my dear friend Dave Zimmer - called and asked if I would be interested in decorating the Irvine Meadows Amphitheater Green Room in Irvine, California in support of their upcoming concert on 8 August 1987. I delightedly accepted.

Along with Dave Zimmer, my friends Ray, Shirley and their son Brian Piantanida selflessly worked all day assisting me decorate the Green Room. The room consisted of five smaller partitioned areas. I decided to dedicate each area to Crosby, Stills & Nash, Neil Young (as always, rumored to be showing up) and CSN/CSN&Y/Buffalo Springfield. About 80 archival pieces were prominently displayed throughout the room, including rare posters, an acetate of CSN's first album with 'Suite: Judy Blue Eyes' listed as 'Suite J', numerous 45rpm picture sleeves, photographs, alternative album cover artwork, and other obscure collectables.

The CSN&Y area included my treasured Henry Diltz poster-sized photograph of CSN's legendary first album cover, using an amazing alternative photograph. Henry had so kindly written on it in large lettering, 'Scott Oxman, Director of the Crosby, Stills, Nash and Young Archives'. Henry was at the concert and generously made the one-off poster just for me. We both smiled the entire time we observed it together.

Just after the 4:30pm soundcheck, one-by-one entered Tolman, then Nash, then Crosby, and finally Stills. Crosby has his infectious smile while viewing his artwork. He said to me that he would someday love to trade some of his memorabilia for some of mine. I said I would like that very much, but nothing ever came of it.

August 8, 1987: Graham Nash and Scott V. Oxman at Irvine Meadows Amphitheater Green Room, Irvine, California, USA. Photo from Scott V. Oxman personal collection

When Nash entered his area, he said, 'Scotty, my man, thank you for keeping the feelin' alive!' I felt his sincerity. Then Stills sauntered in. He walked past Crosby's area with his usual intensity and a half-smile on his face, not knowing what was around the corner. Then he walked past Nash's area, came around the corner and saw his area, including early Buffalo Springfield and CSN&Y memorabilia. His eyes flashed as he observed two large, rare, Atlantic Records posters on the Green Room wall. One with Stephen onstage with Buffalo Springfield playing a Gretsch electric while singing into a red microphone, the second was Stephen standing aside a beautiful, bridled horse. Now pointing at himself in the first poster, he jubilantly exclaimed, 'I still have that shirt!' While pointing to the second poster he said, 'That is one rare poster!'

I humbly asked Stephen if he would sign it in gold to memorialize the concert and Green Room event. He said the unexpected, 'Scott, I would be happy to sign it, but I want to do it justice. Let me warm up first!' He took a large piece of cardboard and began noodling his signature all over the cardboard in his distinct calligraphy-styled signature with very large cursive lettering. Like a confident first violinist warming up, he began practising his signature and after several minutes said to me, 'OK, I'm ready!' He then meticulously signed the poster, smiled, and said, 'This will be worth something someday.' I thanked Stephen for stopping by, sharing his experiences and signing the poster.

The trio then headed to the stage. The concert was unforgettable, as usual. During the last song before intermission, I was backstage enjoying a wonderful performance when I suddenly heard a crashing sound back in the Green Room. I raced to the room to find a piece had been stolen off one of the walls - my precious, signed Henry Diltz photograph. Even though the piece has never resurfaced, this story still ends well.

The good news is that as a result of the Irvine Meadows Green Room display and the quality of the presentation, I was invited by Gerry Tolman, Yves Beauvais, colleague of Ahmet Ertegun of Atlantic Records, and Joel Bernstein, official CSN&Y music archivist, photographer and guitarist, to provide all the memorabilia for the forthcoming Crosby, Stills & Nash boxset.

Once that project was completed, Bill Graham Presents invited me to decorate the foyer of the Warfield Theater, San Francisco during CSN's famed, recorded week-long acoustic concert series in November 1991 in support of their new boxset. I was invited by Graham Nash to stay on his floor of the Pan Pacific Hotel and given access to drive in the hotel's Rolls Royce. Sadly, Bill Graham died in a tragic helicopter accident several weeks prior to the concert series and I never had the chance to thank him for framing, hanging and displaying my collection.

Bio: *Born in Montgomery, Alabama and raised in Southern California, Scott V. Oxman received a B.Sc. Degree in 'Health Science and Safety' from SDSU and has spent his entire career in the safety field. In 1972, he established the CSN&Y Archives, long before the archives concept had been made popular, and has enjoyed many resulting friendships, including with CSN&Y individually and collectively; Francesco Lucarelli; Joel Bernstein; Dave Zimmer; Henry Diltz, and Michael Thomas. Asked to provide memorabilia for the epic 1991 Crosby Stills and Nash boxset and forthcoming Neil Young Archives project, he has never sought compensation because he felt that 'as soon as money was involved, the art would lose its lustre. The value of that collection was in its memories and experiences.' He stopped collecting and saving CSN&Y memorabilia in the late-1990s but 'will long treasure their music, harmonies, tone and images. I still enjoy using my guitar and turntable to play their acoustic wooden music. Their songs shaped a generation and I believe their harmonies and guitar prowess will continue to inspire creativity and musical passion for generations to come.'*

Songs: *'Almost Cut My Hair' (C); 'Johnny's Garden' (S), tied with 'Helplessly Hoping'; 'Teach Your Children' (N).*

SAILING ON THE RAGLAND

by John Partipilo

It was February 1988 and I was at Neil Young's ranch, where Crosby, Stills, Nash & Young were recording songs for a new project, which would be later released with the title *American Dream*. It was the first time CSN&Y had reunited in studio in a long time.

I was mostly working with David Crosby at the time. As a matter of fact, it was the first circumstance that I had worked with all four of them since I started collaborating with them in the late Seventies. At the ranch, everyone had their own room - mine was in the main bunkhouse – and each room had a fireplace, and we all had meals prepared for us daily.

Niko Bolas was recording the album in a sound-truck outside the studio and the goats kept chewing on the cables, causing problems with some of the equipment. I remember it was a Saturday and we had been working pretty hard during the week. I was hanging out with Joe Vitale that morning, when Neil showed up and said, 'We're going sailing on the Ragland. Why don't you come along and bring your camera?' Neil and David were on the boat that day, Graham and Stephen off doing other things.

Me and several CSN&Y crew members went along. I was the only one with a camera and got some wonderful classic photographs of Neil and David. We spent most of the day on the sailboat. Crosby told me that the Ragland used to haul lumber from Japan to California before Neil obtained it.

It was the first time I had ever been on a sailing boat. Neil was a good sailor, and so was Crosby. Neil put us to work, and we actually helped and learned about sailing. I am not sure where we actually went, because I couldn't see much land, but it was a nice cruise and definitely one of the most wonderful, memorable days I spent on that project.

February 1988: Neil Young and David Crosby on W.N. Ragland, Neil's 101-foot schooner. Photo by John Partipilo

Bio: *John Partipilo is an international award-winning photojournalist and fine art photographer. Working as a photojournalist for 40 years, Partipilo has won numerous awards, including National Press Photographers' Association (NPPA) Best of Photojournalism for his essay on gangs in Tennessee. He is also a two-time Pulitzer nominee and finalist for his work on the 2010 Nashville flood. His photography has been featured in national and international publications, including The New York Times, Time Life, and Newsweek; on books; and on album covers.*

PRISON SONG

by Francesco Lucarelli

There are artists who speak to our hearts with a brush stroke, with a verse, with a guitar riff. There are songs to which a moment of our life remains glued forever, a memory as vivid as a photograph. After all, every music lover has at least one reason to be grateful to the artist they love. Me and my friends Mauro and Lorenzo have a very unique one.

Summer 1988. East Coast of the United States. We are here to follow some Crosby, Stills & Nash tour dates. For some years now, I have been running *Wooden Nickel*, a fanzine on CSN&Y, with the help of Mauro and Stefano. Thanks to this magazine, we met Lorenzo and many other fans, in Italy and around the world.

The fanzine, in addition to being a precious news channel at a time when CSN were no longer fashionable, has proved to be a fantastic catalyst for passion and friendships.

'Music is love,' sings David Crosby. For us it is exactly like that. CSN's music has a value that surpasses the artistic one and projects us into a world where those songs become the soundtrack of a journey along the human highway. Those songs that gave us personal pleasure, skin and soul at the same time, speaking to our minds and hearts as teenagers, have increased their power over time: not only a tool for growth but also a way to meet people that we probably would never have met. It is an immense value.

Wooden Nickel, written both in Italian and English, also has another merit, far from secondary: it managed to open the doors of the CSN management to us. Debbie Meister, right-hand of Bill Siddons - manager of CSN, helped us collect information about their concerts and, when we planned to attend a few shows on the East Coast, she organized a meeting with our heroes on 6 August at the Jones Beach Theater, a beautiful outdoor amphitheater on Long Island, the stage right on the seafront. We get to the venue with our friend Lorraine, one of the WN 'foreign correspondents', who over the years has sent us news, concert reviews and a lot of printed material.

We are in front of the gates, excited and waiting for backstage passes. From the box office, they call backstage and put us through to a member of the band's staff: 'Wait for the end of the show. We will send you the passes later. Anxiety. At least we managed to let them know we are here.

The concert is splendid, a dream. 'Wooden Ships', with the suggestive and appropriate setting of the boats anchored in the waters of Zach's Bay, closes the first set with an amazing duel of guitar and Hammond B-3 organ between Stills and Mike Finnigan. The second set brings the surprises: 'Try to Find Me', 'Nighttime for the Generals', 'That Girl, Monkey and the Underdog'. The boys are alive and well. The party ends with 'Teach Your Children' but for us the best is yet to come.

August 1988: the "Crazy Italians" (Francesco Lucarelli, Lorenzo Conci and Mauro Coscia) with CSN on the East Coast. Photos by Francesco Lucarelli, Mauro Coscia, Lorraine Kaczorowski

Somehow, we manage to retrieve the passes and finally what seems to us to be the gates of Heaven open. The first person we meet is Jan Dance, David Crosby's wife. We introduce ourselves; we tell her we come from Italy, show her *Wooden Nickel*. She immediately gets Crosby's attention, who arrives looking at us from head to toe. 'From Italy? Just to see our concerts? ' David looks at us with the incredulous and at the same time amused expression of someone who thinks he is dealing with a group of nutters. 'You must be really crazy!' and greets us and gives us an appointment for the following days. In the blink of an eye, everyone at CSN camp knows us as the Crazy Italians. We try to get Stills' attention, who is coming our way with a cowboy walk and a serious look, but Stephen doesn't even seem to see us and disappears behind a door. Meanwhile it starts to rain. A light summer drizzle. Not far from us, we spot a group of people. They are all around Nash, who holds an umbrella to shelter a girl in a wheelchair with whom he poses for a souvenir photo. That image is enough to make us understand who Graham is.

We approach and introduce ourselves. Nash meets *Wooden Nickel*! He is amazed and happy to meet us. When he hears that we are there to attend six CSN concerts, he wastes no time: he calls Mac Holbert, the tour manager, telling him to make sure tickets and passes are available to us for all the shows we will attend. He adds that, before we leave, he wants to find a moment for an intimate photo session to immortalize the meeting between CSN and *Wooden Nickel*.

On 8 August 1988 in Manhattan, in scorching heat, we meet Nash at the Grand Bay Hotel, on Seventh Avenue, at the intersection with 51st Street. He had promised us an interview and we can't wait. We meet in the lobby and sit on sofas for our chat. We have a fondness for lesser known and unreleased songs and start talking about them. Graham is very helpful and, above all, has an excellent memory. He remembers songs he played live only once, or when and where he wrote them. 'Love is the Reason'? Seattle, 1982. Only performance.' We also ask him about 'Other Side of Town'. He played it in Philadelphia on the 1978 tour. 'Yes, that's right. Only time I played it. But how do you know about these songs, which we performed in concert only once?' He laughs, amused and probably happy not to be in front of someone asking him for the millionth time about Woodstock.

We talk a little about everything, including personal matters. Lorenzo's wife is expecting her first child. Graham talks to us about his family but, typical of this extraordinary man, at the same time he does not give up thinking about others. 'Having children is one of the greatest gifts I've ever had. Knowing I'm healthy makes me feel lucky. When I look around and see people who are not well, I feel a deep compassion. I always think about it when I'm on stage. We should never take for granted how normal it seems to us. Walking, running, playing … We should remember every day how lucky we are. '

Meanwhile, Jan and David Crosby come out of one of the elevators and are heading outside. 'Where are you going?' Graham asks. 'We'll take a stroll and look for a restaurant,' says David. Nash knows one not too far and suggests it, adding, 'As soon as I'm done here, I'll pop into a music shop. I'm looking for a songbook by Simon & Garfunkel. Tonight, I want to sing 'America', if I find the score to review it.' Then he turns to us. 'Can you play it? Yup? Then let's go up to my room.'

Lorenzo knows all the chords and starts showing him them, but we don't remember the complete set of lyrics. 'I'll try to ask Joel. He certainly could fax me the full lyrics. That's Joel Bernstein, photographer and personal friend of Nash. At that moment, however, he is in Europe with Prince for the *Lovesexy* tour. No luck. Graham wants to get those lyrics. A few days earlier, I had been to Colony in Times Square, a fantastic shop specializing in sheet music. There were thousands of them, of all kinds: from classical music to rock, single songs or entire albums. I am pretty sure it would be the perfect place to find it. I suggest it to Graham, and we set off.

Colony does not disappoint us, and Graham finds what he needs. He is satisfied and wants to go back to the hotel to practise the song. We will complete the interview in the following days. 'See you tonight after the show!' says Graham.

We collect our rental car and move to New Jersey. Tonight's show is at Brendan Byrne Arena or, as it is more familiarly known, 'The Meadowlands' in East Rutherford, a few miles in front of Manhattan across the Hudson River.

We arrive at the parking lot of the arena well in advance and decide to promote *Wooden Nickel*, exhibiting some copies near one of the entrances. Alas, we don't know that strict rules apply here. Without permission, nothing can be done. Some security guys seize copies of the fanzine from us and invite us to follow them. We arrive in a booth, where they ask us for documents and photograph us, front and profile. After being identified, filed and scolded, we can go back to our car. We abandon the promotional ambition and get ready for the concert.

The Meadowlands is a huge arena for sport and musical events, with a capacity of around 20,000 seats. Tonight, it is almost sold out and, from one of the rings where we have our seats, the view is magnificent. Nash delivers a beautiful rendition of 'America', that he rehearsed only a few hours ago, and when he starts to sing, 'Counting the cars on the New Jersey turnpike' the audience erupt into a thunderous roar. I have another vivid memory of the concert, when Stills remains alone on stage for a couple of solo songs. Lights go down and everything is dark, except for a huge bull's eye projecting a white beam light, center stage. Stephen grabs a Martin and throws himself into a possessed version of 'Word Game'. He spits out words as if he were firing a machine gun. His fingers fly on the fretboard. The audience watches in awe. Some 20,000 people hold their breath, hostages to a man and his guitar. A breathtaking performance. At the end of the concert, backstage - the most beautiful and best equipped of those we will visit - Stills is visibly satisfied. We are close to New York, so tonight there are many people, many friends who have come to visit them, and we only have time for a short greeting.

On 10 August we are in Philadelphia for the first of two shows at the Mann Music Center, summer home of the Philadelphia Orchestra, a 15,000-seat semi-covered amphitheater in the greenery of Fairmount Park. We are ready for a new dose of emotions. The band, including Joe Vitale, Bob Glaub, Mike Finnigan and Joe Lala, is in great shape. Stills complains about the humid heat, really unbearable, and asks that a fan be placed on his side of the stage to find some relief from the sticky air.

The concert is beautiful but without any particular surprises. When finished, we hurry backstage for a quick goodbye. We have a couple of hours by car ahead of us, our destination the surroundings of Baltimore, to the house of Cathi Henn, another CSN fan and reader of our magazine, who kindly offered to put us up. We meet a hippie couple with a very small Woodstock t-shirt. 'It shrunk after so many washes,' they say and want to have it signed by CSN. Suddenly, a roadie approaches us and, in a peremptory tone, invites us to follow him on Stephen Stills' tour bus: 'Mr Stills wants to meet you! You, the Crazy Italians. At last!' he says, amused to see these guys coming from Italy just for their shows.

On the morning of 11 August, we are on Interstate 95. Tonight, Crosby, Stills & Nash will play the second of two dates at the Mann Music Center. We still carry the emotions of the previous days but today is a special day. So far, we have had the opportunity to spend a lot of time with Graham, a little bit with Stephen, but still nothing

August 10, 1988: David Crosby with his bike, backstage at Mann Music Center, Philadelphia, Pennsylvania, USA. Photo by Mauro Coscia

with David. The previous night he told us to be at his hotel in Philadelphia at 11am. 'I'll make time for you.' It is clear this will be a special day and we are excited, impatient for a meeting that goes beyond our wildest dreams.

When we realize we are still far from the Philly, we begin to speed up. Mauro is driving and we do not want to be late. Not today. When the speedometer reaches 95 miles per hour, we suggest to Mauro to slow down. He laughs, amused, happy to try to get us there on time.

Suddenly, we hear police sirens but don't see any police cars. We realize that - as in the most classic American movies - we are being chased not by one but by four police cars. They quickly reach us and pull us to the side of the road. A couple of cabinet-sized Highway Patrolmen come out of the cars, shouting. Intimidated, we show our ID. Adrenaline rush. We try to minimize our behavior with trivial excuses but are severely cautioned. There is little to joke about. They keep saying they had seen a lot of people come to a bad end when driving at the speed we were going. They are inflexible: they tell us we have to pay a very high fine and follow them to the police headquarters for the administrative procedure.

They escort Mauro into one of their cars. Lorenzo and I have to follow that car, escorted by another car. At the police station, Mauro is invited to take a seat on a bench, next to a couple of scary-looking thugs with chains around their ankles. The biceps are as big as Mauro's thigh, which definitely isn't thin. The officers who stopped us talk to the officials and fill out documents. After a while we are invited to a counter: 'There's a $255 fine. If you can't pay now, he stays here.' They point to Mauro, who in the meantime has bleached.

We have barely $100, and a few traveller's cheques we have in our wallets are not accepted as payment. We notice a sign where it says payments can also be made by credit card. Lorenzo and I don't have any cards, but Mauro started working at Diners Club a few weeks previously. We breathe a sigh of relief, especially Mauro, who approaches the counter, pleased to be able to get out of this nasty mess with his new piece of plastic. He opens his wallet, takes it out and asks, 'Do you accept this?' 'Everything but Diners', the employee replies, aseptically. Panic!

Mauro is increasingly pale. They allow us to see if we have anything in the car. We open the trunk, rummage in the suitcases, in the pockets of the jackets. We also collect the loose change scattered in the storage compartments of the car. By putting together all the cash and coins we find, we are able to pay the fine, $255, definitely not a small amount of money.

In the meantime, we have lost more than an hour which, added to the delay accumulated previously, rules out the appointment with Crosby. We call him at the hotel to notify him. I talk to Jan. She asks if we're okay and calms us down, saying we can meet David in the afternoon at the Mann Music Center.

We get into the car and resume our journey. We turn on the radio to look for some good music to cheer us up. Suddenly, we hear the familiar voice of Nash. It sounds like a live interview. FM station 93.3 WMMR in Philadelphia. It's DJ Pierre Robert's radio show and there's Stills in the studio, too. In silence, we continue to listen to the interview. At one point, Pierre asks a question. We seem to have not understood well but then Stills and Nash start talking ... about us! Even on the radio they affectionately call us the 'Crazy Italians', and they still can't understand why we came all the way from Italy just to attend their concerts. This moment of radio 'glory' brings a smile back to our faces.

When we enter the CSN hotel in Philly, it seems that everyone already knew what happened to us. Musicians and crew guys greet us, ask us what happened, pat us on the back. The news spread like wildfire, everyone taking the episode to heart.

In the hall we meet Nash, fresh from the radio interview. In the meantime, he had heard about our misadventure too. Having no other commitments, he invites us up to his room to talk about the concert the previous evening and continue the interview that began in New York. It feels like Graham has taken us under his wing, as if he wants everything to go well on our journey. We spend a couple of hours together, which helps us get rid of the stress of the morning. He asks what we think of his version of 'America', which he has now included in the set after presenting it at Meadowlands. Lorenzo loves it but tells Graham he played the wrong chord the night before. Graham smiles and says he thinks he did it right. 'Shall we bet a beer?' asks Lorenzo, jokingly. Nash doesn't know we recorded the concerts and have evidence.

It's almost soundcheck time. We follow the band's tour buses through the streets of Philadelphia to the Mann Music Center. We have the chance to watch the entire soundcheck, photograph Crosby riding his Harley-Davidson, and be guests on his tour bus to listen to a preview of his beautiful new album, *Oh Yes I Can*, due to be released several months later in early 1989. David is eager to play the record for us. He invites us to sit comfortably, inserts an audio cassette into the hi-fi system of the coach and, when the music starts, he too sits and watches us. After a day full of emotions, 'Tracks in the Dust' and 'Distances' definitely knocks us out with its acoustic, rarefied splendor. They are certainly among the most beautiful things Crosby has ever recorded. He gloats, proud and pleased, at the expressions of wonder painted on our faces. Then it's time to take the stage.

By now we know the set-list quite well, which usually unfolds without surprises until the acoustic set. After Crosby, with the recent and unreleased song 'Compass', it is Nash's turn. He begins his solo set talking about some fans who have come from far away to attend some CSN shows, and that a few hours before the concert they had a little mishap with the Maryland traffic police. We look at each other in disbelief and a second later he dedicates 'Prison Song' tov us, a song rarely performed live and never played during that tour, except that night.

The girls sitting next to us, whom we had made friends with before the show begin, shouting 'These guys! These guys!', pointing us out to the band and the rest of the audience. We are petrified by emotion. This man is incredible, as incredible as his passion, his humanity, his compassion, his generosity. There was no need for that public dedication but probably Graham wanted to exorcise our morning adventure in his own way.

The concert ends with a rousing version of 'Carry On', followed by the inevitable collective chorus of 'Teach Your Children'. As the audience starts walking home, we show our passes and head backstage. David, Graham and Stephen hang out with fans and friends who are gathered in the room. Then a curfew is called. 'Time to close!' Everyone is accompanied to the exit, while we are invited to move to another room, near the area where the trucks with the equipment are loaded.

We are dumbfounded. There's the complete CSN crew lined up in front of us: the manager, the musicians, the technicians, the roadies, the drivers. Nobody is missing. Graham has an envelope in his hands and invites us to come over. He hands it to me, saying: 'We heard what happened to you today. We are very sorry and thought about making a collection. Here's $250. The five bucks missing will remind you not to speed next time.'

Bio: *Roman, Capricorn, dreamer, traveller. Natural light photography, EEEEBE, blue, sea, football, red wine, Crazy Horse, friends, harmony vocals, AS Roma, kindness, curry, knowledge, strong passions, California, ginger, Rawstars, wildlife, guitars, Moon, freedom, apricots, respect.*
Rod says blondes have more fun, but I love my brunette.

Songs: *'Laughing' (C); 'Suite: Judy Blue Eyes' (S); 'Wind on the Water' (N).*

VINTAGE WINE

by Shirly Ambrose

Over 20 years ago, Graham Nash arrived at our Yukon regional airport with bags, a family of four, and four friends. They left for a wilderness camp about 50 miles south on Nares Lake. A beautiful little camp vista surrounded by a mass of poplar and evergreens at the base of a rugged mountain called Nares. Most of the summer canoes would be dotting the shorelines and animal bone mobiles swinging from the trees.

June 21, 1989: Graham Nash and Shirly Ambrose at Nares Lake, Yukon, Canada. Photos courtesy of Ambrose Arts

In reality, it was the camp of a common occultist, promoting himself as a wilderness guru, and his campaign was relentless. This is where Dick Person entertained them for 17 days with yogurt, yoga, tepee, and talk. And a whole lot of inka thrown in to replace coffee. It was a unique experience for anyone who was secretly self-masochistic, and I kid no one. Dick had three American boys as assistant, handyman and bread-baker, by the names of Roger, Rick, & Seth. There were 18 people in camp, all eating blue corn chips and drinking substitute coffee surreptitiously, from as far away as Sweden and Germany. The following account is of the 19 hours I spent with Graham, his wife Susan, sons Jackson & Will, and their daughter Nile.

Over near the makeshift shower, Susan was vigorously working out the imaginary kinks in her tiny body on a gigantic trampoline. She was possibly the healthiest person in camp.

Somewhere in the distance, the boys practised with Jack's bow and arrow, fizzing over the edge in delight. Something new and adventurous that city life could not deliver.

When Graham was introduced to me, it was spontaneous. Very spontaneous. The three of us coming from different directions; Graham from the west, me from the north, and Dick from the east. It was almost like Graham and I were making an effort to get by one another to see how much longer we could stretch our introduction. A crazy mind game. Maybe all morning if it had not been for Dick intervening. We had conversed, we had laughed, we had sat beside each other, but we had not met. I know I sat beside him because I remember what he had for breakfast: cinnamon oatmeal in a stainless bowl. I remember he didn't really feel like being around everyone, but how good he was at hiding it.

He spent many long hours collecting stones and driftwood from the verdant shorelines of spring. A favorite pastime while there. I saw him at the campfire only a few times that morning. When he was there, he went about his needs quietly and consistently. He was Graham: so pure and original. The one you want to know when he is playing on the other side of the world. The one who managers, roadies and personnel would prohibit someone from meeting if they did not have proper connections. Normally this man was off limit. Suddenly, he was one of us in the middle of nowhere.

I stepped into the cook-tent that afternoon, where there were boxes and cans of things like raisins, grains, nut butters, and dreaded inka to keep us all happy and healthy. In the midst of four walls ready to collapse was a man leaned over his work. Busy with interest. Busy with his fingers. With his thoughts. I have no idea what his thoughts were on. They could have been on the antler box he was making. They could have been on Cros in the Caribbean. They were intense.

I should have felt guilty for watching him. Somehow, I did not. I wanted to make use of the opportunity to see him in those unique surroundings. I never had and knew I never would again. Quiet moments of observing his introverted creativity finally passed when I stepped outside and remembered to breath once again. All of this was caught somewhere between the real and the surreal. While it was certainly happening, in another sense it was not. It seemed that time was going by very fast that morning, yet it also felt like time completely stopped.

Most of the work around camp was done by Roger, Seth, Graham and Bill, who cut wood daily with the Swedish saw and packed gallons of water. Susan baked her first pie. I think it was rhubarb with whole grain crust. Something like Neil Young's favorite (with strawberry), but Neil wasn't there! When supper was finished, 'the' Jackson would personally instruct me on the dangerous delight of axe throwing. Certainly, something he had just gleaned from the guru. He was 11. I was 17. His younger brother, nine and their sister, young enough that I could pack her around. A story has been recited that the very first time she started to walk, they and the rest of the band were in Rome on tour. So, her first steps were in the Italian capital.

When their father sang that evening, one held his mouth organ, the others sang harmony. They were inseparable. They were an embroidered unite. Though there remain no pictures of that miniature concert, to this day, it remains impossible to forget those sweetest and quintessential moments.

That night the sun would not go down. We stayed up very late. It was summer solstice. Past midnight. I left with family by boat in the twilight hours and only recall the cool air on my face, coming from the surface of the lake water. I recall how the air was so fresh. It was a peaceful and exquisite evening in the land of the midnight sun. I was an emotional person and was attempting to keep my composure. Inside I was overflowing like fermenting wine. After years of nothing happening in our lives, I was feeling invigorated, and I was fuelled.

That next morning, I would hear giggling and laughter everywhere. It sounded as though most of them had managed a longer rest than I, still zapped from going to sleep so very late. I was nearing an emotional crash. It was now about noon. I remember Graham offering to order me some food along with everyone else. I remember Bill pulling up a chair for me to sit down beside them. A small hotel diner, nonetheless we had a triple table and 15 chairs. Crazy time, a good time never to be forgotten. At one point, Graham got up and went out to use the phone around the corner, calling a ship in the Caribbean. David was sailing merrily with his crew. Obviously quite content to think it was Graham in the far North and not himself.

After a very late breakfast, we toured the historic paddle wheeler. An extensive tour, it was, taking in everything from the captain's office and bunk to even the boiler room. Graham absolutely loved it and doubtlessly had the greater appreciation for ships than any one of us. I still hear him calling down to the boiler room through the pipes, his children hyperventilating in sheer delight. They were having a lot of fun and no intention of it ending. Somewhere along the line I became their village tour guide, and certainly I was a willing guide.

They wanted to meet my grandfather. A man who was not actually my grandfather, but many people thought he was, and I figured I would not be the one to burst anyone's bubble. He was the one who lived at the end of the road, the very last cabin in town. When we arrived, he had apparently just finished in the kitchen. He was bustling around as usual with a bee in his bonnet, apron on crooked. Perhaps an overdose of oven heat. On the table sat some kind of overly embellished dessert made of chocolate, whipping cream, and Graham's cracker.

We stayed about three hours. I watched Graham shake hands and embrace with everyone. Then I watched him walk up the stair again and shake hands with my father. They had got along well, and I had absolutely known they would. Now Bill and I stood at the back of the truck. Everyone was trying to decide where to ride and if they could even possibly fit. Twelve to cram in. I asked Graham if he was going to walk back down to the waterfront. I'll not forget his perfect humor. He said he would be unless I was going to pack him. When Seth, Bill, Graham, and I set off to the water, everyone else was still arguing, carrying on over their places. We were halfway down before the little truck went thundering past, arms and legs flailing out the back, signaling victory on us. They were shouting something, but it was beyond us. They were shouting nonsense.

The street we were on, I would often stop and try to visualize what it would be like to see one of the famous four walk along on the opposite side. And if they did, whether or not I would manage to actually recognize them at that distance. There were certain times that I could absolutely envision them here in this mountainous village of magnified splendor. I remember thinking that as I walked along on the right of Graham, my favored one. He pointed out the churches and asked about them. One on our right and one at the very end of town. One blue and white. One green and white. One Catholic, the other Anglican. Just before my years of theological study were to begin. Religion was a continuing study for him, and I really had no idea how theology would soon become mine. Five years later I would end up sharing with him my own spiritual discoveries that would in fact take a stark contrast. God knows how to surprise us.

I stood and watched the three men get their coats on and untie the canoe, pushing it into the water without effort. A few moments later I saw them grow smaller and disappear underneath the bridge on their way back to camp on Nares. Overhead, very high up, mares tails danced across the sky like they were stretching the circumference of the clock. Never again. When I closed my eyes, I could remember the little things. Like the book he read from. He was not a man for fiction. Or the blue speckled enamel cup he drank (smuggled) coffee from. His favorite color was winter green. He gave people the benefit of the doubt, yet he was no one's fool. A sage for his age yet incredibly youthful in the same degree. His beauty and reassurance. His genuine interest in other people. He could be so funny, yet he was so serious. The seven songs in the tepee the few nights before. If his time and graciousness was not enough, I don't know what was. The greatest realization that I have come to is that he is always there. Somehow always obtainable. He is wine. He is vintage.

Bio: *Shirly Ambrose is a passionate lifelong artist, author, graphologist, theologian, fresh water sailor, and unapologetic conspiracist. She is a 1970s girl who was raised in the Yukon wilderness near Alaska and really likes to visit Western Europe where her ancestors came from. It was in the wild isolation that she discovered her creative side, as well, the songs and musicians of her life. She has produced two 75-minute albums of her own songs after many years of waiting. http://ambrosearts.myfreesites.net*

Songs: *'Wooden Ships' (C); 'Southern Cross' (S); 'Wasted on the Way' (N).*

DAVID CROSBY FOR PRESIDENT

by Ray Haley

Ray Haley with Crosby & Nash, backstage at H. Ric Luhrs Performing Arts Center. Photo from Ray Haley's private collection

I cannot remember not having 'David Crosby for President' painted on my vehicle during a Presidential Election year. Sometimes, I wore hand-made buttons or had it written on my cap as well. In the mid-1980s, I first took an American flag to a concert in Toronto, Canada for a CSN show at Massey Hall. Right after the opening song, I unfurled my flag over the front of the balcony in front of David. Stephen immediately pointed and said, 'Look, they're here!'

Something very magical happened to me the night before in Darien Lake Amusement Park, in New York State. I was noticed from the stage by Crosby, Stills and Nash! I showed up in Darien Lake with two banners. One read, 'This is my 49th CSN show'. CSN was interwoven and painted on in full color. I was wearing a denim coat which had a CSN interwoven emblem in the center of my back. I hand-embroidered the coat earlier that spring on the way to a CSN show in Tangle Wood, Massachusetts. About two years later, denim shirts with a similar emblem was available at the shows. I like to think I started that trend.

Anyway, Stills spotted my banner and announced, 'Hey, there's a dude here that has seen us 49 times as of tonight. Thanks for putting our kids through college!' David, who had put his hand up his shirt and was making pumping motions like it was his heart chimed in, 'Real nice sign, dude, thanks.' I didn't let the opportunity slide by and replied, 'If you all like it so much how about signing it?' David gestured for me to come to the stage, and, as they say, the rest is history.

First thing the next day, I called and bought tickets for that night's show at Massey Hall, showing up with a plain American flag. When Steven noticed it and commented that we were there, I wanted even more to interact with these guys. I have always known that they are superstars and that their audiences feel like they know them, mostly because of how much they have shared with us and what we hear through the media. Sometimes you just have to remind yourself, 'Yeah, but they don't know me from Adam.'

I held the flag up as high as I could before the show, and everyone cheered and clapped. I felt pretty proud of my handiwork, but when CSN got a look at it and praised it from stage I was ecstatic. David motioned for me to give my flag to him. I was so excited. David and Graham held it high in the air and danced with it, while Stills jammed out his solo in 'Woodstock.' I felt even more connected that I had previously. Unfortunately, I was so taken in by the moment I never even took a picture of what in my lifetime was an historic event!

I have sewn the CSN flag, a Crosby Nash flag, a Crosby Stills Nash & Young 'Freedom' flag, a Nash flag, and a Croz flag. I have covered my brand-new Mini Cooper with a huge vinyl CSNY 'Living with War' flag, painted the hoods on my VWs and new Chevy pick-up trucks, and always supported my personal 'David Crosby for President' banners as a viable alternative to what the establishment has had to offered. More than anything, I love being The CSN Flag dude. It has allowed me to interact with these superstar musicians and human beings on a level so many others have only dreamed of. I have been blessed.

Ray Haley with his CSN flags. Photo by Susan Haley

Bio: *Ray Haley was a fan of CSN&Y long before CSN was an entity. He has followed them and their music since about 1966. Years ago, he headed back to college to get his teaching credentials, explaining, 'I convinced my American History professor into letting me teach the decade of the 1960s, and used mostly CSN to address The Sunset Strip riots ('For What It's Worth'), Woodstock ('Woodstock' - CSN&Y version), The Manson murders ('Revolution Blues'), and Kent State ('Ohio'). Not too long ago I approached Graham asking to do an interview after a show. At first, he did not recognize me. I opened my coat and pulled out my 'CSN Flag.' He immediately asked, 'What the fuck happened to your hair?' As I explained, I cut my hair and beard off to enhance my getting a job teaching.'*

Ray's biggest personal accomplishment took place over the last 41 years. 'While continuing to attend a ton of great CSN&Y shows, I helped raise my daughter Heather. In the process I have taken her to close to 20 CSN&Y shows, and she has managed to convince me to take her to see Michael Jackson and Pink Floyd. After all these years, we both still love CSN.'

Ray is originally from Lockport, New York (42.8 degrees North latitude), and is currently retired and living in Gillam, Manitoba, Canada (56.3 degrees North latitude), and adds, 'There has been quite a climate change for the two of us!'

Songs: *'Almost Cut My Hair' (C), 'Suite: Judy Blue Eyes' (S), 'To The Last Whale' (C/N), and 'Wind on the Water' (N).*

AN ACOUSTIC BENEFIT CONCERT FOR THE SEVA FOUNDATION AND IT'S 3rd SPIRIT OF SERVICE CONFERENCE

seva

WAVY GRAVY, M.C.
BRENT MYDLAND
BONNIE RAITT

INTERMISSION

BOB WEIR
DAVID CROSBY & GRAHAM NASH

SEXSON AUDITORIUM
PASADENA CITY COLLEGE
SATURDAY APRIL 16 - 8:00PM

PRODUCED BY AVOCADO PRODUCTIONS

RAINBOW WARRIOR MUSIC FESTIVAL

AVOCADO PRODUCTIONS AND CONCERT PROMOTIONS PRESENT
A BENEFIT

JACKSON BROWNE
NEIL FINN
HERBS
GRAHAM NASH
TOPP TWINS
NEIL YOUNG

SAT. 5 APRIL., 12 NOON,
MT SMART STADIUM AUCKLAND.
GREENPEACE
ADMISSION $18.50

PLUS SPECIAL
SPLIT ENZ REUNION

LA PENCA PROJECT

A BENEFIT CONCERT TOUR
CHRISTIC INSTITUTE
AN INTERFAITH CENTER FOR LAW AND PUBLIC POLICY
JACKSON BROWNE
SPECIAL GUESTS
DAVID CROSBY
GRAHAM NASH
BARRY CRIMMINS

SAN DIEGO CIVIC THEATRE
SAN DIEGO, CALIFORNIA
NOVEMBER 5th • 1988

BY BILL SILVA PRESENTS AND AVOCADO PRODUCTIONS

THE CRANE SCHOOL

CROSBY, STILLS & NASH

TEACH YOUR CHILDREN WELL

A SPECIAL ACOUSTIC BENEFIT CONCERT
FOR THE CRANE SCHOOL SCHOLARSHIP FUND
SUNDAY AFTERNOON, SEPTEMBER 20, 2:00PM
SANTA BARBARA COUNTY BOWL
805-969-2007
Produced by Pacificoncerts, Stephen Cloud, and Avocado Productions

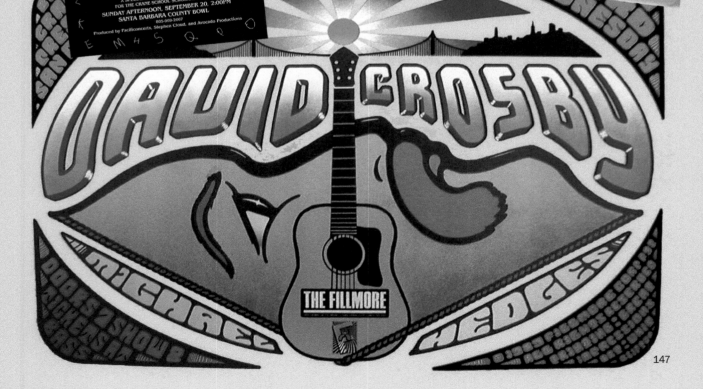

DAVID CROSBY
MICHAEL HEDGES
THE FILLMORE

147

90's
The American Dream betrayed

PRESENTS

STOP HANDGUN VIOLENCE

CROSBY STILLS & NASH

Great Wood
June 30, 1996

FORWARD

BE COU

CSN TOUR PROMO

CHOICE
FRIENDS OF FAMILY PLANN

CROSB STILL

1994 SUMMER TOUR

END WAR

MAKE LOVE NOT WAR

CSN
Crosby Stills & Nash
25th Anniversary Tour
WITH VERY SPECIAL GUESTS

FLEETWOOD MAC
FEATURING: MICK FLEETWOOD JOHN McVIE DAVE MASON BEKKA BRAMLETT JERRY WILLIAMS

GRAHAM PRESENTS IN SAN FRAN

LAUGHTER LOVE & MUSIC

TO CELEBRATE THE LIVES OF BILL, STEVE AND M
SUNDAY · NOVEMBER 3 1991 · 11 AM
THE POLO FIELDS, GOLDEN GATE PARK

An Evening of Acoustic Music with
David Crosby
Graham Nash

VIP 9/19

CSN TOUR 1990

DIRTY DOZEN BRASS BAND
BOBBY McFERRIN
JACKSON BROWNE
ON NEVILLE
EVELYN CISNEROS
EL SMUIN
PATRIANI FRIENDS
LYONS
NTANA
OBOS

ROBIN WILLIAMS
JOURNEY
TRACY CHA
NEIL YOUN
DAVID CROS
STEPHEN ST
GRAHAM NA
GRATEFUL DEAD
JOHN POP
JOHN FOG
JOAN BAEZ
KRIS KRISTOFFER

ROYAL ALBERT HALL

ASGARD PRESENTS
AN ACOUSTIC EVENING WITH
CROSBY STILLS & NASH
THURSDAY OCT. 08/92 AT 8:00 PM

ALCONY
OOR   5
ROW   T3
SEAT   65

EVENING
INUTES BEFORE PERFORMANCE

RS TO THE CITY OF SAN FRANCISCO MAYOR ART AGNOS, THE SAN FRANCISCO POLICE DEPT.
AND THE SAN FRANCISCO RECREATION & PARK DEPT.
DUCED BY THEIR FAMILIES AND FRI
THE BILL GRAHAM

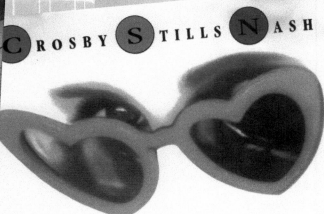

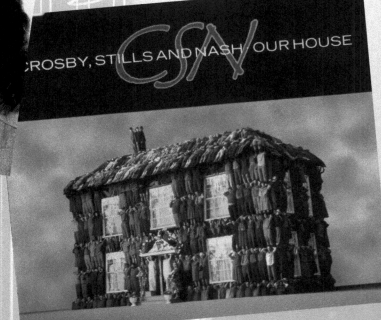

THE GLUE

by Rod Sims

How does one encapsulate over 45 years of listening pleasure into a few lines? I first became aware of Crosby, Stills & Nash through Neil's first album around 1970. At this time, the movie of *Woodstock* appeared in cinemas and, like many of my peers, I was awestruck by 'Suite: Judy Blue Eyes'. From that moment my record buying focused more on Crosby, Stills & Nash and my first bootleg purchase was the amazing *A Very Stoney Evening* on blue and yellow vinyl - which I still have to this day. From then on, without the internet and only the music press (*Rolling Stone*) and AM radio stations, the search for CSN was often unsuccessful, until *4 Way Street,* and again I was rewarded with the magic of the solo work and the harmonies. Music that continues to live in my every waking moment.

Over the years, I was always on the lookout for anything related to Crosby, Stills & Nash (and Young) and my collection grew and grew to the extent that, at the time of writing this, I have a very eclectic collection of CSN&Y music and memorabilia: hundreds of CDs and vinyl, as well as diverse videos, books, songbooks, cassettes, t-shirts, memorabilia and merchandise.

Sadly, the performances of CSN&Y were rarely reported Down Under and only a few bootlegs emerged, such as the 1974 reunion bootleg. Of course, I snapped up any new release, although it was not until 1991 that CSN first toured Australia.

After almost 20 years of waiting, my first CSN concert was in early April 1991 at the beautiful State Theatre, Sydney, with balconies and statues reminiscent of the Beacon Theatre in New York, where I saw CSN in 2011.

The boys were in great form and I was able to see them close up. At one point in the show, doing a solo set, Crosby discovered that the floor had been glued by Graham and Stephen and his shoe was stuck, so he couldn't tap in time. This of course caused great hilarity amongst the audience and the band, a very funny moment which David alluded to when I saw him perform solo at the Honoka'a People's Theatre on the Big Island of Hawai'i in December 2016.

Since then, I have been fortunate to see CSNY in various configurations across the world, and - as the internet made knowledge of touring and schedules more available - it has become easier and easier to see performances by combinations of CSNY more and more frequently.

There are of course some special memories, like on 28 September 2015 in Paris when Graham and Shane sat about one metre from us and sang a song written for L'Olympia. And in 2007 in Brisbane, when Stephen came out and played '4+20' - one of my all-time favourites - or in 2010 in London when I stood just below Stephen as he blasted out 'Love The One You're With' for the encore.

There have been so many moments when the sheer magic of harmonies ('Guinnevere' in 2000) or the magic of the playing (Neil supporting David in 2006) makes you glad to have witnessed the performances. Then there are the songs; I never tire of hearing them, especially those where David's voice hits new highs – 'Long Time Gone' or 'Almost Cut My Hair'.

Another of my favorite songs is 'Cathedral' – it's always special to hear it in concert. And of course, having been to both Stonehenge and Winchester Cathedral, I was curious to see if the gravestone Graham sang about was real or part of a musician's creative license. So, when I visited the cathedral, I paced up and down the aisles and almost gave up, until my partner Sharon found the stone. The inscription reads, 'Hugh Foulkes, Esq., Lieutenant in the Royal Cheshire Militia, died Febr. 2nd. 1799, aged 26 years.'

Crosby, Stills & Nash have been with us for decades, and it is their accompaniments to our life's journey that make them so special and so enduring.

Bio: *Rod Sims was born in Scotland and moved to Australia as a young boy. His career was in academia and the effective use of computer-based education. He lived off-the-grid in the bush for 15 years, building a house and commuting via the internet. His love for all things CSN&Y began in the late 1960s and Rod loves to sing and play at amateur nights when the opportunity arises. He has now retired to Hawaii, enjoying the aloha spirit, golf, and sunset music.*

Songs: *'Games' (C); 'Black Queen' (S); 'Fire Down Below' (N). And as CSN, 'Delta'.*

THE TWO DAVID CROSBY GUITARS

by Pat Lennon

I was 17 when the *Crosby, Stills & Nash* album came out. It's still one of my favorite albums. I remember sitting for days figuring out 'Guinnevere'. In the early Nineties we used to play in a nice little club in Santa Monica and would play 'Guinnevere'. One night, Jackson Browne heard us sing it and said David would love it.

He invited him and David showed up next time, coming backstage after and saying he had never heard anyone do it justice like we did and how he would love to sing it with us next show. He also asked what tuning I played it in. I said I thought I had figured out his tuning, and he said I was one string off and it looked too hard the way I played it.

He shows up next show, borrows one of my guitars and says on the microphone, 'I can't believe Pat is playing such shitty guitars'. Anyway, the three guitarists played it in three different tunings: Michael, my cousin, in standard, I play it in mine, and David in his. And it sounded really cool that way. We became friends after that, and he came to see and sing with us often.

He was going to record one of our songs on a solo album and asked us to play all the tracks in the studio. He said I could use one of his guitars that he would have there. He was recording at Jackson's studio, we showed up, and he had a dozen Martins there and told me to try some. They were all beautiful guitars and he picked one out especially, told me to play it. Unbeknown to me, David had told my other bandmates he was going to give me a guitar, and they were all there when he said, 'That guitar is yours, because I am sick of you playing shitty guitars.' It was a 1985 Martin D-28 Herringbone, a 150-year Anniversary model. It was and still is my touring guitar and my favorite acoustic.

This story leads me to another. Around the year 2000, we were touring the Netherlands, where we have a very loyal following. We had just finished singing a song with four vocals and just Michael playing guitar. I was expecting my guitar tech to give me my guitar when I heard a 'kabong' behind me. I knew it was my Martin. I turned around and there it was with the neck broken off! He had dropped it! We brought it home and took it to Billy Asher, David's and Jackson's luthier. He looked at it and said he would have to think about how to fix it, and it would take a little while.

One month later we were doing a show and David came backstage before. He had a brand-new guitar case with him. He was excited because Martin had just come out with his signature model Martin D-18: only 250 made! He opens the case and brings out this beauty of a guitar and says, 'Try it!' Of course, it sounded rich and I loved it. Then he says, 'Number one I gave to James Raymond, number two I gave to Graham. And this is number three, and it is yours!'

Two weeks later he gave Michael number four. My D-28 was repaired, and I think sounds better than before and is back on tour. That's how I have two David Crosby guitars, and he remains to this day a great musical inspiration and a generous, wonderful friend.

Bio: *Born and raised in Venice Beach, California, Pat Lennon's family had lived there for 100 years but he now lives in El Segundo, a beach town near Los Angeles Airport. In the band Venice since 1980, he has a second career as a woodworker/ furniture builder, doing considerable woodworking for Jackson Browne and building studios for Patrick Leonard, Danny Kortchmar, JD Southern, and Tom Petty. He adds, 'I am now building reproduction surfboards from different eras, and touring Europe twice a year with Venice.'*

Songs: *'The Lee Shore' (C); 'Bluebird' (S); 'Just a Song Before I Go' (N).*

November 1991: CSN harmonizing at The Warfield, San Francisco, California, USA. Photo by Raymond Foye

DAVID AND ME

by Adolfo Galli

David Crosby means many things to me. Great music, first of all, then extraordinary personal and professional satisfaction, tiring challenges and lastly, friendship.

David's music - and the music of Crosby, Stills, Nash & Young or, more generally, the music expressed in their different combinations - actually represented my musical guiding light as a boy, along with a small circle of other American and English artists and bands who made their mark on me. Indelible traces of beauty that I always carry with me, and songs I still enjoy strumming.

At the beginning of the Nineties, as a promoter, together with my partner Mimmo D'Alessandro, I tried to bring the musicians I loved to Italy. David was a dream that seemed out of reach. For reasons beyond my control, he was reluctant to return to Italy and never included it among the destinations where he was to perform. I did not know it at the time, but he had been so burned by his previous experience in our country - which took place amid a thousand personal, logistical, technical and economic difficulties in 1983 - that, when it came to planning tours in the 'old continent', he always put a cross on our beautiful country. Not aware of this diktat (Crosby himself would tell me years later, when we became friends), when at the end of 1991 the possibility of a tour in Europe the following spring leaked out, I decided to give it a try with Paul Charles, who was David's agent at the time. I don't know how, perhaps the competitive side of the association was provoked, but I managed to convince him that a show in Milan would be crucial. So, we set the date – 2 April 1992 - in what was at the time the Milanese venue par excellence, the PalaTrussardi, plus one concert in Rome.

The preparation of the event was particularly laborious. In addition to the normal tensions that accompany the organisation of a live show, I would be finding myself in front of one of my idols, and I would be unable to maintain the usual detachment. As the concert day approached, I felt even more charged and involved.

Then came 2 April, an unforgettable day, which unfortunately did not begin under favourable circumstances. An idea by local promoter, Ferdinando Salzano, contributed to making the climate electric. He wanted to take Crosby out for dinner before the show, to a trendy restaurant, the 'Dixieland', which served American food. They agreed to open earlier just for the famous guest. What was intended to be an explicit homage to the artist, with the conviction of making him feel at home, turned into a complete disaster. The place was known for 'Southern food' from Texas, but Crosby associated images which were anything but pleasant to that State, having frequented the notorious prisons there at the worst moment of his addiction to alcohol and drugs. I remember as if it were now, David's cold gaze when he realised where we had taken him; and I remember just as well the insults that followed that he threw at me, up to him leaving the place outraged. I stood at the door of the club, dazed, incapable of any reaction: I could only think that I had been insulted by a musician I was crazy about. I came round when David's wife, Jan, put her hand on my shoulder, and explaining the reason for her husband's reaction, told me not to pay too much attention to it. 'He'll get over it,' she said.

I think anyone can imagine the state of mind I was in when I went back to the PalaTrussardi. However, despite everything, I was still determined not to ruin the evening. After so many years I was attending a David Crosby live show again, and I wanted to do it with a light heart and a clear mind, open only to music.

The concert was a success. If before the concert I had got onto David's personal blacklist, probably by arrogance, at the end of the evening he adored me. The reason for this sudden change was simple: I had reserved the entire front row of the hall for me, my wife and a group of friends, people who had the same passion as me for the songwriter from Los Angeles. Contrary to what I usually do - that is, to live the shows I organise without allowing myself a fixed position, moving nervously between the audience and backstage, this time I sat down five minutes before the beginning of the concert and got up only when the curtain fell. I sung every song in the setlist at the top of my lungs, with the accompaniment of my friends. I could feel David's amazement, standing in front of me with the guitar on his shoulder (the show was acoustic, as a trio), occasionally looking at me, and perhaps he even saw himself reflected in my own competitive trance.

At a certain point, towards the end, something terrifying happened: Crosby asked for a round of applause for me, the organiser of the evening. He said: 'In so many years of career, I have never seen a promoter sitting at the foot of the stage listening to me with such attention; nor, least of all, have I seen one singing my songs word for word, from start to finish'. More than applause, there was a standing ovation, the thought of which still gives me goosebumps.

That was the moment my acquaintance with David Crosby went to the next level; and over time it became friendship, fuelled by numerous encounters, especially in the States. It is something that goes well beyond the professional relationship, and that has also had the opportunity to extend to Stephen Stills, Graham Nash, and Neil Young, bringing together what remains one of the most fascinating folk-rock bands in the history of music. I have anecdotes for each of them: from Young's singular combinations of luxury and Franciscan lifestyle when he is on tour, to the need for a constant supply of novels and essays for Stills (tireless reader, over a volume a day), to the artistic kindness of Nash, of which I treasure, among other things, an autographed text of the song 'Teach Your Children' with his self-portrait incorporated.

But we are talking about David Crosby in particular, so I prefer to reveal two other anecdotes from the many I have experienced.

The first concerns an element that David cannot do without: air conditioning. He loves it, he expects it all the time, even out of season. In fact, most of the times I've seen him angry or heartbroken was when the cooling system wasn't working properly or not at all: if you want a raging Crosby (but I wouldn't wish it on anyone), turn the air conditioning off.

Adolfo Galli with CSN backstage at Luglio Suona Bene, Auditorium Parco della Musica, Rome, Italy. Photo by Francesco Lucarelli

The second is a very personal, absolutely romantic memory. I met my wife Luisa for the first time in California, in 1982; and I saw her again the following year, by chance, at a David Crosby concert in Italy, and we've been together ever since. When we became friends, I told David this story. To which, smiling under his monumental moustache, he said to me: 'So then, in that disastrous period, of which I have many negative memories, at least one thing I got it right: I helped you meet her.'

Yep: the power of music, and of David Crosby.

Bio: *When Adolfo Galli was 14, he played in a band, the Horizons. 'We did Southern rock and West Coast music, which is still my go-to music. A few years later, I moved to London for a while. One morning in August 1979, I left Charing Cross, with my tricolour flag, bound for Knebworth, where Led Zeppelin, the greatest rock band ever, would play. In Italy, there was no such thing. It was important to be at that festival. It was unforgettable. A couple of years later, still in London, I was struck by McLaughlin, De Lucia and Larry Coryell, whom I met at the end of the concert. The following summer, August 1982, I was on vacation in Los Angeles and met Coryell at a club. We had a drink together and he asked if I wanted to try to find him some dates in Italy, where he couldn't get a gig. Thus began my career as a promoter.'*

Songs: *'Long Time Gone' (C); 'Suite: Judy Blue Eyes' (S); 'Lady of the Island' (N).*

STORY OF A COVER

by Guido Harari

The Byrds were the American Beatles. I loved them right away, ever since 1965 when I listened to their electric version of 'Mr Tambourine Man' pouring from the stereo of a record shop in Jesolo Lido, a little beach town not far from Venice. How can you resist their irresistible vocal mixes and McGuinn's 12-string jingle-jangle? There was folk, rock, Indian exoticism, and the rising wave of psychedelia.

David Crosby was the restless soul of the Byrds, in the mood for reckless adventures. Everyone knows the saga he wove together with Stephen Stills, Graham Nash and Neil Young, but it was his first solo flight, *If I Could Only Remember My Name* in particular that wove a magical sound network gathering the illuminati of the best rock music made in San Francisco and Los Angeles. That record invented a visionary country rock, under the banner of psychedelia, civil commitment, and unbridled freedom.

In 1989, after years of existential drift and chemical alteration, Crosby resurfaced with a second solo album, *Oh Yes! I Can*. On this occasion, he also promoted it in Italy. I was able to interview and photograph him for the magazine *Rockstar* and it was a truly dazzling encounter. I absolutely wanted to capture the rebirth of one of my favourite artists in

February 1989: David Crosby and Guido Harari. Photo by Neri Oddo

December 9, 2014: David Crosby and Guido Harari, Teatro del Giglio, Lucca, Italy. Photo courtesy of Guido Harari

February 1989: David Crosby's press tour in Milan, Italy. Proof sheet by Guido Harari

a photograph, which I did with a very narrow cut on the face, a direct look at the camera and nothing else. We shot in Crosby's hotel room, the cramped dimensions shaping the light.

Throughout the interview he looked at me with great suspicion, even more so when, in the end, I revealed myself to be the die-hard fan I was, and presented him with his entire discography, including LPs and singles, from The Byrds up to that moment. I stared at him without saying anything and he exclaimed, 'Don't tell me you want me to autograph them all!' As I nodded, he widened his eyes and exclaimed, 'No! No! I know you will sell them to collectors!' 'David,' I replied with a smile, 'if I'd ask you to write me a dedication as well, do you really think I would sell them?' After a long haggle, Crosby agreed to sign one single and one LP for each line-up in which he had played. We parted only after I solemnly promised to send him the photos for reviewing.

A few months later I received an enthusiastic fax from him. In those days, there were no text messages, no e-mails, and obviously no internet. According to him, even Graham Nash, a refined photo collector, congratulated him on what he believed to be *the* definitive photo of Crosby.

David decided to use it on the cover of his next album, *Thousand Roads*. In 1992, in Milan for a CSN concert, Crosby confirmed his choice, showing me his favourite shot on the proof sheets I had sent him, and thanked me for having been able to capture that particular moment of his rebirth to a new life.

When Bill Siddons, his manager at the time, contacted me, it was not easy to come to a financial agreement. Indeed, in an interview with Laura Putti for *La Repubblica*, Crosby did not hide the fact that the cover of *Thousand Roads* almost fell through due to my ridiculous financial demands. When the stencil of the preview cover arrived, I was shocked: my original black and white photo had been heavily photoshopped, destroying its original magical atmosphere.

December 9, 2014: Guido Harari photographing Crosby's soundcheck at Teatro del Giglio, Lucca, Italy. Photo by Francesco Lucarelli

Over the years, however, that cover has sealed a relationship of esteem and affability. A few years ago, I proposed to Crosby to sign a special edition of that image with me in fine art print, and he happily accepted. When I offered to reward his kindness, David wanted nothing. He simply said, 'I should be the one thanking you for taking that picture!'

Bio: *Guido Harari started out in the early Seventies as a music photographer and journalist, also exploring reportage, fashion, advertising, corporate photography and the graphic design of his books. He's produced countless record covers for such artists as Kate Bush, David Crosby, Bob Dylan, B.B. King, Ute Lemper, Paul McCartney, Lou Reed, Simple Minds and Frank Zappa. In Italy he has collaborated with many major stars, from Claudio Baglioni to Luciano Pavarotti, from Fabrizio De André to Maestro Riccardo Muti and La Scala Philharmonic Orchestra. He has published books about Vasco Rossi, Fabrizio De André, Tom Waits, Kate Bush and many others. In 2011 he launched his own photographic gallery. Wall of Sound Gallery, and his publishing company for limited edition books and catalogues, Wall of Sound Editions, both totally focused on music imagery, in Alba, Italy, where he's lived for many years.*

Songs (CSN solo): *'Laughing' (C), 'Love the One You're With' (S), 'I Used To Be a King' (N).*

THE GREATEST EMOTION OF MY LIFE

by Massimo Rossetti

If I didn't have videos and photos, I would have thought my amazing adventure was just a dream. And yet, thank goodness, it was all true.

Spring 1992, nine years after the concert at the Capannelle Hippodrome cancelled last minute due to a furious storm, Crosby, Stills & Nash had finally returned to Rome to play.

Together with my friends Stefano Frollano, Mauro Coscia and Francesco Lucarelli, editors of the *Wooden Nickel* fanzine, I had the opportunity to meet three-quarters of the artists who had released one of the records I have listened to and consumed the most in my life, *4 Way Street*. I must have bought it at least ten times.

Rome was the last stop on a short European tour and CSN had a few days off in the city. We had the opportunity to meet them several times, different memories linked to each moment. A visit to St Peter's Basilica with Crosby, Nash, their families and manager Bill Siddons. A chat while having lunch with them at I Tre Scalini restaurant in Piazza Navona. What really impressed me was to perceive that Crosby and Nash were like one family. They had been from the beginning, and I believe they will be forever. I took advantage of the intimate atmosphere and suggested Nash sang, 'I'm flying in St. Peter's Cathedral' during the performance of 'Cathedral' the next day. Believe it or not, he actually did.

On the day of the show, we arrived at the Tendastrisce Theater in time to attend the soundcheck. Crosby had fun changing lyrics to 'The Lee Shore', using funny words while I filmed the scene. Suddenly, a guy rushed towards me, kind of threatening, with the obvious intention of seizing my camera. Fortunately, Nash saw the whole scene and reassured him from the stage, 'They are our friends. There is nothing to worry about.' This is how I met Chris Rankin, son of singer-songwriter Kenny, with whom Croz had recorded a duet a few years earlier on the album *Hiding in Myself*.

Soon as the soundcheck was over, we were invited backstage. We started talking about open tunings and Graham showed us the correct tuning of 'Lady of the Island', playing it for us. At the end, smiling, he told us, being the last date of the tour and the last date of each tour always being a bit special, he would like to invite us on stage to sing 'Teach Your Children' with them, the final encore. We barely believed what we'd just heard but there was no time to recover from the shock: it was showtime. Back into the audience, we managed to keep the secret and didn't say a word to our girlfriends, making the surprise even bigger.

The concert began and it was a wonderful evening of hits and hidden gems. It was only the three of them on stage with their acoustic guitars. From time to time, Stephen grabbed his Telecaster to unleash some killer guitar solos. During the intermission, Chris brought us passes and, during the first encore, Stefano, Francesco and I sneaked backstage, climbed some stairs, and we were on stage. We waited behind a curtain as CSN began singing 'Teach Your Children', hearts pounding. Suddenly - in the middle of the song - Graham Nash called us on, shouting 'These are our friends from *Wooden Nickel*!'

Stefano and I headed towards Crosby's microphone. Francesco shared the mike with Stills. Then Stephen joined Nash, who now had his daughter Nile beside him.

I still remember the roar from the people at the end of the song and the hugs and smiles backstage. What a joy, what a thrill! After the birth of my children, it was the greatest emotion of my life.

Bio: *Massimo Rossetti was born and lives in Rome, where he works in the marketing sector of an oil company. Family, friends and music are the most important things in his life. He adds, 'The greatest emotion I felt, apart from the birth of my two children, was singing on stage with CSN, and I owe this to the benevolent folly of some dear friends among whom the editor of this book is counted.'*

Songs: *'The Lee Shore' (C), 'Suite: Judy Blue Eyes' (S), 'Chicago' (N).*

CLOSE ENCOUNTERS OF THE THIRD KIND

by Stefano Frollano

... 1, 2, 3, 4, 5, 6, 7, 8, 9, 10, 11 ... 1, 2, 3, 4, 5, 6, 7, 8, 9, 10, 11 ... so he marked the 11/8 of 'Low Down Payment', in front of me, then starting to sing the song with the Martin, tuned to the low E, down one tone. Vocals, harmonies, guitars, experimentation, melodies, rhythm. In a close encounter of the third kind, I was facing a living legend of West Coast music. Both sitting on the same sofa holding guitars and playing together with him. David Crosby.

It was 17 May 1993. In that period, the Californian artist was releasing his album *Thousand Roads* and was on an interview-only promotional tour in some European cities. That morning, me and my friends from *Wooden Nickel* (the fanzine dedicated to CSNY created by Francesco Lucarelli and Marco Martella, later joined by me and Mauro Coscia) met David in a warm and sunny Piazza di Spagna, where we spent some time chatting, before reaching the French Academy, where a photographic exhibition was in progress. After having lunch with the promoter, our friend Adolfo Galli, we went to the Regina Carlton hotel in Via Veneto in Rome, where David was staying, where a press conference with the specialist press was to be held that afternoon.

April 3, 1992: CSN live at Teatro Tendastrisce, Rome, Italy.
Photos by Marco Tomassetti

The walk we took from Via Veneto to Piazza del Popolo was a real crowd-pleaser, with many people who stopped David asking for autographs and handshakes. Outside the hotel, we took pictures and talked about Harley Davidson. Then we invited David to Francesco's house to celebrate the new record with a small circle of friends.

When we got to his house, guitars ready for the party, we didn't hesitate to invite him to play with us, and for us, David generously performed a beautiful set that slowly turned into a lesson about the open tunings of some of his songs.

It was truly incredible. This miracle had repeated itself, albeit in a different form and in a decidedly more confidential way. The year before, in April, we had been guests at the Tendastrisce in Rome during the encores of the Crosby, Stills & Nash concert, and now we were at home with one of our heroes, sharing songs and emotions, stories and - why not - good Italian food and wine.

In October 1992, after the Italian leg of the tour, I followed CS&N in Europe with my friend, musician Stefano Fedele from Udine. We travelled through Holland, Germany and Denmark, where we often spent time backstage with musicians, before and after concerts. Nash's generosity, and the fact that we had sung with them a few months earlier in Rome and had driven them around the city, sightseeing, in the days following the Roman concert, automatically created an aura and amiable relationship. We were rewarded with admission to concerts and reserved areas, thus enjoying memorable shows and songs, sometimes even surprising acoustic versions or unpublished versions of classics. One, above all, was a two-voice version of 'Triad', performed at the Falkoner Theater in Copenhagen. There was no shortage of dedications for us during the concerts, and we were delighted by the warmth with which, especially Crosby and Nash and the technical staff, welcomed us everywhere. The same intimacy returned that afternoon in May 1993.

It was a feeling I did not understand but at the same time helped me live those hours fully because that voice, those songs, those guitars had been part of our life for many years, accompanying us when we were teenagers, and taking us by the hand up to that day.

The musical festivities began with 'Guinnevere'. Who would have thought that one day I would be able to play it with its author, and receive his compliments? Crosby did not believe that Massimo could sing Graham's vocal line, but he did not know we had been addicted to CSN&Y's music for years. And so, after a brief mention of the song, David accepted the challenge and Max and I played and sang the song with him from the beginning till the end.

Realising we were able to do it, David introduced us to a song he was writing at that time, 'Till It Shines On You'. He pulled out a leaflet where he had written the lyrics and started playing and singing the - at the time – unreleased song. We immediately added guitars and vocals in full harmony. In the meantime, another dear friend and guitarist joined us, Roberto Pezzuoli, leaving his camera for a guitar, leaving the honour and pleasant burden to Mauro to film these precious moments for posterity.

Crosby launched into a blues classic, which had been part of his repertoire in his early folk years, 'Motherless Children', followed by 'Drop Down Mama'. We were having fun, not fully aware of what was happening but, at the same time, realising that opportunity could be truly unique.

Between one song and another, Francesco took care of dinner and in the meantime some friends joined us to party with the famous guest. After so many years of music, we certainly had learned many secrets of CSN songs, but having Crosby available was an irresistible chance to learn more: starting from 'Distances', then 'Laughing', 'Kids and Dogs' and 'Dancer', which David performed in front of us, start to finish, with that very unusual tuning, DGDDAD. Then we sang together: 'Laughing', 'Music Is Love', 'Naked in the Rain' and 'Low Down Payment'. We all sat there learning from the Maestro: tricks and counter-times, alternating tunings and harmony vocals.

The magical evening continued with spaghetti, mozzarella di bufala, wine, laughter, obscure CSN footage from our archives, autographs and photos. Cunningly avoiding calling a taxi, Roberto offered

May 1993: David Crosby and Stefano Frollano, Rome, Italy. Photo by Paolo Golini

himself as a chauffeur and off we went with his dark grey, vintage Fiat Uno. We took David on board and the wonderful day ended with a return trip to Via Veneto, talking about stolen and found guitars, songs, traffic and more. A night in Rome with David Crosby. A dream come true.

We left Croz in front of the hotel and said goodbye. We stood there while he slipped through the hotel doorway. Adrenaline flowed through the body, and we were unable to sleep. We talked about it for days. I would see Crosby four years later, in Las Vegas, in Los Angeles and on other occasions in Italy and the USA. However, out of all the adventures and experiences, the image that will remain forever impressed in my mind and in my heart, more than any song, more than any word, more than any hug, was the moment when David stood still in silence for a minute contemplating an evocative image, a black and white photo of a sailing ship, in navigation. While I stared at him, I got lost in my thoughts, in the songs he had written while at sea. The minute was as long as all the times he had me daydream with his music, and I remembered the first time I 'met' him: it was a photo in a newspaper clipping, taken while he laughed under his legendary moustache, sitting under the sail of a boat, anchored, who knows where, under a coast sheltered from the wind.

Bio: *Stefano Frollano (Rome, 1962) is a composer, guitarist and singer. He has released two solo albums to his name (SF and Sense of You), an EP ('One More Cup of Coffee'), as well as records with Blackbirds, Skydog, and Polankaren. Alongside his main activity, he works as a writer (some essays and biographies on CSN & Y) and journalist, as a contributor to various periodicals of the specialist music press (Jam, Raro, Satisfaction, Mucchio Selvaggio). His latest editorial efforts can be found in the volume, The History of Rock Guitar (Hoepli).*

Songs: *'Guinnevere' (C), 'Dark Star' (S), 'Carried Away' (N).*

OUR HOUSE IS A VERY, VERY, VERY WHITE HOUSE

by Melinda Bates

I remember a special visit on a Saturday morning in our first year. It was a magical moment for me when Graham Nash sat at the state piano in the North Foyer and - with David Crosby looking on - played and sang, 'Our house is a very, very, very White House'.

This is the kind of thing that happens at the White House almost every day, but it never gets old or ordinary. You just look around and say to yourself, 'I can't *believe* I'm here with this person, and this just happened!'

1993: Graham at the piano as David looks on with Jan Dance at The White House. Photo by Melinda Bates, the Ultimate White House Insider

Bio: *Melinda Bates is a Washington, DC native whose career in Visitors Services began at the National Gallery of Art and culminated with the title of special assistant to the President and director, White House Visitors Office. After the White House years, Melinda wrote a funny, surprising, candid memoir,* White House Story, *a Democratic memoir, and created the first and only recorded tour of the White House,* A Walk Through the White House.

Songs: *'Love the One You're With' (S); 'Our House' (N).*

April 5, 1993: President Clinton greets Stephen Stills in the Oval Office. Photo from the William J. Clinton Presidential Library – courtesy of John Keller

ALL ACCESS PASS - GRAHAM NASH

by Lorenzo Conci

I arrived in New York on the evening of 16 August 1994. It was a typical summer night - hot and sticky weather, humidity so high you keep sweating. I was taken by the lights of the city, by the air filled with smells and fumes, walking to my first stop, a hamburger joint.

I was staying with Ermanno Labianca, Italian editor of Bruce Springsteen fanzine *Follow That Dream*, at an apartment in the Village, and our plan was to see as many concerts we could. Before the internet, our only source of information was *The Village Voice*, that you could pick up for free at various outlets, our favorite being - of course - Tower Records.

I was excited and had dreamed and planned this escape for months, but when I woke up the following morning melancholy overtook me. I was missing my kids, four and six at the time, so much that I burst into tears while in the shower. The whole thing, being away from home just to catch some shows, seemed meaningless compared to the value of the time I could spend with them, their laughter still ringing in my ears. So, I said to myself, 'Ok, just this one: let's see CSN tonight and leave tomorrow'.

Strengthened by this resolution, I started planning the day. The show was to be held at the Jones Beach Theater in Wantagh, Long Island, so early in the afternoon I took the LIR train and a bus from Merrick. Feeling grateful, I picked up a complimentary ticket and after-show pass, courtesy of Debbie Meister of the CSN Management, the friendly voice we would talk to over the phone to have this arranged.

I was happy to be there but worried I would not get to see either Croz or Nash after the show, because I was told the band would leave immediately. The ocean was dark grey, the sky threatening. It seemed the perfect fit with all my worries.

Through Raymond Foye, a fan like us and a close friend of Graham, I was admitted backstage before the show. Nash was getting ready. Always a gentleman, kind and concerned, when hugging me he said, 'See you afterwards'. A bit shyly, I replied: 'Oh, I don't think I can. Your bus is supposed to leave right after the show'. I still can feel the warm feeling his reassuring voice gave me. 'Why?' he said. 'Come with me. I'll take you back to Manhattan'.

The show was excellent: the new songs from *After the Storm*, their latest release, sounded fresh and clear. 'Unequal Love' and 'It Won't Go Away' stood out. Sometimes I was taken by a feeling of disbelief and feared that Graham would forget to look out for me. What if I missed the bus? What if he'd left without me? What would I do? Sleep on the beach?

Maybe these thoughts conjured up a storm, because toward the end of the concert, it started pouring. They ended with 'Woodstock' and I was drenched, but happy and a bit anxious. I feared the crowd of friends and guests backstage to greet them was going to be so big I would never make it close to him and would end up stranded.

But no. All my hopes were met. Graham was alone in his dressing room. There was no meet and greet because of the downpour, and he was welcoming and reassuring like an older brother. He offered me a glass of red and gave me a hair dryer. He was in great spirits. I began to melt, taking it all in.

On his tour bus, it was just him, road manager Bob Stern, me and the driver. I felt so happy. They were talking away and I sat and listened like a kid on the back seat during a trip with the parents. It felt like being part of a family and I didn't think of me as a tourist anymore. In Manhattan, billboards and record shops windows were promoting Pink Floyd's *Division Bell* and I told Graham I had just seen them in Europe. He referred to David Gilmour as a good friend and a neighbour in Hawaii. He had helped when the two of them fixed the Nashes' plumbing and was the one who, in the midst of a bad divorce, answered the phone with 'house of broken dreams', the line Nash turned into a song.

Then he asked about my plans. I had tickets and passes for Holmdel and Philadelphia but wasn't sure about New Jersey and renting a car to drive to the Garden State Performing Arts Center. He looked at Sterne and said, 'We'll take you down, you can ride with the kids, and I'll meet you there in Holmdel.' Two days later CSN were supposed to fly to DC in the morning, sing at a White House surprise party for President Clinton and fly back to Newark for the show. I was supposed to be at the Plaza at 2pm, meet Stern, and ride to Holmdel with him, Willy and Nile.

As if that shouldn't be enough of a service, while hugging me, 'Good night! See you', he stopped and gave me his laminate, saying 'Take this. If you have troubles, use it and give it back to me there'. On the train to the Village, I kept looking at it, I could hardly believe it. It served as a reminder that everything was real: 'All Access – Graham Nash'.

Guess what? I stayed.

Philadelphia, 20 and 21 August, last stop on the 25th anniversary tour. After the show in Holmdel, I rode with Graham, the kids, Susan and Sterne on Graham's bus down to Philly. They let me have a room at the band's rate at the Four Seasons, where they always stay when in Philadelphia.

I hung out in the lobby around 4.30pm to be ready to ride with them to the venue for the soundcheck. Crosby was not feeling good but I had not perceived anything at the recent shows. On stage there was no sign something was wrong, but I noticed how everybody treated David with love and tenderness. He had spent all the time secluded with his wife Jan, so I was a bit surprised when he appeared in the lobby, briskly looked at me and nodded my way, 'Come with me.'

I followed them and felt embarrassed when, in a typical swift change of mood, he reacted pretty rudely to a few fans asking for autographs. When we got to his tour bus, there was no driver waiting for us and unexpectedly David sat at the wheel. Later I found out Nash was upset because Croz had given the day off to his driver.

Not surprisingly, he was running late and, in the traffic, he drove a bit aggressively. He grinned and his face showed the fun he was having, disregarding the rules. I don't believe his licence allowed him to drive a bus. At a major intersection, he didn't yield to oncoming traffic and came close to an accident, Jan shrieked, I froze, and he grinned, 'Intimidation by the size, that's how you drive these things.'

The Mann Music Center is a beautiful venue, surrounded by the green of trees, and I sat by myself, listening to the soundcheck. Such a privilege. The show was wonderful, Nash sang 'After the Storm', which they haven't done yet on the tour, and I tried to prepare myself for returning to real life the next day.

It was only afterwards that I found out from the crew that David's liver was collapsing. He was in great pain and if an organ donor was not found within weeks, he may not have made it through. It froze me to hear it. Saying goodbye, he invited me to come to New York in October when they were supposed to play a string of shows at the Beacon. I was scared I wouldn't get to see him again.

Bio: *Born in Trento, taking on classical studies, Lorenzo Conci is an eclectic man: engineer, CEO of Residencehotels Spa, ski instructor, International Ski Federation technical delegate, and president of the organising committee of the 3 / Tre of Madonna di Campiglio, World Cup slalom race. For him, 4 Way Street was the spark, in 1973. His first concert, at the age of 15, was Genesis in Reggio Emilia (4 February 1974). In the fourth year of high school in California, he saw concerts by Santana, Fleetwood Mac, America, The Beach Boys, Country Joe Mac Donald, and John Sebastian. He's witnessed more than 200 CSNY concerts, in all possible combinations – from Stills in 1980 at San Siro, to Crosby in May 2017. Since 1999, he has not missed a tour, together or separately.*

Old songs: *'Where Will I Be/Page 43' (C), 'So Begins the Task' (S), 'Another Sleep Song' (N).*
New songs: *'Somehow She Knew' (C), 'Don't Want Lies' (S), 'Myself At Last' (N).*

STEPHEN STILLS 'SOUTHERN CROSS' D-45SS SIGNATURE EDITION

by Dick Boak

In August 1995 I received a call from Martin's California district sales manager Dan Gulino concerning Stephen Stills. Dan had become friends with Tom Lowrey, Stephen's guitar technician and assistant at that time. Tom suggested Stephen might be interested in a signature model collaboration. We were certainly interested in Stephen.

From our perspective, the whole Crosby, Stllls, Nash & Young band was immensely significant, but we had to start somewhere. Very early on in our discussions it became clear that doing a CSN&Y model was going to be a real challenge. It would mean negotiating with an assortment of managers and agents, and it began to look like a licensing nightmare.

So, conversations focused logically on Stephen, after all he is the most fervent Martin aficionado in the group, a serious Martin collector, and incredibly astute in his knowledge of Martin history and instruments.

Initially, Stephen centered in on the herringbone D-28 as the basis for his signature edition. Actual detailed specifications were

Stephen Stills' Southern Cross D-45SS Signature Edition

developed for an HD-40SS model, but gradually Stephen's love
of higher end vintage models persuaded him in the direction of a
Brazilian D-45.

He was so excited about the project that he booked a flight just to
visit the factory, Nazareth in Pennsylvania, arriving with a yellow
tablet in hand, upon which he had enumerated a lengthy list of
details relating to the model. He knew what he was talking about
and by the end of the day had had an in-depth factory tour and
had carefully stipulated all the specifications for a Stephen Stills

*Graham Nash with Chris Martin IV at NAMM 2003, Los Angeles, California. David
Crosby playing his signature Martin D-12 model (photo by Emily Boak). Dick Boak
with CSN. Photos courtesy of Dick Boak's private collection*

'Southern Cross' D-45SS Signature Edition of just 91 special instruments. That was exactly the number of Martin D-45s produced before World War II.

During that visit, Stephen also fell in love with a Jimmie Rodgers 000-45JR Signature Model along the tour route, and for his daughter, a 00-16DB Women & Music model caught his eye. We arranged to ship these instruments out to California and concurrently, we initiated the prototypes for Stephen's model.

In researching the Southern Cross constellation on the internet, I found the Australian flag and quickly digitized the star configuration for Mother of Pearl inlay into Stephen's pickguards. After a significant amount of labor, Pearl Works sent the first samples, one of which I forwarded to Stephen with great anticipation, only to be quickly informed there were in fact five stars in the Southern Cross constellation, not six as the flag represented. The large white seven-pointed star in the lower left quadrant is not part of the constellation but represents the seven states of Australia and is known as the Commonwealth Star.

In spite of this, the error was easy to correct, and the prototypes gradually reached completion. We shipped one to Stephen for his comments, and he had many. The top was too white and needed toner, one of the bindings was too tall to be indicative of 1930s' styling, and he wanted the model to be offered with hexagon inlays as well as Style 45 snowflakes (as were the original 91 D-45s of the pre-war era), depending on the taste of the customer.

Though we were frustrated at not getting everything right on the first pass, it certainly was a testament to Stephen's great knowledge of our instruments. His fastidious input ensured the model possessed accuracy and integrity. Stephen had ordered several edition guitars for bandmates. One for Neil Young had a customized pickguard with an abalone inlaid broken arrow. Stephen customized his own prototype with his name in large pearl script lettering in the fingerboard. It is certain that Stephen's signature models caught the attention of David Crosby, himself a longtime D-45 owner.

The edition was unveiled at the Nashville NAMM Show in July 1998. Stephen attended and signed a great deal of autographs, after which we took him out to a great dinner at Morton's to thank him for making the trip to Nashville. The details of that memorable dinner are reserved for another book entirely. We came away from Nashville pretty elated, about half of the edition sold – not bad given the retail price of the Stills model was $19,000.

In the meantime, Stephen earmarked the Tides Center Foundation as the recipient of the charitable contribution from the project. Those royalties would go a long way in bringing music education to children.

It was a very interesting experience from a professional point of view and exceptional from a human point of view. Suffice it to say, although Stephen has 'paid his dues,' he is a marvellous talent with tremendous personality, humor, and character.

Bio: *Dick Boak has worn many hats at C.F. Martin and Company over 40 years. From design draftsman to director of artist relations, from company historian to director of the company's special projects. Dick also became director of the C.F. Martin & Co. Museum and archives. Currently living in Nazareth, Pennsylvania, Dick retired in January 2018, celebrating in full style with a concert featuring Steve Miller, John Mayer, Marty Stuart, Jorma Kaukonen, and David Bromberg.*

Songs: *'Guinnevere' (C), 'Southern Cross' (S), 'Simple Man' (N).*

1995: CROSBY/NASH AT WESTBURY MUSIC FAIR, LONG ISLAND, NY

by Roy Abrams

A Crosby/Nash show was always unforgettably unique; an entity of its own related to but by no means dependent upon the 'mothership' of CSN. On this particular evening, I came to the concert bearing gifts to present to each artist. For David, whom I knew was travelling with his wife, Jan and son, Django: a bright red jogging suit-type outfit that was exponentially too small for Crosby but the perfect size for his infant son, with an accompanying card. For Graham, a new issue of *The Music Paper* featuring a major interview with Nash that focused on *Life Sighs*, a technological marvel of a performance concept he had been working on with collaborator Rand Weatherwax.

My original plan was to deliver these gifts personally backstage after the concert; I knew after-show passes were waiting. However, upon speaking with the road manager, I learned that there were simply no available passes; Crosby, having just returned to the touring life after a lengthy recovery from liver transplant surgery, had a large number of family and friends from the New York area who had not seen him since before his illness, each of whom received a pass. I was told that even Graham Nash had to relinquish his remaining personal guest passes to accommodate the sheer volume of familial well-wishers who came to celebrate their relative's return to his normal life. There were simply no passes left.

Disappointed but understanding the situation, I handed the aforementioned gifts to the road manager, asking him to please deliver the items to their intended recipients. Making our way to our seats, we no sooner had sat down than my companion tugged on my arm, saying she saw the man I was just talking to heading in our direction. I turned and, sure enough, the road manager saw me and beckoned me to join him. Unbelievably, he held out two after-show passes, with the words, 'Graham saved these two for you.' Humbled and honored that Nash would be so thoughtful I made my way back to my seat, somewhat stunned.

After a show that can only be called – in a favorite term of Crosby's – a stunner, we made our way backstage and were greeted with a sight that, to this day, retains the surreal nature of the moment. The only other people in the room were David, his wife Jan – holding Django on her lap – and Graham, who was standing in a corner, reading the very issue of *The Music Paper* I brought for him. On a long, rectangular table situated in front of an L-shaped couch upon which David, Jan, and Django sat, was the opened gift box containing the bright red jogging suit, and the opened card stood nearby.

Graham walked over and told me he was glad the passes had found their way to me. He enjoyed reading the interview and asked how we enjoyed the show. As if rehearsed, we replied in unison, 'We loved it!' Nash chuckled, and at that moment, another familiar figure entered the room: John F. Kennedy, Jr. had stopped by to say hello.

Then David stood up, walked toward me, looked me dead in the eye, took my right hand in both of his, and asked, 'That gift is from you?' Answering in the affirmative, he replied, 'That was very, very, kind of you. Thank you very, very much!' I could not help noticing the tears in Crosby's eyes as he said this, and I felt the need to crack a joke to lighten the atmosphere. 'I tried finding a matching one in your eyes, but they don't make them that big,' Corny, undoubtedly, but enough to bring a sunny smile to Crosby's face.

November 11, 1995: Crosby & Nash with Jeff Pevar live at Valley Forge Music Fair, Devon, Pennsylvania, USA. Photo by Francesco Lucarelli

CAPE LOBSTERS AND GUITARS

by Marc Maingard

It's 1995. I'm sitting in a stadium in Cape Town listening to Paul Simon and his band. It was at a time when I knew I was making a great guitar, but had no idea how to get it out there into the real world:

January 25, 1996: Marc Maingard with Stephen Stills, backstage at Good Hope Centre, Cape Town, South Africa. Photo by Jeremy Dowson - from Marc Maingard's private collection

USA, Europe, etc. As I sat there, I thought to myself, 'Now here is a great musician and guitar player, why did I not make a plan to show him my guitars? I am considered the best in South Africa. So, what's my problem?' I walked away from that concert promising myself I would somehow connect with the next famous guitar player coming to South Africa.

Towards the end of the year, I heard Crosby, Stills & Nash were coming to play. 'My chance!' I thought. I found out Dave Marks of Third Ear Music was the promoter. I had known Dave for many years, so called him. 'Sure, we can try to do something, but it's not so simple. You have to get past the manager, the minders, etc. before you get close to the band.'

I replied, 'Cool, how many are there?' 'More or less 20 people,' he said. 'How about a fresh crayfish dinner for them all?' I suggested. 'Great Cape wine at my house at the seaside in Scarborough. They can come for dinner, chill out, talk guitars, and move from there.'

So that's what we did. I personally dived out thirty or so lovely Cape Crayfish, ordered some great Boschendal Chardonnay, made a big bowl of French mayonnaise as my mother had taught me, a huge salad, lots of snacks and things, and we were ready.

They arrived just in time for sunset in front of my house, and what a great crew they all were! Lots of fun and laughter. A fantastic evening was had by all. They loved my guitars and suggested to put four or five guitars in their dressing rooms, at the venue where the band was scheduled to play and see what happens. Done deal! I was so excited. Stephen Stills and the band had been my heroes since Woodstock. What a treat to be able – maybe - to meet them.

Next night arrived and I went to the venue with my sons Nathan and Joshua, and my partner Tracey. Dave and the crew put my guitars in their dressing rooms, and CSN played a stunning concert. More amazing was the fact that Stephen had that terrible fall in Durban and was in a lot of pain and discomfort.

At the end of the show, when everyone was chilling, we were all sitting in the crew section, and Graham Nash walked in, holding a D model guitar of mine, asking, 'Who made this guitar?' They all looked at me and I said, 'I did.' He said, 'This is a fantastic guitar! You must come through and hang with the rest of the band. They want to meet you.'

I could not believe it. I went through with my boys and Tracey and met Stephen - who was playing my Grand Concert model - and David Crosby with his wife and young baby. An instant party. David said, 'This is one of the most accurate 12-string guitars I have ever played. Accurate way past the 12th fret!'

An hour or so later Stills wanted to go back to the hotel and we tagged along. Stephen and I played 'Teach Your Children' on my guitars. I felt like I was in Heaven!

We hung out again at the venue and hotel and discussed the way forward for a guitar, leaving it that I would be in touch once he had returned to the USA.

At the venue, on Saturday, a *Sunday Times* reporter took a picture of us together and Stills said to him, 'I came to South Africa to play a series of concerts, never thinking I would find one of the world's best guitar makers here. He really is amazing. His guitars are everything I could wish for.'

I was walking on cloud nine, after those moments, really looking forward to getting a guitar into his hands. Unfortunately, that proved to be impossible, as – for a number of reasons - I could not get hold of him in the USA. Great artists are often so protected by their managers and staff that in the end it is just not possible to get in touch with them.

However, his comments really helped launch me and my guitars worldwide. And as CSN are such respected musicians, many people got hold of me due to the comments in the newspaper. And to this day I am incredibly grateful to Stephen Stills, Graham Nash and David Crosby for the time they spent with me, for the laughter and good vibes.

Bio: *Born in Durban, South Africa, to French immigrant parents, master luthier Marc Maingard traces his family lineage to 1350. It is a legacy of craftsmen musicians, lute and viol makers to the French court. Marc performed as a professional musician in South Africa and Europe. Unable to have his guitar repaired in the early Seventies forced Marc to attempt the work himself and he subsequently flourished as a repairman. As an avid surfer he lives in Cape St Francis, Eastern Cape. For the last 45 years, he has devoted himself to guitar construction and restoration, following his dream of making trees sing again.*

Songs: *'Woodstock' (CSNY version); 'Teach Your Children' (N).*

NORTHERN MAN

by Ian Astle

I come from York, in the northern part of England. I was introduced to CSN's music at high school in 1969: Crosby, Stills & Nash's first album blew me away. I've followed their music ever since. Seeing the *Woodstock* movie at the cinema confirmed my feel for hippie music and long-haired look! I wore neck beads through college, denims and long sideburns. Crosby, Stills & Nash, and Neil Young had become the soundtrack of my life.

During my 1972-76 college years, I had all their albums and played *4 Way Street* loudly in my college digs. That's how I introduced many students to their music. Attending a CSN&Y concert at Wembley Stadium in 1974 was fantastic, but I had to wait 23 more years before meeting them in person.

Fast forward to 1997, spending a week at the Fillmore Theatre in San Francisco: it was seven evenings of bliss! Graham Nash supplied me with photo and after-show passes. I had the chance to chat to him throughout the week: what a great guy, the glue that holds them together. During those days, Stills and Crosby were a little more reserved, but it was nice to have a few moments with them too. And Neil Young turned up one night and joined in on the encores. What a moment!

I had the privilege of attending Nash's private party at the Triton Hotel on the Wednesday night and an opportunity to photograph one of the most beautiful rooms of the hotel: the CSN suite, 'Suite: Judy Blue Eyes'. Again, Graham looked after me. He has the ability to make you feel important and appreciates your efforts to meet him. He always has time for you and loves to chat. A real gentleman. He is a northerner, after all!

Bio: *Born in 1952, Ian Astle lives in York, England. A retired high school teacher, his main hobby is photography. He adds, 'I was a live concert photographer from 1979-95 and since then I've covered a few gigs for pleasure. Over the past five years I have had a few exhibitions in local galleries. I'm currently archiving my collection of rock-stars gigs and my website is in working progress: www.rockandrollshots.co.uk. My current activity is photographing York, using mainly iphone 7+, and celebrating its glory!'*

Songs: *'Homeward Through the Haze' (C); 'Cherokee' (S); 'Another Sleep Song' (N).*

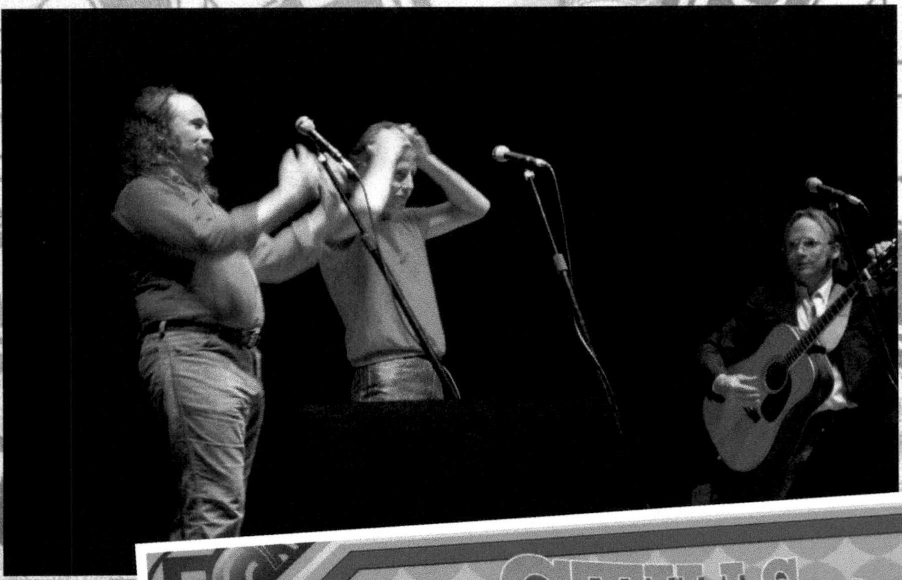

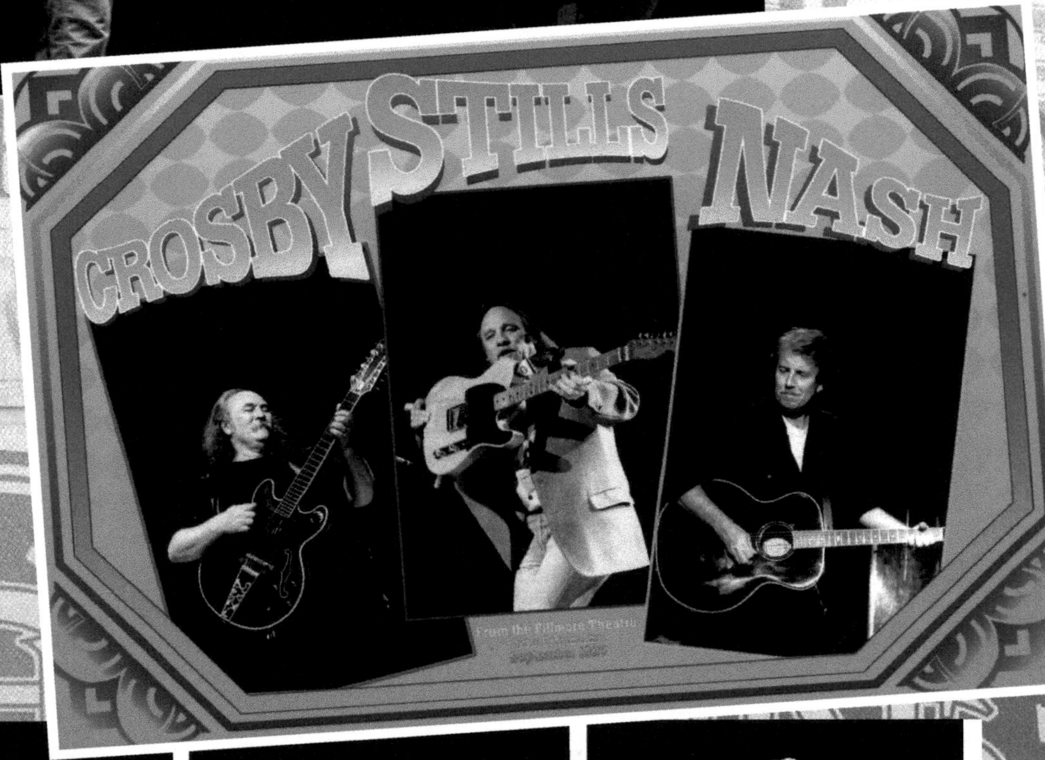
CROSBY
STILLS
NASH
From the Fillmore Theatre

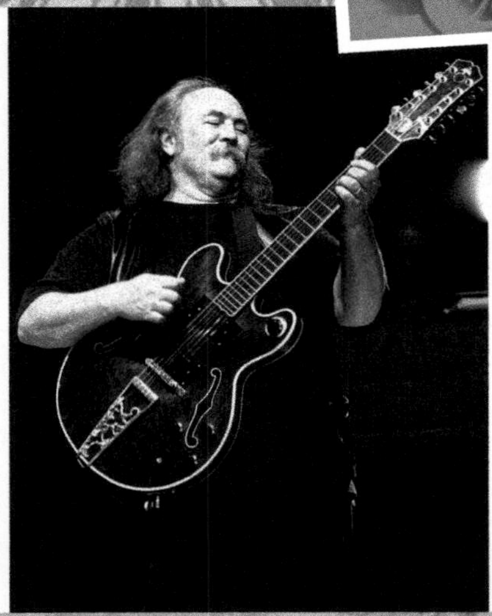

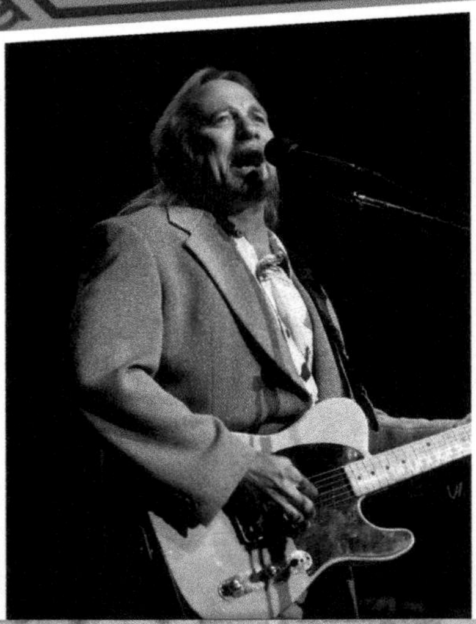

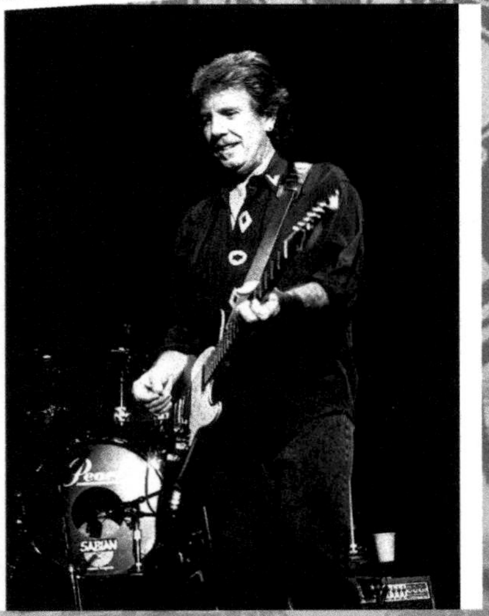

July 9, 1983: National Exhibition
Center, Birmingham, England;
September 14 - 20, 1997: The
Fillmore, San Francisco, California,
USA. All photos by Ian Astle

January 26, 1997: Crosby / CPR tour live at The Wild Duck, Eugene, Oregon, USA. Photo by Tim Owen

August 19, 1994: CSN at President Clinton's birthday party. Photo by Robert McNeely (courtesy of William J. Clinton Presidential Library)

WHAT A FUCKED-UP WORLD!

by John Braun

In 1970 I was fifteen, still broken-hearted that The Beatles had broken up. I had three older brothers in Vietnam, one of whom brought some LPs home with him for me, because he knew I was a music fanatic. I played them all, then put on one that entirely changed my life: CSNY's *Déjà Vu*. As soon as I heard 'Carry On/Questions', I was hooked. I hadn't even heard the first CSN album, but went out and bought it the next day. It blew my mind. These guys were amazing. I had heard of Graham Nash and had several Hollies albums. I had heard The Byrds, but that was McGuinn's band. I'd never even heard of Buffalo Springfield up to that point. FM radio was just beginning in the US, so I started hearing them too. I was on my way!

The music kept flowing - Jefferson Airplane, Jimi Hendrix, The Doors … but there was nothing like those magical voices of CSN. Of course, after *Déjà Vu*, they all went their own way: Crosby's *If Only I Could Remember My Name*, Nash's *Songs for Beginners*, Stills' *Stephen Stills 2*, and Young's *Everybody Knows This is Nowhere*. I was blown away again!

Now able to drive, I went to see these guys. At the time it was solo shows or Crosby/Nash shows, the Stills Young Band, then the CSN 1977 reunion tour, a couple of Graham's shows, and Neil with Crazy Horse. I was totally hooked. I couldn't get enough. Then there was silence for about four years. The *Daylight Again* album was pretty good but lacked Crosby's songs. 'Might As Well Have a Good Time' was good but not written by David. 'Delta' was excellent but had to be pulled out of him by Jackson Browne. Then, as we all know, the bottom fell out.

I first met Graham at an art show in the mid-Eighties in Youngstown, Ohio. I was scared shitless to talk to the man and I didn't say anything intelligent to him. I again met him in 1997 in an art gallery in Cleveland, Ohio. Croz was there and Joe Walsh too. I took my son Graham, of course named after Nash, and after I introduced myself and my son. Graham kneeled down to speak with my son, who was eight, and asked him if he played music and had any instruments. My son told him yes, he had a guitar and a set of keyboards. Nash talked to him for about five minutes, basically telling him to stick with it and maybe he could be a rock'n roll star as well. Nash then stood up, looked at me and said, 'What a fucked-up world!' I asked him why he said that. He replied that anybody that would name a kid after him was fucked up!

Fast forward to 2014. My ex-wife, myself and my son Graham, 24 by then, went to New York City for a visit, our last night being a show at the City Winery, a very cool venue. Before the show, we had a 'Meet and Greet' with Nash. I bought his new book, *Wild Tales*, and purposely planned on being the last group to meet with Graham before the show. I figured this would give us more time with him. As it turned out, I was right. We spent a half hour together, talking about everything from the new CSNY 1974 CD about to be released to asking Graham about the possibility of a CSNY reunion tour.

Then I asked him to sign the copy of the book I had just bought. When I asked him to sign it 'What a fucked-up world!' he picked up the story about halfway through and finished it himself. His notes inside the cover says, 'To John, Jackie and Graham … what a fucked-up world.' He remembered the experience from 17 years earlier. What a guy!

Bio: *John Braun grew up in a small town in Northeast Ohio and has lived there ever since. He adds, 'I was fortunate enough to hook up with some very cool musicians and became their roadie for a while, when I wasn't working my day job. I collected albums, had a nice stash, but CSN&Y were always in the front of the cantaloupe crate. I attended every show I could, solo and in various combinations. I couldn't get enough. Then I started saving ticket stubs, set-list, picks, whatever I could get my hands on. As time went on, and my career became more successful, I became more mobile, and somehow have seen them, again, in various combos all over the country. Thank you, Francesco, for making me go thru a lot of my memories for you to share with the world. It was an amazing experience and has taken me back in time on many occasions as I searched through 8-tracks, cassettes, 45s, albums, CDs, bootleg tapes, and on and on.'*

Songs: *'Cowboy Movie,' 'Tracks in the Dust,' 'Through Here Quite Often' (C); 'Don't Want Lies,' 'There Was a Place,' 'Think I'll Go Back Home' (S); 'Liar's Nightmare,' 'Lost Another One,' 'Myself at Last' (N).*

WELCOME TO THE SHOW!

by Gareth McNair-Lewis

I met Graham Nash on Remembrance Day (known as Veterans Day in the US) at the Vietnam Veterans Monument Wall in Washington DC on 11 November 1998. He was there because he was scheduled to sing 'Live On', a new song he had recently written about the Vietnam Veterans Wall, which was part of the soundtrack of TV movie, *The Wall*.

Nash was talking to a few official looking people but no one else in the crowd seemed to recognize him. A few minutes later, when he stood alone facing the wall which honors the name of 58,000 service members of the US armed forces who died in the Vietnam War, I approached him, introduced myself and we shook hands. I said I had written a few concert reviews for *Wooden Nickel* fanzine over the years and regularly corresponded by mail with the editor.

I reminded him of our brief meeting at the CSN Great Woods concert, near Boston, in 1990 during the *Live it Up* tour. I had walked in late to the show after the third song, and Nash was just finishing a piano song when I walked down the center aisle to the front row. He saw me holding up my new copy of the *CSNY Wooden Nickel Photo Special* book and he leaned over and shook my hand as if to say, 'Welcome to the show,' with the class that has always distinguished him and the friendliness of the landlord.

I told him how much I had enjoyed the 1991 CSN boxset and about some unreleased songs they chose not to include. He said they all had so many songs and they couldn't fit everything they wanted on there, but future solo boxsets would meet the demand for lots of lesser-known songs. In fact, over time, he was the engine behind the three boxes dedicated by Rhino to Stephen Stills, David Crosby and himself. And it was Graham, along with Joel Bernstein, who was able to bring to the light the beautiful boxset with the recordings of the 1974 CSN&Y tour.

As we said goodbye and parted company, after a very kind and cordial conversation, I was impressed by something very unusual for someone used to meet so many different people each day: he remembered my name!

Bio: *Born in Cardiff, Wales, Gareth McNair-Lewis lives in Bryantown, Maryland, USA. He works at the Maryland Archaeological Conservation Laboratory in St. Leonard as a conservation technician.*

Songs: *'Carry Me' (C); 'See the Changes' (S); 'Cathedral' (N).*

YOU PICKED THE RIGHT INSTRUMENT

by Vasken Gurdjian

September 1999. I received a shipment to my home in France of my very own Stephen Stills Martin D-45 SS, 'The Southern Cross.' Mine was number 26 out of 91 instruments made for this special limited run. I think I learned about the guitar on the Martin website, as I frequently visit it. As a long-time fan of Stephen Stills and his music, and being a musician myself, owning the instrument was very important to me and has a special meaning. The first song I played when I got it was 'Bound to Fall' from the album *Manassas*.

April 13, 2002: CSNY live at National Car Rental Center, Sunrise, Florida, USA. Photo by Tom Davis

I already had a D28 autographed by CSN in Atlantic City in 1996, if I am not wrong, thanks to Hans and Lorraine. I remember waiting at the door with Danny 'Mouse' de la Luz, one of their long-time roadies – sadly not with us anymore - when Stephen opened the door sweating, wearing a bathrobe. He yelled, 'Get me a sharpy!' He signed it and I couldn't even say 'Hi'. I was so speechless. That was my first encounter with Stephen Stills.

When I heard about the 'Southern Cross' guitar, I called Mandolin Brothers and booked that D-45 SS. The waiting was long but worth every penny. I am not a guitar pro, but the sound and the feelings were out of this world. At that time, I met Stephen Barncard in Paris. We went together to Chris Stills' showcase at Virgin Megastore Paris and I got Stephen's email address from Chris.

I wanted to send a message to Stills and let him know how honored I was to own this limited-edition guitar. Among other things, I wrote, 'I want to thank you for taking such good care of us all, by letting us dream a little by touching this wonderful piece of art.' I thought I would have never got an answer but - boy - the day I got his mail I was nuts. Really nuts! I couldn't believe my eyes. I was rewarded with wonderful correspondence back from Stephen, discussing the guitar and its creation at length. That message really shows his love for music and for guitars, his attention to details, his intelligence, wit and humor. What can I say...the man is my hero.

I waited for a few years and on 7 June 2005, when CSN played in Paris at Le Palais des Congrès, Joe Vitale had it autographed by Stills. He said Stephen didn't want to damage the top, so he put a very little tidy autograph besides the bridge. A couple of years later, Joe helped me to meet Stephen in NYC during a SS solo show at the Concert Hall of the New York Society for Ethical Culture, on 14 May 2007. We took a picture and Stephen yelled at Joe, 'Come on, click before we get older!'

Bio: *Born and raised in Beirut, Lebanon to an Armenian family, Vasken Gurdjian met rock at 12 through The Beatles' red double-LP (1962-1966), and used to sing 'She Loves You' all day, so the neighbours complained to his parents, and 20 years later, 'Suite: Judy Blue Eyes,' playing it in Paris, France, the neighbours starting to send letters. He adds, 'CSN...every one of them fed my soul. I was lucky enough to meet all of three. Hope to see them back on the mothership again. Carry On.'*

Songs: *'Wooden Ships' (C) – 'transports me to the indefinite future'; 'Suite: Judy Blue Eyes' (S) – 'the most beautiful love song I have ever heard'; 'Chicago' (N) – 'shouts for justice.'*

VASKEN GURDJIAN'S MESSAGE FROM STEPHEN ...

Way to go, bud. You picked the right instrument. All the people at Martin worked very hard on it, and I think CFM is quite frankly glad to see the last of me. I pretty much drove them crazy over the minutiae as well as the initial structure. At any rate, Chris Martin decided to get up off his best edelweiss spruce and Brazilian rosewood for this run.

I am flattered beyond measure that it carries my name. This project was never about money. It has, from the start, been about replicating the best qualities of the craftsmanship that went into the pre-war D-45's. As a former luthier and guitar shop dogs body, I learned just enough to bust their balls over the details once I got the chance. I am very proud of the result. I have played 12 of them so far, and every one of them has a) a unique voice and b) comes out of the case sounding like an old guitar.

This is not by accident. Once I saw the proof in the other models that they were serious about reproducing and adhering to the space devised by the makers of the pre-war era, I was able to hold their feet to the fire and get the shop to pay attention and get it right. They also proved themselves correct in the modern advancements.

The truss-rod assembly (which I would never have believed could be successfully incorporated into the design without destroying the resonant qualities of the neck and body interact), works wonderfully and the updated size and placement of the bridge and saddle has introduced a mathematical precision to the intonation that is flawless. The sucker stays flat in tune all the way up to the neck, which is something that cannot be said for the old ones.

The scalloped braces are of a similar density of wood type, and only slightly adjusted to accommodate the placement of the bridge. The size of the binding is back to the older, smaller specs, and the joining and finishing most exact.

These are but a few of the reasons yours and every other instrument that has come to life during this limited production run, sounds and plays so amazingly, and remains true to the original formula. One is hard pressed to imagine the qualities they will attain with age.

I used the neck design most comfortable to me: a bit fine with very little crown to the fingerboard so as to accommodate the demands of an experienced player who is able to employ a wide variety of techniques, from fingerpicking, to flat-picked bluegrass to big handfuls of chords, as well as defined, precise lead melodies.

This instrument is not intended for the faint of heart. If you can make it, it will react with all the delicacy and passion you require. But you have to get there, because its very precision is such that it does not respond well to being sawed upon with the heavy hand of a folk poet sage content to bash out a few chords in support of their latest tome.

There were 91 D-45's made before WW II. Many of them were not that great, intended to satisfy the glitzy showmanship of the cowboy star, the band lead-singer, the front man in need of a prop. So they had lots of abalone inlay and fat necks and looked good and played terribly at first.

The herringbone was the player's guitar; a big version of the finesse pieces of the 00 and 000 types. That's what Hank Williams and Doc Watson and Lester Flatt and so many others had.

But people getting hit records eventually got the attention of the old boys down in Nazareth, and these craftsmen were never going to be satisfied with the idea of their top-of-the-line guitar as a prop. So, it wasn't before long before they got down to business and put everything they had into constructing the finest instrument they could imagine. All their best wood, resins, and the lessons of having been at it awhile already. By the mid-Thirties they had it down, and we have not seen or heard its equal since.

Anyway, that's what I wanted to have copied, with a few minor adjustments in realistic deference to modern science, and that is exactly what they have done. And a damn fine job of it, too. Don't you think?

Kindest regards,
Stephen Stills

May 10, 1997: CSN at Fox Theatre, Detroit, Michigan, USA. Photo by Michael Curcuru

October 11, 2018: Graham Nash live at The Theatre at Ace Hotel, Los Angeles, California, USA. Photo by Gary Goltz

00's

Things We Do for Love

6th ANNUAL
VALLEY MUSIC FESTIVAL
a special benefit for arts outreach

NEIL YOUNG
DAVID CROSBY
& CPR

SEPTEMBER 28, 2003
FIRESTONE CROSSROADS MEADOW

ALL ACCESS

CROSBY
STILLS
NASH
2001

CROSBY NASH 2005

2/20/2005

Crosby
Stills &
Nash
10/4 CLUB

KONOCTI HARBOR
3/29/03

MILITARY MADNESS
MARRAKESH
LONG TIME GONE
LAY ME DOWN
IMMIGRATION
IN MY DREAMS
JUST A SONG
CARRY ME
JESUS OF RIO
THEY WANT IT ALL
CATHEDRAL
DEJA

COLD RAIN / THE WALL
GUINNEVERE
MILKY WAY
PUPPETEER
USE TO BE A KING
DELTA / TRIAD
DON'T DIG HERE
WASTED ON THE WAY
WIND ON THE WATER
WOODEN SHIPS

OUR HOUSE
CUT MY HAIR

TEACH

CROSBY STILLS NASH

AFTER SHOW ON

ONTARIO
CSNY2K
YOUR

CROSBY STI
& NASH

8 LUGLIO '05
VILLA PISANI

PLATEA
Posto 3
Settore 3

nome
cognome _ZUCARELLI_
ruolo

NO BACKSTAG

SN
CROSBY, STILLS & NASH
LIVE
2004
ALL

PASSPORT

CROSBY STILLS NASH & YOUNG
MERCHANDISE COLLECTION

North American Tour 2000

RJ600
30/99
WA
VALID FOR

ADMISSION
IF ATTACHED
DULT

76.00 PRICE
5 TAX1 7

02
105 27 9

CONTR

PRESENTED BY VH1
AMERICA WEST ARENA

CROSBY STILLS NASH YO

NO CAMERAS/RECORDE

MON FEB 21, 2000 8:0

SEC 105 02 A

SEAT

a special benefit for arts outreach
...SIC FESTIVAL

MUSIC IS LOVE
CROSBY, STILLS AND NASH

PHOTO...

1st 2 SONG
ONLY
NO FLASH
...RO 3-7-10

NEIL YOUNG
DAVID CROSBY
& CPR
SEPTEMBER 28, 2003
ONE CROSSROADS MEADOW
VIP

CSNY 2000
DC 4/5 MSG VIP

SPECIAL CSNY 2000 GUEST

CROSBY, STILLS &

...CCESS

...LLIE

WOODSTOCK
LOVE THE ONE M
HELPLESSLY HOPING S
49 REASONS STARTS SLOW W/ MOMENTS OF UPBEATS & ENDS W/UPBEAT
MAKE LOVE TO YOU S BUILDS ON CHORUS
ACADIENNE CAJUN STYLE
CAN'T GET NEXT TO YOU - KEYS LEAD VOCAL UPBEAT BLUE
JOHNNY'S GARDEN NICE MELLOW M.
DEATH LETTER - KEYS LEAD VOCAL ROCK BLUES
SEEN ENOUGH M TREETOP FLYER
SOUTHERN CROSS
FOR WHAT ITS' WORTH
DARK STAR - DRUM INTRO / PERCUSSION
MAN of CONSTANT SORROW - SOLO ACOUS
(CARRY ON)

*Belterra, IN
11/15/2001*

MW0716   3   T   2   AD
EVENT CODE   SECTION/AISLE   ROW/BOX   SEAT
$100.00   MAIN FLOOR   1
CONVENIENCE FINANCE
$11.85   *** **** ***
SECTION/AISLE
3   CROSBY STILLS & NA
ticketmast
JI   11X
ROW   SEAT   MOUNTAIN WINERY
T   2
715AZUS   14831 PIERCE RD/SARA
WED JUL...

CSNY 2000

by Lorenzo Conci

It was really cold and there was a lot of snow on the ground when I landed in Detroit, late afternoon on 22 January 2000, excited about the CSNY tour about to begin. I remember the drive to Auburn Hills, the radio tuned to a classic rock station, 'Comfortably Numb' engulfing the car. The night was black and the snow whitish on the side of the highway.

The United States felt like home. The year I spent as an exchange student in high school did the trick, that and my love for music and American literature keeping me attached. This time I couldn't miss the opening night of the CSNY reunion tour.

It was a dream I'd had since seeing pictures of the 1974 show in London. I was too young and had heard of it after they played it. I grew up on *4 Way Street* and whatever it took, I had to be here. I had sent an email to Graham a few days ago, simply saying, 'I'm coming to Detroit'. He must have been online, the reply coming immediately, 'See you there'.

The show was on Monday, 24 January, and I was a little concerned about killing a Sunday in Detroit, not a place you would probably choose for a day off. But I was lucky, the end of January marked the time of the Motorshow, world famous, and I was interested to visit. Seeing the Detroit Pistons beat the Dallas Mavericks at the Palace of Auburn Hills, the same venue where my dream was to come true, made it a full day.

Monday morning, I couldn't wait, anxiety growing, like if I was playing the gig. What if in the end it didn't amount to much, what if the myth wa bigger than the real thing? Maybe they were huge just for us kids in Europe, just because they were far and unreachable.

The parking lot was already full when I get there. It wasn't even dark and it was an eight o'clock show. Wow! Signs of affection. People loved them over here, too. I felt less lonely. The merch stand was surrounded by prospect customers, I wouldn't be the only one buying all the different t-shirts.

Lights off, 'Carry On' and 'Southern Man', 'Pre-road Downs', 'Cinnamon Girl', the sound very similar to *4 Way Street,* bass and drums the only addition to the foursome. It was so potent. If I closed my eyes, I was back in my room, listening to the vinyl and dreaming ... maybe one day... which was here now!

For the acoustic set they sat on barstools. 'Helplessly Hoping', 'Our House', 'Only Love Can Break Your Heart', 'Looking Forward'. The carpets and the old lamp were there, and it was, 'Welcome to our living

April 19, 2000: : CSNY live at Kiel Center, St. Louis, Missouri, USA. Photo by Tom Davis

room!' once again. After another electric set, they closed the concert with a soulful 'Long May You Run'.

We were among a group of about 30 with backstage passes, still thrilled, over-excited, deeply satisfied with what we'd seen. Tour manager, Mike Sexton – Coach, as everyone in the CSNY family called him – came over and reported that the guys were tired and they apologized that there would be no meet and greet. A little delusion hung in the air. Then Coach turned to me and said, 'Just him. Lorenzo, come with me.'

Graham was in his dressing room. He looked super-happy, exhausted, but still excited. He had many things to do and told me to come along. First, over to drummer Jim Keltner and bass player Duck Dunn, to say thank you, and it's a very kind thing they appreciated a lot. Then he had an interview, together with Stills, and I sit there in a corner, like a puppet. I had to pinch myself … was I dreaming?

They told them they were very happy. First CSNY tour since 1974. They were not sure - would the magic still be there? Would the fans show up after so many years? Everything was there, the magic and the crowd. And from the next day there were 50 more shows.

Afterwards, Graham went around, expressing gratitude to everyone in the crew. The load-out was a big thing: amps and cases with the CSNY 2K logo, I was so thrilled. Then, turning to me, he told me how grateful I'd come from Italy, even more so when I told him I was flying back tomorrow. Deep within myself, I was melting.

Before the tour ended, I would be back for two more shows, in New York at the Madison Square Garden, 3 and 4 April. Together with Francesco Lucarelli and his wife Isabella, we visited Graham in his suite. He was still so happy. The tour had been a great success and great fun. Egos were in check, they let Neil be the artistic director, they acknowledged his strength and focus. 'My career could be over, I'm 60…. instead, I'm doing the thing I love the most. This band is still alive and well, we have fun playing together and people still love us. How could I not be happy, excited and grateful for my faith?'

Well, it's hard not to agree with him. Francesco, Isabella and I, looked around this suite at the Carlyle Hotel, Midtown Manhattan. The three of us alone with Graham Nash. How could we not feel grateful?

TRAVEL NOTES

by Isabella Cattan

Thirty years of encounters, unrolling lives, changing paths that come and go. Emotions, words, notes, glances, and joking around. The background made up of theatres, arenas, historic villas and auditoriums. In the middle of it all, three guys who were often the reason for the travelling. Sometimes they were one person, sometimes two, sometimes three together: fit, tired, enthusiastic, ironic, poetic, wise, capricious, alive.

When I talked about my life with Francesco, I always started with a premise, a *lectio vitae*, if you like. To follow and uphold the passions of the person you love is not always easy, or even simple. But once you shake off the jet-lag, the hours spent listening to the same tunes over and over again, the half-hour conversations about a single song, interminable solos, concerts in improbable clubs, days spent between hotels and theatres, soundchecks, interviews and travelled miles, what remained made you weak at the knees, just like the first time.

A network of friendships around the world offering you their lives and feasting on yours. A continuous osmosis of languages, passions, places, stories. It is music that brings everything together through a single ball of yarn, full of sensations and mutual enrichment. Like a tireless postman, it covers daring trajectories and styles and is able to unite people so different from each other, yet so close, in an endless party.

A tape, a package, a dedication on the cover of an album, a postal order subscription, a review in a newspaper, a CD sent by priority mail, a video, an email, a text message, a post, a tweet. A last-minute train, a lost flight, a bike ride on an island in the middle of a river, a music tour in a redwood forest, a

April 13, 2002: CSNY live at National Car Rental Center, Sunrise, Florida, USA. Photo by Tom Davis

play, a painting, a photograph, an unforgettable dish, an afternoon of Trappist beers, a missed concert, an unexpected encounter. Above all, the palpable, thick, enveloping sensation of a single soundtrack, like a lifelong hug.

This is the best gift of music: the world, its lives, its people and their passions. Everything close at hand, everything at your fingertips. And, in the midst of this plot, the myths, the musicians, their friendship, the memories.

Nash, who refuses to try tiramisu at a restaurant in Rome - 'It wouldn't do justice to the best of all, yours', who asks you in NYC where you bought your candy apple shoes, who takes you to eat Creole in Los Angeles. Every place and every moment bring

Robin Williams backstage at Fillmore Theatre, San Francisco, California, USA (CSN 6-night residency - September 1997). Photo by Ian Astle

back something precious, be it his genuine envy of a Beatles t-shirt worn by my son Andrea backstage at the Royal Albert Hall in London, or his enthusiasm as he emptied his suitcase on the ground in the middle of the road, in front of an astonished driver, just to give you a preview copy of his new CD in the parking lot of an auditorium.

Stills appears gruff and shy. But he's also cheerful, irreverent and free. Like a huge burp (oops!) which hypnotizes your seven-year-old child, Filippo.

Then there's Crosby. Crystal and magnetic eyes. As soon as he sees you from a distance, he points at you, and you are magnetized. His eyebrow rises, he smiles under his moustache, stares at you, then grumbles to Francesco yet again: 'How the hell did you do that?!'

I could write a book as long as a lifetime together. My life with Francesco. But let me just choose one memory. Vivid and alive, like it was yesterday.

CSNY 2K Tour, Madison Square Garden, New York. After the concert, we joined 'our friends' in the beautiful backstage: rugs, candles and lots of warmth. Each guy had his own room. We came to Crosby's and he was talking in a corner, in the dim light, with a little man all dressed in black, a black hat and the poise of a modern Charlie Chaplin.

Crosby saw Francesco and me out of the corner of his eye and opened his arms to welcome us with a resounding, 'Hi Francesco! My Italian friends!' His friend looked up at us with two blue penetrating transparent eyes, like sea water hit by light. He smiled as Crosby proudly showed us the curly-haired, chubby baby in Jan's arms. David's friend peered at us curiously as we chatted about the concert and Crosby cracked his usual joke about Francesco and me.

Suddenly, in silence, the little man disappeared into the darkness.

I've always believed in goblins. Mischievous but good. Unpredictable, just like children. Ready to amaze you and drag you into the mysterious hole of a tree or into the thicket of a bush. You are always a little scared as you follow them, but you can't resist that contagious laugh and those starry eyes. All children grow up, all but one …

Bio: *Born in 1967, Roman by birth and life, but with Lebanese blood in her veins, the traces of which reside in a surname she is both proud and protective of, Isabella Cattan graduated in Statistical Sciences, and has juggled the liquid profession of marketing and communication for more than 25 years. Her life would have been condemned to the yuppie dullness of commercials, press tours, conventions and aperitifs, had it not been for a fateful meeting, on the Roman coast, with the curator of this work, Francesco Lucarelli. From their union, two duplicates of their father were born, Andrea and Filippo (but the mother claims they are much more beautiful than him), a common passion for photography (creating a photographic exhibition together in 2009, Spheres), travelling, writing, good food and wine, and - guess what? - music. Her children say of her, in the highest expression of affection, 'Mom, you are useless!'*

Songs: *'Almost Cut My Hair' (C); 'Helplessly Hoping' (S); 'Our House' (N).*

A BACKSTAGE PASS AND 12 GOLF BALLS

by Dave Champagne

In early 1998, I settled a lawsuit after being broadsided by a drunk driver nearly two years before. The proceeds went to paying off a bunch of bills, setting up a college account for my son, and with the couple of thousand dollars in 'mad money' that remained, I treated myself to a trip to Las Vegas.

The day tickets went on sale for the CSN stop at Caesar's Palace, I was on the phone to the ticket office at exactly the time it opened. I managed to come away with an 'elbows on the stage' seat right in front of Stills, at which I eventually ended up with my bucket of Coronas perched on the stage at

August 22, 1996: (L to R): Stills, Nash, Rance Caldwell, Howard Cotner, Jeff LaRocca, Bill Evans at Highland Springs Country Club, Springfield, Missouri, USA. Courtesy of Bill Evans

Stephen's feet. After the show, I hooked up with some online folks for a bizarre trip around the town, the most noteworthy result of that particular excursion being that I came away with an e-mail address for Graham Nash.

Not wanting to simply inflict myself on someone I admired and respected, I waited to send a note, wanting to have something more substantial to discuss than a rather lame, 'Gee, I love your stuff.' Surprisingly, an opportunity for contact came up shortly thereafter.

As I sat in my recliner, half asleep, a celebrity golf tournament from Hawaii on the TV in the background, I sat bolt upright in my chair as Graham Nash lined up a chip shot, which he managed to skull through the green into the nothingness beyond. Then they showed him once more, hitting an approach shot from some fairway that he also skittered into an uninhabitable place. From there the telecast broke to a commercial that featured, incredibly, Graham Nash yet again, practice swinging a $400 driver in much the same manner as I'd just witnessed live.

Off I went to my trusty PC and hammered off an urgent e-mail to the address I'd been hanging onto since Vegas. A quick two-line note was the result, saying something like, 'Gee, I love your stuff. And by the way, you're picking your head up on your downswing. You even did it in the TV commercial when there wasn't even a ball there. Try watching the clubhead when you hit the ball. Best regards.'

No sooner had the send button clicked my pearls of golf wisdom off into cyberspace, the thought entered my mind that receiving an unsolicited message from some moron I didn't know, telling me elementary stuff about the game of golf, might not be at all endearing. However, the deed was done, and I comforted myself in the knowledge that if Graham thought I was a moron, at least I was a relatively anonymous one.

Several days later, a much nicer return note than I'd anticipated showed up, thanking me for the tip and telling me I'd actually been of some help. Occasional messages back and forth followed, not too often to be a pain in the neck, but often enough (I'd thought, anyway) so my name would be recognisable when things from me appeared in his mail, and that maybe what I'd sent wouldn't get systematically trashed.

This pattern continued for most of 1998, until my son (10 at the time) got word that he'd won a contest sponsored by a major book publishing house, and his prize was a trip to LA along with a guest role on a Nickelodeon kids' programme. Checking dates and making plans for the trip, it looked at first glance as if our dates in California would fit in with a March 1999 CSN show in Thousand Oaks, not at all far from where we were staying.

Armed with this info, back to the PC I went, explaining to Graham that my son and I were headed west, that it looked like we'd be there for the show and that I'd be extremely grateful if Graham could point me at someone I could approach to beg for backstage passes to the Thousand Oaks show. Once again, a very nice note came back in return, Graham saying he had absolutely no clue who I should contact, so he'd see about handling backstage passes personally. This was fabulous! So naturally, something *had* to go wrong.

And it did. Not two days later, word came from the TV folks that our trip dates had been changed, and now there'd be a couple of weeks between our trip there and the show I'd hoped to get my son and I into. So then came another note to Graham, explaining the change in dates, how I felt like an idiot writing this, but was there any chance of him giving us a raincheck on the backstage passes for the next time CSN were in the northeast? And yes, at this point I'm figuring I'm being a royal pain in the neck.

Another very nice return note showed up, saying I should wait a couple of months and get in touch again, since a tour was in the works for late summer 1999. After several more postponements, the tour was finally cast in concrete on calendars, and the bonus for all fans was the inclusion of Neil Young in the mix. I logged onto the Ticketmaster website the day tickets went on sale and scoffed up three floor seats.

Tickets in hand, I e-mailed Graham yet again, hoping to set the backstage pass deal up for the Hartford tour stop, and heard … absolutely nothing. Figuring I'd been blown off, I consoled myself (and my son) with the knowledge that we'd see a great show, at the very least.

In mid-January 2000, an unsolicited note showed up indicating the 2000s might actually be better than the 1900s. The passes would be waiting at the Hartford will-call window on the day of the show!

This put me back into 'begging mode', since I'd only asked for two passes, and my niece had been added to the mix. The only thing to do was offer a bribe, since it would have been extremely bad form to leave my niece waiting in a rapidly emptying venue as my son and I ventured backstage after the show wrapped

April 13, 2002: CSNY live at National Car Rental Center, Sunrise, Florida, USA. Photo by Tom Davis

up. Back to e-mail I went, offering Graham a dozen golf balls (brand of his choice – big of me, huh?) in exchange for the third backstage pass. Again, a positive response … and we were set to rock 'n' roll.

So, on April 12, we were off to Hartford on a nice smooth three-hour (each way) excursion to the show. Having already seen the guys in Philadelphia a few weeks earlier, I had more than a clue as to how great the show was going to be, but managed to keep my mouth shut as we played a tape (courtesy of our own CSN website hostess Lorraine) of the Hartford tour stop from a couple of years before.

Arriving at Hartford Civic Center about two and a half hours before show time, I headed expectantly to the will-call window and found that … the backstage passes weren't there! OK, so I *had been* told to wait until 6.30 to pick up the tickets, but since my best-laid plans almost universally tend to hit snags, the three of us headed for dinner with my stomach still somewhere down around my ankles, figuring we were basically screwed. And of course, things only got worse at Wendy's when my son managed to dump the better part of his Biggie orange soda all over his lap. As an aside, orange soda on tan jeans does not an attractive combination make. Grateful for the uncommon foresight I'd shown in buying my son's tour T-shirt about three sizes too big, we got him cleaned up as best we could, pulled the shirt down to what looked like knee length, and headed back to find that the passes had finally been delivered. The night might actually work out after all!

Taking the stage shortly after 8pm, the guys proceeded to simply blow us all away for almost four solid hours. A notable occurrence took place as Stephen launched into the 'Suite', my son watching his incredible finger work through binoculars, his jaw dropping open wider and wider as the song progressed. I finally told him that when someone that played *his* music could do something like *that*, I'd start listening to bands like LimpBizkit right along with him. All he could do was gape and nod.

Late in the show, Neil launched into a 20-minute version of 'Down by the River' that he wowed everyone with throughout the tour. As the song opened, my son (standing and singing along for over three hours by now) collapsed into his seat, definitely running out of gas. He asked, 'How much longer?' as his eyes drooped down to about the length of his T-shirt. I explained that there were only a few songs left, but *this* one would go quite a while. With a yawn and a 'Wake me when it's over', he was out like a light on my shoulder. As the song ended, my son regained consciousness and yelled, 'Let's rock 'n' roll!' and sang every word of the rest of the show along with everybody else. 'Rockin' on the Free World' turned into something I think we'll both remember for a long, long time.

As the show ended, we joined the group waiting to be escorted backstage to meet whoever'd left passes for us. We were escorted into a TV green room type setup, complete with drinks, finger food, and padded chairs circling conference room or cafeteria style tables. No sooner had I got each of us a drink when a young fellow walked into the room and called out, 'Is there a Dave Champagne here?' Obediently raising my hand, I was greeted with a 'Hello … Graham wants to see you *right away*.'

It looked to me like we had the best of the arrangement, everyone else there waiting for Croz in a larger area, and only the three of us there to see Graham. We were ushered further back, into the bowels of the building. A few steps further and we emerged into an area with four separate curtained-off areas, one for each guy, and instantly there was Graham, pumping my hand, saying, 'Well, it's only been a couple of years talking online. There really *is* a Dave Champagne.' Not to be outdone, my niece came right back with, 'There really *is* a Graham Nash. We all thought Dave was just BS-ing us all this time.' A priceless icebreaker, and one for which I'll always be grateful – definitely worth the cost of her ticket!

April 13, 2002: CSNY live at National Car Rental Center, Sunrise, Florida, USA. Photo by Tom Davis

What followed was a really nice 10 minutes, only a few seconds of which involved music. The rest of our time together was spent in golf talk, of all things. As good as my word, I passed along the dozen golf balls that procured my niece's pass, and we stood there talking about stances and ball position and weight distribution amid all the ruckus around us, like a couple of possessed fanatics.

As this was going on, I glanced over at my niece, whose eyes had just gotten as wide as silver dollars as someone I couldn't see entered the general area. Still talking with Graham, it only dimly registered when he acknowledged the new guest with a quick 'Hi, Jackson.' Only able to see from behind, it was still readily apparent (hell, *nobody* else has hair like that) that now we had Jackson *freaking* Browne there with us too.

Saying good-byes, shaking hands, thinking the evening was just about complete except for the long-haul home, making our exit, my niece and I were talking on our way out how wild it was that Jackson Browne was there, and my son chimed in with an extremely loud, 'Who the heck is Jackson Browne?' From right behind us came a voice. 'Is someone talking about me?' The night was *too* perfect. I couldn't resist. Spinning around and grabbing his hand, I proceeded to blather on about the night, almost 30 years ago by then, I'd seen him in Saratoga, New York. Of course, I just *had* to add that it was the only night I could recall that a woman had ever attacked me affectionately in public (I've heard he seems to have that effect on women). As we were chuckling about that, my son pounded me on the back and said urgently, 'Dad… you're making a fool out of yourself.' Browne dissolved into full-blown laughter. Hey, so what, I was entitled.

A final impression: the time was so great, the show was so good, and Nash and Browne were such regular guys, I didn't even remember to take photos or get autographs from either of them. Figures, right? But I rode a pretty good natural high all the way home, one that lasted through all the overnight road construction on our route and stayed … well, pretty much until right now, as a matter of fact.

Bio: *Originally from Cohoes, New York, and currently living in Red Hook, New York, Dave Champagne retired from IBM (their idea, not his… as Croz wrote, 'They want it all'), currently working in IT for New York State. Into horse racing (with several pretty good hits), casinos, and golf (winning several local tournaments and club championships).*

Songs: *CSN: 'Long Time Gone' (C), 'Carry On' (S), 'Teach Your Children' (N). Solo or other projects: 'Carry Me' (C), 'For What It's Worth' (S), 'Right Between the Eyes' (N).*

TRY TO FIND ME

by Pierre Robert

I didn't meet Crosby, Stills and Nash until they came out to the Philly area in 1982, playing at The Spectrum on 11 August. The *Daylight Again* album was out, and they were touring behind that. At the time, Croz was not in good shape, but Atlantic Records arranged meet and greets. I have a picture of me with Steven and Graham, my eyes wide open. It looks like I'm on coke. I was like, 'Oh my gosh, I am not worthy', like that scene from *Wayne's World*. Actually, it was just the thrill of being with the two of them. Just a quick meet and greet, and they were on their way.

I met Graham again at Live Aid, July 1985, but it wasn't until he put out solo album *Innocent Eyes* that I started getting little interviews with him. In the summer of 1986, Graham came on my radio show and played a couple of songs live. That's when we formed a bond, because I was playing songs which were not usually played on the radio, and he was impressed by that.

A few months later, in December 1986, he and Crosby played at Valley Forge Music Theatre. Graham came in and played again on my show. It was at that time I started to realize it wasn't Neil for me

February 18, 2016: Pierre Robert and Graham Nash on Graham's tour-bus after the World Cafe Live show in Philadelphia. Photo by Dallyn Pavey

anymore, it was Graham. I was beginning to realize what they were really like, as opposed to what I thought they were like.

And then - time, after time, after time - that proved to be true with how decent and how nice and how caring he is and how considerate he is of, not only the band, but the fans and even the crew. They have their own travelling crew, but then they also have a crew in each town which are local. And I would see him go around and shake hands with the local crew at the end of a show going, 'Hey, thank you for helping us out tonight.' Nobody does that!

Time and time and time, and time and time and time again, I've seen him do just extraordinary things. Sadly, to me he doesn't get the acknowledgement for it that he should. Everything from Peace Sunday, which started as a dream as you probably know, to No Nukes. I love Bono, but long before Bono and people of his echelon were doing benefits, Graham, David and Stephen - and Neil to some degree - Bonnie Raitt and Jackson Browne, they were playing benefits a long time ago and they kind of don't get the credit I think they deserve.

Graham's desire to truly change the world in a positive way was reflected to me over and over again. And when I'm trying to think of one thing in terms of my knowing him, I'm not quite sure what it would be, because there are so many cool moments. Nevertheless, there is a thing that he did for a handicapped kid that I loved.

He had written a song called 'Try to Find Me'. CSN were playing it a lot on that acoustic tour, and he would set it up and explain it, do a great job, and people loved it in concert because he was saying that this was a song about handicapped kids. He saw a handicapped kid at the Bridge School Benefit, the annual concert organized for years by Neil and Pegi Young. He knew that kid was okay inside, but the kid wanted to be reached. That's what the whole thing of the Bridge School was: let's build a bridge of technology and whatever else it takes, because these kids are living in these distorted bodies, disfigured bodies at times, but they are all here. They have heart, they are all here; so how can we reach them? He totally got that from one of the first times they played it. Nash was in a market somewhere, within the next year or so, and a lady came up to him and said, 'I saw your show recently with CSN.' Graham thought she was going to ask about 'Teach Your Children' or 'Our House' or something like that. Instead, she said, 'I love that song 'Try To Find Me'.' He said, 'I'm glad you liked it,' and she replied, 'I have a handicapped son, he is in a wheelchair and I've always wanted him to hear that song but don't see it in any of your catalogue releases, solo or group.' Graham said, 'It was never recorded.' 'Oh, that's too bad,' she commented. When they were about to say goodbye, Graham asked her address and her name. That afternoon he went home to his new studio, recorded the song, put it on tape or CD or whatever, and mailed it to this lady.

To me that is the essence of Graham Nash, right there.

Bio: *Pierre Robert has been a rock DJ on WMMR-FM in Philadelphia since 1981. The radio station itself arrived at its 50th anniversary on 29 April 2017. Both of those stats are highly unusual. In today's radio world, that's almost unheard of, but it's true. Pierre has played all types of music over the years, from Jimi Hendrix to The Killers, and firmly believes all styles of music should be represented on the air. Along the way, he's also interviewed everyone from The Kinks and the Rolling Stones to Green Day, the Foo Fighters, and many more.*

But his favorite group is Crosby, Stills, Nash and Young, who he's seen in concert (in all their incarnations) since 1974. The members of CSNY, especially Graham Nash, have been interviewed on his programme more than any other artists. His hope is that they'll do one more tour together, but he's fully aware of their fragile, inter-person connections, and how easy it is for that chemistry to break down. However, he's been in the audience many times when those connections are firing on all cylinders, and knows there's nothing like it!

Songs: *'Wooden Ships' (C), 'Helplessly Hoping' (S), 'Soldiers of Peace' (N).*

DAVID'S TUNINGS

by Rickie Lee Jones

So I sat on a bed in a hotel room with David Crosby playing his beautiful songs to me and teaching me open tunings. I wrote them down on a hotel notepad and called it David's Tunings. I have it here.

I tried to call to the girl I was, who imagined one day she would meet these guys (CSNY) and sit with them on some kind of level other than 'let's fuck!' and would be liked by them and they would sing. I tried to call to her and say, 'Come, here we are, sit here with me and take it all in.'

You know, when dreams come true, it's not possible for them to collect the big prize that exists only in the invisible world. If it is played out almost exactly as you saw it, almost prophetically, you could not derive anything out of it. You just live it. It's like it's a story being read: it's not real, you are flat somehow,

April 13, 2002: Crosby live at National Car Rental Center, Sunrise, Florida, USA (CSNY tour). Photo by Tom Davis

standing outside yourself watching yourself while having to be there in the room, being whomever you have grown up to be. It has already been written, and somebody skipped ahead when you were a kid, so you heard the whisper of what was to come (one day you will sit in a room with David while he sings this song to you...) but now they are reading the book out loud, and you aren't really there. It's fiction somehow. That's my way of saying it way a big thrill, I think.

He played a little of 'Triad' for me, and I sang it with him a little, but I think I was too full, inside, in my heart, to really sing. I was just relishing the moment, you know. In high school, I played that song over and over, and in fact, it was probably the vehicle for some amount of high school promiscuity, thinking that we would all start an earthly commune and all go to bed with whomever without any religious/moral punishment type repercussions, like 'Stranger In A Strange Land', water brothers, you know, many of us were that way.

It was rather sensual and sweet, the cold gray sky, high up in the middle of a Midwestern town, he had knocked on my door after calling first. In the course of talking, he told me he was almost 60. How can this be? I don't know. Yet here we are, and the years are just colors, really, to a picture that stays in one place. Time has not moved, we are the same, just the more colors on the canvas, the more understanding of what is taking place. Vanity made us disdain getting old. But now as we approach it, I can tell you, it is kinder, and just as sensual, and in better control. Well, I am a lot younger than David, but not too far.

Maybe he thinks he has drugs in common with me, but he does not. What he has in common with me is a journey well travelled. Maybe one day I will get to sing some beautiful harmony together. I love harmony, and not many peole do it these days. It's a game of solitaire, this life. You never know what cards are underneath the one you are looking at.

I sense he is really self-sacrificing, as far as his career goes, though he is driven to play music all the time. I wonder if he feels like golden days have passed him by, the old majesty of being the kings, CSN,

July 19, 1998: Crosby live at Testaccio Village, Roma, Italy (CPR tour). Photos by Francesco Lucarelli

March 10, 2005: Crosby & Nash live at Auditorium Parco della Musica, Rome, Italy. Photos by Francesco Lucarelli

those days. But, you know, their music will endure and redefine the times, as history does, and the boldness of beautiful harmony, I think, will be most cherished again soon, and people will listen to those records, and try to learn from them. Try to relearn the innocence and sense of belonging to a time.

He is always trying to bring a little hope to people, I think. That is my impression of him. I have only met him three or four times, though. He's a nice guy.

Bio: *Born in Chicago, Rickie Lee Jones was uprooted and dragged to a new home soon as she had got settled in the last one. In 1969, while living with her father, she went off with some friends to a rock concert in California. She never returned home, instead beginning a hippie road life and finally settling down in Los Angeles, where she fell in with friends Tom Waits and Chuck E. Weiss. She began working as a waitress and club singer in Los Angeles, 1977. In 1978 Rickie Lee signed a recording contract with Warner Bros. and began a recording and performing career which now spans over four decades.*

July 6, 2005: Stills & Nash live with CSN in Piazza Napoleone, Lucca, Italy. Photos by Francesco Lucarelli

April 13, 2002: Stephen Stills live at National Car Rental Center, Sunrise, Florida, USA (CSNY tour). Photo by Tom Davis

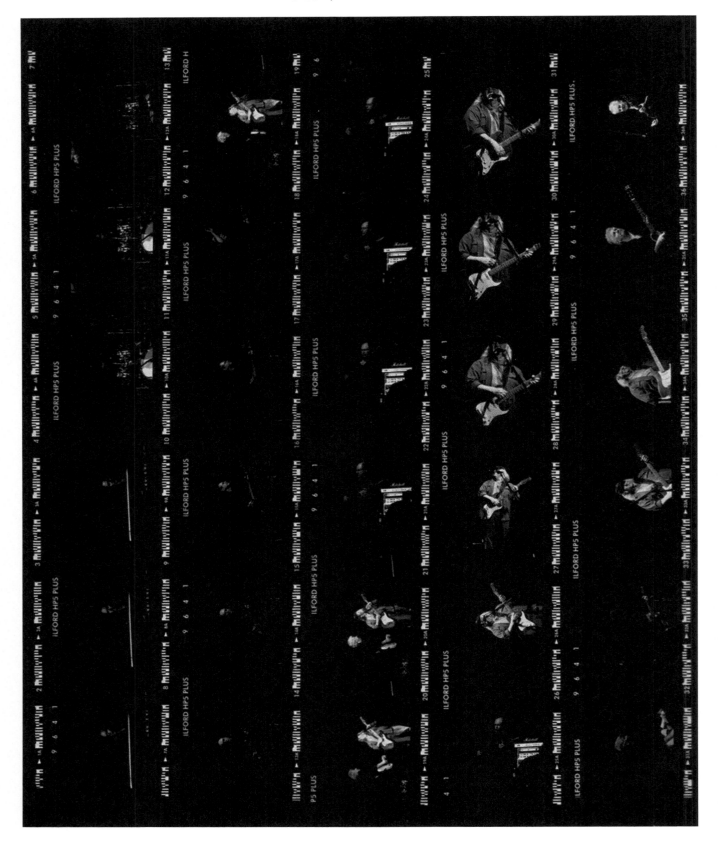

March 10, 2005: Crosby & Nash - Sala Santa Cecilia, Auditorium Parco della Musica, Rome, Italy. Photos by Francesco Lucarelli

207

I HATE SOUTHERN CROSS!

by Lorenzo Conci

It was 13 August 2001 in Detroit, Michigan, a hot summer's day. Having been there the previous January, I couldn't help thinking of the snow and freezing temperature that welcomed me then. Now everything was so green. I was amazed at the difference. It was the tour's opening night and I arrived in Clarkston in time for the soundcheck. CSN were already on stage. Everything was pretty loose. It must have been a while since they'd seen each other. Crew members moved around the stage, Nash going through a list of songs. He wanted to start with 'Wild Tales', have it flow directly into 'Love the One You're With'. They tried it. Graham was taking charge, Stephen in a bit of a world of his own, David looking lazy and unwilling.

In July he had toured Europe with CPR, the group he started in 1997 with Jeff Pevar and son James Raymond. They were there to promote their second album. Crosby was obviously still totally immersed in this adventure, not so happy to be here. He had enjoyed

April 6, 2000: Stills and Young at MCI Center, Washington, D.C., USA (CSNY tour). Photo by Francesco Lucarelli

making new music and playing his own material. 'Food for the soul', as he refers to it.

Nash was putting together a set-list, pretty much the one they ended with the last time they toured as CSN, which was 1997. He had new songs too, but there wasn't much time to rehearse, and he only picked out one. David, none.

When Nash calls for 'Southern Cross', David can't help it: his outburst comes out uncensored. 'I hate 'Southern Cross'!' Nash was petrified. Stills, shocked and taken aback by such a lack of respect, appeared to recover immediately, and conceded, 'Let's drop it.'

Nash glared at him, and Croz understood he may have gone a bit too far. 'No, I hate them all,' he admits. He looked like a kid who just didn't want to start school again.

The show would be good, especially the second set. Enjoying the atmosphere, the loving crowd, the smell of freshly mown grass, and the fireflies, they let it go a bit and Nash offered a solo version of 'Simple Man' that was not on the set-list and which he would not play on the tour again, while Stills took the spotlight to strum his 12-string guitar and dedicate 'The Dolphins', also not on the set-list, to its writer, his late friend Fred Neil, who had recently passed away.

After performing 'Guinnevere', Crosby was moved by the reception and looked like he was enjoying himself again. The loving crowd was made of real fans, no one would complain for a mistake. Thirty-five miles north of Detroit, Clarkston is a little town and there is not the pressure the artists feel when performing in New York, Boston or Los Angeles. After the show David looked tired and complained a bit about the length of the concert. Considering the break between sets, it was a three-hour affair.

The next day they would be in Chicago – 14 August, David's birthday. The show was shorter and there was time to celebrate backstage. Turning 60 with a CSN tour to go through for the rest of the summer, a boy of six at home, a happy marriage and his own band, he smiled, his eyes twinkling. There were plenty of good reasons to be happy.

April 3, 2000: CSNY at Madison Square Garden, New York City, New York, USA. Photo by Francesco Lucarelli

PLAYING TOGETHER

by Michael Curcuru

It was a summer afternoon when I visited one of my friends, who happened to be listening to the new JBL speakers. I was treated to the crisp sound of an acoustic guitar and clear distinct harmonies. That was my introduction to 'Suite: Judy Blue Eyes', and it was like I had discovered music for the first time. My friend had just bought a new album, called Crosby, Stills & Nash. We listened to it, marvelling at the depth in sound and the merging of the harmonies.

I fell in love with CSN and their songs. In 1974, I journeyed to Toronto at the Canadian National Exhibition to see CSN&Y, The Band, Chicago, and The Guess Who. It was in an outdoor stadium, and during the CSNY show it was pouring with rain. The temperature dropped about 30 degrees and I completely lost my voice from the cold. I didn't stick around for the encore, fearing I was going to get really sick. That concert marked my introduction to taking concert photos. Although they were hardly close enough to tell who was who, I learned a lot about what equipment I needed and began what would become an interesting hobby.

Each member of CSN has 'classic' songs that would make most musicians very happy. Each one has his own identity but together there is that sound that only a few groups ever achieve. The same success that

The Beatles had, and resulted in their breakup, has plagued CSNY through the years. They talk about it openly, and finally realized they were great together if they just learned to play together.

I was fortunate to get a surprise photo pass in 2001 from Jeff Pevar. I was conversing with him on the internet when he emailed me to stop at the box office the day of a show CSN was playing in Clarkston, near Detroit. Of course, I did, and was really surprised to find out he left a photo-pass for me. When you are sitting up in the first few rows, you see and hear different things than you would in row 20. After one of the first couple of songs, Graham looked over at Stephen and said, 'Fuck you, Stephen!' And I heard a reply, 'Fuck you, Graham!'. It seems Stephen had altered his playing for a little longer solo, and it didn't go over very well with Graham. It obviously wasn't a big deal since a couple of songs later, Graham was praising Stephen about a great solo Stills had just done.

It made me think of a CSN show I saw in 1978. Stills was doing a solo song with his acoustic guitar,

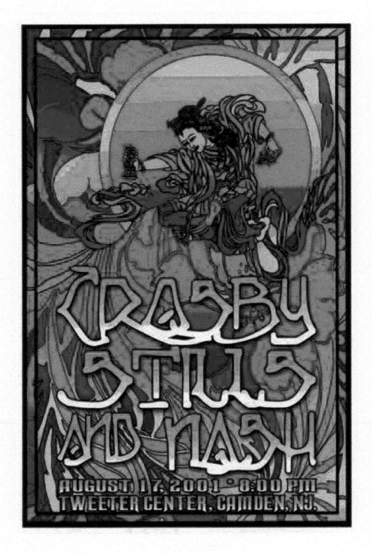

and the chord to the guitar was stuck under his stool. As Stephen tried to free it, you could see he was losing his patience and his temper. Luckily Crosby, smiling the whole time, came out to help Stephen free his guitar chord and prevented an ugly incident. The boys were acting like a team. I guess they have learned to *play* together.

Crosby, Stills and Nash aren't just musicians. They are very political, and the things they write about are personal to me and have meshed with times in my own life. At various times, my favorite has changed from Stephen Stills to David Crosby, to Neil Young, to Graham, back to Crosby, then back to Stills ... you get the idea. Their music has paralleled my generation from the beginning in 1968. If a musical group had to define the rock 'n' roll culture I grew up in, I am happy to say it was Crosby, Stills and Nash. Thank you, boys!

Bio: *Michael Curcuru was born in 1952 in St Clair Shores, a suburb of Detroit, and still lives there. He uses an Argus 35mm camera with an 85-230mm zoom lens. Michael worked in a supermarket for 39 years and for Comcast for four years, while attending over 200 concerts, taking photos at about 80 of them. Living near Detroit left him 'exposed to all the major acts'. He has a blog called Music 101 on Facebook. Married with no children but loving his two grandsons, he adds, 'One of my proudest moments was listening to my nine-year-old grandson singing the refrain from 'Hey Jude.'*

Songs: *'Almost Cut My Hair' (C); 'Wooden Ships' (C/S); 'Lady of the Island' (N). 'Ask me again tomorrow and I'll probably have three different ones.'*

DREAMS CAN COME TRUE

by Cathryn Hendel

I finally got to meet my hero Graham Nash on 19 September 2001, after a Chronicle Pavilion show in Concord, California, just a few days after the NYC terrorist tragedy, with the death of my father not long before that. I first made contact with Graham shortly after he broke his legs. I sent him a gift of healing and got a thank you. When the CSN2K1 shows were announced I was so excited and managed to snag center-row 11 seats. I wrote Graham that I would be there and wondered if he was willing to arrange a meeting for us. He said he would take care of it. So, tickets in hand, trying not to get my hopes up too high, I steeled myself and approached 'the window'. The passes and two tickets were at will-call, with my name on them. I about fainted.

The show was awesome. We enjoyed every minute. It was so cool knowing that soon we would actually be backstage with such an incredible person, and maybe a few of his cohorts. While waiting for my name to be called to enter the 'dungeon', we visited with other fans and a bit with Michael Finnigan. Then, Graham's road manager, Bill Long, called my name and off we went down the stairs to a narrow hallway with small rooms off to the sides. There was Graham, having a glass of red wine, his hand stretched out to greet us. We exchanged 'nice to meet you's, but that wasn't enough for me. This was my big chance. I was going to get every little bit out of it I could, so I said, 'A handshake isn't enough' and asked for a hug. I got one. We took pictures and chatted for a bit more. In the meantime, some idiot (me) set a drink down on the floor to take pictures, and I kicked it over, making an awful mess. Gasp! Graham said, 'Good one, Cathryn' and I was pretty embarrassed but still determined to hang in there. I brought gifts for Graham (hand-held special Angels), and a few extra just in case.

David and Stephen were hanging out right by us. I wasn't about to let that pass. I approached each separately, introduced myself and asked if they would accept a gift from me. David said, 'It's not drugs, is it?' Of course not, I reassured him. I asked him to share with Jan. He said he shares everything with Jan.'

Then Stephen comes by, and I walk up to him to say hi. He looked at me like I was from Mars or something. I asked if I could give him a gift. He paused and said, 'I guess so'. He opened his Angel and asked if Graham had one of them. I said 'Yes, he has seven!' Stephen thanked me and said he could really use an Angel at this point in his life, but one was enough for him. Good feelings all around, so I went for it and asked for a hug. Again, that, 'What, are you crazy?' look flashed across his face, then he said laughingly, 'Why not? Everyone can use more hugs!' An unexpected pleasure.

To top things off, Bill Long came up and said, 'Graham wanted you to have this'. He handed me a little piece of plastic and I had no idea what it was, barely looked at it and stuffed it in my pocket with a polite thank you. After about 20 minutes of hobnobbing, it was over. Time to get the show on the road, as Graham put it. They had 600 miles to go that night. We emerged from the 'tunnel' in a blissful state. Only then did I retrieve the bit of plastic from my pocket: it was a guitar pick Graham had used in the show. What a great way to end the evening. I feel lucky to have had that night. I will always cherish it. Dreams can and sometimes do come true!

Bio: *Cathryn Hendel came onto this planet at Kaiser in Oakland, California. Most of her growing years were spent smack in the middle of the two US coasts. Happily married to a fantastic guy for more than 40 years, they have a beautiful and ever so intelligent daughter who loves CSN too. In second grade she moved to the St Louis area but soon realized she wanted to be a hippie … 'and was always a hippie at heart.' Sweet, innocent and very into what was going on in her culture, she moved to Tiburon, California, 'on the water straight from middle America,' experiencing 'culture shock and loving every moment of it.' Years later she was lucky to have the opportunity to exchange emails with Graham Nash and brief after-show visits. Today she has some wonderful, magical memories, adding, 'Rock on, Mr Graham Nash, and compadres. You lifted the world in so many ways. Namasté!'*

Songs: *'Camera' (C); 'Thoroughfare Gap' (S); 'Myself At Last' (N).*

BARNEY AND CROZ

by Gary Goltz

On 1 June 2002, I met David Crosby backstage at a CPR special benefit show on the Pasadena City College campus, CPR and Joe Henry headlining Harmony - The Concert to Benefit The Walden School's Commitment To Diversity.

I was sporting my new Simpsons CSNY caricature t-shirt. When Crosby saw it, he was mesmerized. He apparently had never seen it and asked where I got it. I told him I found it on eBay.

He was so enamoured with it, I asked if he wanted it. He said, 'I can't

take it right off you, man! What would you wear?' I thought about it for about a second then literally gave him the shirt off my back! My friends who were there were elated and provided me a blue jean jacket.

I asked Crosby if he recalled the scene he was in on *The Simpsons*, but he didn't. So, I shared it with him, as my son had refreshed my memory prior to the show. It entailed Crosby encountering Barney as he entered Moe's Tavern. Barney the drunk exclaimed, 'David Crosby, I love you!' Crosby response was 'You like my music?' To which Barney said, 'You make music?'

Croz cracked up, we hugged, and he thanked me profusely for the shirt. It was a moment I will always remember, and hopefully he will too!

Bio: *Gary Goltz was born in Pittsburgh, Pennsylvania, in 1953. As a child he loved listening to the Everly Brothers and their harmonies. 'No doubt this was behind my becoming an avid fan of CSNY.' He became heavily involved in judo after a failed attempt at learning to play guitar. After graduating the University of Pittsburgh, a career in business took him to Chicago, eventually settling in the greater Los Angeles area. In terms of judo, he started his own dojo (club) in 1988 and it grew into one of the largest in the US. He's also served as president of the US Judo Association. He saw his first show with Crosby, followed by Manassas in 1973. Then while on a cross-call country road trip while living in the Bay Area of California, he got to see the whole group perform on 13 July 1974 at the Oakland Coliseum.*

Songs: *'Wooden Ships' (C); 'Suite: Judy Blue Eyes' (S); 'Chicago' (N).*

July 8, 2005: CSN live at Villa Pisani, Stra, Italy. Photos by Francesco Lucarelli

July 6, 2005: Stephen Stills live with CSN in Piazza Montenapoleone, Lucca, Italy. Photo by Fabio Gaffurini

October 1, 2008: Stephen Stills live at Auditorium Parco della Musica, Rome, Italy. Photo by Filippo de Orchi

ALL THE WAY FROM ITALY?

by Lorenzo Conci

Solvang, California, in the Santa Ynez Valley, near Santa Barbara, is a small town - the Danish capital of America, in the sense of the pastry ... as a billboard greets on-comers.

David Crosby and his wife Jan had been hosting a beautiful event called Valley Music Festival, to promote the arts for the schools of the district, so the kids can have more music classes, more art and instruments, and more chances to develop their talent, skills and taste. This year, at the fifth edition, 18 and 19 October 2002, the guest artist was Graham Nash, with David and Graham playing a set each with their own bands. It had never happened before ... a must for me, of course!

My friend Peter and I get into LAX early that Friday afternoon and drove up the coast on 101, and inland to Solvang. After a quick shower, they were at the outdoor theater.

Finally the time to relax a bit and enjoy the atmosphere at a beautiful small venue, round and intimate, we sitting to a side, very close to the stage and were welcomed by the lonesome sound of a harp, played live, the air still warm and full of flagrancies. It was like the gathering of a clan. Fans from all over the States and parts of the world had convened there.

CPR took the stage perfectly on time and Croz looked super-happy and excited. They celebrated the evening by starting with something never tried before, with 'So You Wanna Be a Rock and Roll Star' given a brilliant rendition. The show moved on, and towards the end of the set David stopped to look around at the crowd and acknowledge the 'loonies' who had come from a bunch of places like New York, Chicago, Phoenix, Italy. He must have seen me, I think.

After a short break, a few songs with Graham, David introducing his guest with pride. Nash was accompanied by a host of great musicians: Russell Kunkel on drums, Dean Parks on guitar, Larry Klein on bass. They had been touring to promote *Songs For Survivors*, the first solo effort put out by Graham in 20-plus years.

Their sound, full clear and refined, shone over the familiar tunes, dressing them like the new ones. It was pitch dark by now, the air cooler, and I began to feel a little tired after the long flight and the drive, all adding up to the nine-hour time change. And song after song, I felt so lucky.

While I entertained those thoughts, I was shaken by surprise. Nash turned to the side, took a few steps toward me, came over and said, 'Lorenzo! How are you? All the way from Italy? Are you on your own? Are you coming back to see us after the show? Are you sure? You are a crazy SOB!' I don't believe I answered any of those questions, but a feeling of being welcomed and loved showered over me.

Graham walked again towards the centre of the stage, went to the microphone and to a crowd that was laughing, mumbled, 'Oh, nothing' and started the next song, 'Marrakesh Express'.

After the show, there was a lovely reception, with wines offered by local producers. Graham and David were both very warm and kind, and between the exhaustion, the wine and the affection, I felt life could not be any better and I could die there and then.

Next day it was show number two, all the loonies back. Relaxed and restored, we enjoyed every note, the details of yesterday lost in dreamlike stupor. That Sunday night Crosby and Nash played the Lobero Theater in Santa Barbara, for a benefit to help the county supervisor not to be unjustly ousted. We got there at the end of the soundcheck and Graham showed me the printed set-list, like asking for my approval. How could I possibly not give it? It was a fan's dream come true, including 'Page 43', 'Immigration Man', 'Lady of the Island', 'Tamalpais High', 'Carry Me', 'Taken At All', and 'Find The Cost of Freedom'. A beautiful, warm, passionate evening, also highlighted by the appearance of Jackson Browne for the encores.

A glass of wine at the reception afterwards, hugs, thank yous and goodbyes and it was late at night when we headed back to LA. Driving down 101, I knew I wanted this to last forever, but our flight back was leaving at 7am. Back to Europe, via New York. We had 15 hours to readjust to the idea that it was going to be a Tuesday morning in Munich, late October, rainy and cold, but with us 'California Dreaming' for the rest of the fall, into the winter.

ALMOST CUT YOUR THROAT

by Mark Lennon

We have known David Crosby and been singing off and on with him for over 20 years. Through him we have met and sang with Graham and Stephen as well.

'We' is our band Venice: me, my brother Michael, and our cousins Kipp and Pat Lennon, with CSN one of the most inspiring bands we grew up listening to, covering many of their songs at parties, family reunions and our own live shows.

David has always been one of my top singers I've been influenced by. So, whenever he'd come to see us live, perform a show with us or sit on with us, we are always honored but still a little nervous that one of our favorite vocalists is going to be listening to us sing for a change. We knew he probably had high standards...to say the least.

Once our band was performing at the Lobero Theater, Santa Barbara, and we had just finished our encore. We were waving goodbye to the crowd and walking offstage to head to our dressing rooms. No sooner had I stepped past the curtains, out of the stage lighting, into the dark side-stage, I felt someone jump out from behind the curtain, quickly grab me in a very, firm choke-hold and whisper loudly in my ear, 'Hey you, motherfucker! I'm gonna slit your throat and steal your goddamned voice!'

It was then that I noticed the very real, very sharp, exquisitely made, wooden-handled switchblade at my throat. Luckily, I knew that voice anywhere and was quite relieved to find it was just li'l' ol' prankster David behind this horribly, thrilling joke that made me almost crap my jeans and my boots. He eventually released me, we laughed, I checked for any blood on my neck, and we both walked to the green room after-party.

Twice now, at a couple of our gigs, he has scared the hell out of me like that, as we'd come off stage at the end of our gigs. The third time it happened I was on the ocean, on his sailboat, off the coast of Santa Barbara. David had invited me and my partner Jeffrey to go out sailing on the boat with him and his family for an all-day picnic. As I went down into the galley kitchen to go help David's wife Jan make lunch, David was letting Jeffrey steer the boat and telling his stories.

Mid 00's: Mark Lennon and Crosby's family sailing on the Mayan off the coast of Santa Barbara, California, USA

David waited for me to get out of earshot, then proceeded to tell my partner that the reason he invited us out sailing on his boat was so he could slit my throat, steal my voice, and dump me overboard.

Jeffrey didn't know what to say at first, but then the laughter kicked in as Jan and I walked up and out with the huge lunch-tray of awesome sandwiches, drinks and snacks. We asked what was so funny and they told us. My response was, is and always will be, with a trembling, shaky voice, 'B-b-b-but gee! It was always *you*, Mr C-c-c-crosby th-th-that I modelled my voice after... P-p-p-please, don't kill me!' His response was, is and hopefully will always be a huge hug, followed by his awesome laugh.

Nearing the end of our sailboat picnic, we had the ship's deckhand take some photos of us to remember that wonderful, overcast, autumn day on the ocean. By the third picture, I said, 'Okay, everyone make a very sad, crying face, like you're having a miserable time at sea, just for the hell of it!' We all did, and that ended up being the one photo we all wanted a copy of, and it has its place in a frame on our huge photography wall in my family home in Venice.

Bio: *Born and raised in Venice Beach, California, Mark Andrew Lennon is best known as the blond-haired lead singer of the band, Venice, although his list of musical credits is lengthy and versatile. Mark has toured with Cher and Phil Collins, and joined Roger Waters of Pink Floyd on the highly successful world tour of The Wall. Venice's signature sound is distinctly 'Californian', reflecting early influences from another So Cal band of brothers and cousins, The Beach Boys, as well as Crosby, Stills & Nash, and The Eagles.*

Songs: *'Guinnevere' (C); 'The Lee Shore' (C); 'Lady of the Island' (N).*

THE GUY WHO GETS TO CREATE MUSIC FOR A LIVING

by Roy McAlister

I grew up in the Sixties in the San Francisco Bay Area, the youngest of five siblings – one of four brothers and a sister who were anything but quiet and reserved. Our home also became a sanctuary for kids in need, and we took in any stray child or refugee who needed a roof, a meal and some love. My mother was a compassionate, wise and very funny woman who oversaw the chaos with minimal control. It was a crazy household, but I'm proud of who we were and the values and compassion my parents instilled in us.

CSN&Y at the White River Amphitheater, WA, 2006. Photo: Dan Wilson

My father was a gifted Boogie-Woogie/ blues pianist who played with more passion and soul than anyone I've heard. My earliest memories are climbing onto his lap while he was at the piano. His knee bouncing wildly with me on it, I'd laugh and squeal trying to hang on through whatever song he played. We dubbed this a 'piano ride'.

The 'piano ride' began with me sat on my father's knee, him uttering through a cigarette to hold his drink and not spill it. His left hand would start pounding out bass lines, his right followed with riffs and fills. He'd start singing 'Caledonia', me bouncing on his knee, grasping a tumbler of gin, his cigarette smoke drifting around us both until the song and ride came to a stop. These are the greatest memories I have of the man.

His old upright piano sat silent and lifeless while he worked his corporate job to support us all, including the strays and refugees we'd taken in. But as soon as he sat down in front of it, both he and that piano came to life and us kids would come running toward the music. Piano rides were my introduction to people creating music, and the relationship between musician and instrument.

So for me, music was a simple function of life that is tangible and inclusive, not just a hobby or tunes piped in through the radio. Playing music is visceral. It's what people do. I wanted so badly to participate in that creativity and held musicians who do in high regard. I still do. But when I grew up in the Sixties, the people who played the music we heard on records and radio were far less accessible than today. Their lives and interests were limited to spoon-fed profiles and anecdotes contrived by recording labels. What we knew about them was written on the back of album covers … and later maybe the occasional *Rolling Stone* article. We thought we knew who these people were, but in reality had no idea. I don't know why, but it seemed relevant for me to understand who these people are who get to create music for a living. Lucky them.

David Crosby was one of those people whose music captivated me. I loved his music and wanted to know as much about him as I could. But David was an intangible and inaccessible celebrity in every sense. He's a musical icon and large influence in the music I enjoy and how I listen to it. But I had no idea who he was and what committed him to a life of playing music. I'd read articles the press wanted me to read, but I was aware someone else controlled those stories. If I read something I didn't want to hear, I would stop reading it. Simple as that. Don't tarnish my heroes, I can make up my own mind…or at least insulate myself. This served me well, but the stories of David and other musical influences who fell prey to the culture of the Sixties and Seventies were unavoidable. Regardless, no article could erase David's contribution and how his music revealed to me the complexity of harmonies and depth of lyric.

The guitar entered my life by my oldest brother Mark, who played very well and made it look so cool. He later taught me to play when I was ten, after I got my first guitar for Christmas. I loved that guitar and played it every chance I could. I spent years trying to become the musician I wished I was but came to accept I was not a gifted musician. However, I later discovered I was gifted at facilitating music, becoming a guitar builder - the tool maker for the musician.

I began my woodworking career as a part-time job after high school when I was 15, and soon began dissecting guitars. It would be a long time before I could build a functioning instrument, but the pursuit began when I became a woodworker. Building a musical instrument greatly satisfied me and filled the creative void. I didn't need to play music to contribute to music. Making the tools that inspired musicians made more sense to me, and it became my purpose. I slowly established my own shop of machines, tools, jigs and fixtures for building guitars, but couldn't resist an offer from a friend to work for the Santa Cruz Guitar Company. In this shop, a small team of luthiers hand-built amazing guitars and I loved it … all of us who worked there loved it. I got to make guitars for those people who get to create music for a living.

Passions in life don't often cross paths, but when they do, it's noteworthy. I got word that David Crosby was coming to our shop to order a 12-string guitar and it would be my job to meet and work with him. I was excited, but also cautious about the meeting. What if David was an asshole? What would I think if my perception of who he was ended up destroyed by this meeting? What if the media who relished his indiscretions were right? I would find out soon enough.

It was a Saturday when David was scheduled to arrive, so not much activity in the shop other than us who were there to meet him. I got to the shop early to prepare and waited for David's arrival. Without any fanfare, the outside door eventually swung open and David stepped in. There's no mistaking him. It's David Crosby. I've seen him many times on album covers and from the nickel seats in arenas and auditoriums, but this time he was only 20 feet away. He stepped into the shop, stopped, looked around and took in a deep breath of that distinctive rosewood and spruce guitar making atmosphere. David grinned like a kid in a candy store. Perfect start. I walked over and introduced myself. This man was a legend, but the David Crosby now in front of me appeared to be a normal guy without a trace of arrogance. No cape, no entourage, no air of superiority. He seemed as excited to talk to me about guitars as I was to meet him. I don't recall the initial exchange, but I remember David making a humorous remark…a truly funny remark. He put me on level terms and I reciprocated as comfortably as I could. He had respect not just for what I did, but who I was. David Crosby the legend became a very real human in no more than five minutes. He'd never be the abstract celebrity again.

We spent a few hours talking guitars, looking at wood, discussing the building process and listening to David play various guitars around the shop. He then brought out the famous 12-string he had converted by a luthier at Lundberg's Fretted Instruments, a shop in Berkeley, from David's '59 D-18. David told me it was the first guitar he purchased with money earned by playing music. This was the guitar he used to write and record 'Wooden Ships', 'Déjà Vu', etc., an exceptional instrument with much provenance.

He told us stories about the guitar, how 'some young guy' with a shard of glass tried to scallop the bracing to improve its tone. The look on his face confessing that the 'some young guy' was him. He'd strum the guitar and discuss the complexity of overtones produced by his guitar. He pointed out unique features and techniques Turner had incorporated into the guitar. David also asked a lot of questions and listened intently. He knows more about guitars than most players ever will, but he was not above asking questions, eager to learn more.

During our afternoon together, I had a chance to show David a guitar I was building. Not a production guitar, but a guitar I was personally building with my own approach. He held my guitar and looked it over before putting it in his lap. David played it for a few minutes then looked up at me to say, 'That's one scrumptious axe! Very nice!' I like this guy, I thought. Honest, funny, and as unpretentious as humanly possible. But most of all, he just complimented me in such a meaningful way.

David left the shop late in the afternoon, me feeling grateful that my perspective of him had improved, not diminished. Over the following months, we built David two 12-strings at Santa Cruz Guitar Company. I would contact him now and then with questions and updates until his guitars were completed and shipped off to him. The experience came to an end, and I filed it away in my memory, assuming I wouldn't interact with him in that context again. I was accepting of that fate, but I was wrong.

Two significant events happened to me a couple of years after my experience with David. My daughter Natalie was born, and I left Santa Cruz Guitar Company. Not because I didn't want to work there any longer, I left to be a home dad. The birth of my daughter was so profound, I knew I had to make changes in my life. My wife Lucy was a schoolteacher and had the benefits and schedule that worked well for us. So, I stayed home to watch our daughter during the day and build guitars at night when Lucy returned from teaching. Tough times. I wasn't selling any guitars and paying our bills was very difficult. But for us, it was right.

During this time, I would recall David's words …'That's one scrumptious axe!' It was validating to me and kept me motivated to keep building despite no paycheck. I wanted to quote David to boost my credibility as a guitar builder but wouldn't do so without his blessing. I liked the 'regular guy' David Crosby who spent a day with me at Santa Cruz guitar, but could I bother David Crosby 'the legend' to endorse my guitars with his words? It didn't feel right to me, but neither did struggling to support my family.

It was no big deal to call David about his 12-strings, so I thought I'll just call and ask if I could use his kind words. We were desperate to make ends meet and we needed help, so it was time to call. David answered his phone right away and I reminded him who I was. He was the same affable guy I remembered - straightforward, honest, funny and completely accessible. He told me he was about to leave on a CPR tour, and I could sense his excitement. He talked about a few new songs he'd written and rehearsed to perform on tour. CPR was booked to play a concert at Palookaville, a venue in Santa Cruz that no longer exists. I told him I was looking forward to it and would definitely be in the audience as it was close to home. I don't know why, but the CPR song, 'Somebody Else's Town' came to mind. I eventually got around to telling him why I was calling and asked if I could use his quote. No problem. 'I meant what I said, that was a great guitar.'

Very cool! I was relieved and optimistic to get permission to use David's quote. We continued to small talk for a while when David casually mentioned wanting a Martin OM someday. Okay, I thought, I'm gonna make him one but not tell him. I did use David's quote, his words did boost my credibility, and I did build him a guitar without his knowledge. A Brazilian rosewood, German spruce OM-ish size guitar braced and voiced for David's use of alternate tunings. It was built for David and had to respond to his music. I'm proud of that guitar: it did what I wanted it to. I could only hope now that David would like it too. I kept it safe until time came to drive down to Santa Barbara to present it to him.

With my wife Lucy, our young daughter Natalie and the Brazilian rosewood guitar, we drove the three hours from Watsonville to the Crosby house. We arrived at his gate in the early afternoon and David was perplexed at first, but graciously invited us into his home. Jan came from another room and greeted us with such warmth. We all walked through the kitchen and saw jars and labels on the counter ... we learned about Jan's homemade salsa. Amazing! Natalie became fascinated with toys she saw in their living room belonging to young Django Crosby. Jan allowed my Natalie free rein to play as she wished.

We sat down in the Crosby living room where David set the guitar case on a coffee table in front of him. He unlatched the case, opened the lid and removed the guitar. He looked it over and nodded in approval before setting it in his lap. David tuned it up and then strummed it one time. His eyebrows raised and he looked over at me sitting on his stone fireplace hearth. That smile of a kid in a candy store returned to his face. He looked back at the guitar and strummed it again ... then again. Smiling, David looked over at me and simply said, 'Stunner!'

That moment changed my life. It changed my entire family's life.

Much has been written about that guitar and David's enthusiasm for my work. He became my biggest advocate and believed in me. What hasn't been written is how much his support and loyalty has affected my family - my wife and children. With David's support for my work in articles, interviews and stories on stage, I was flooded with guitar orders. I was no longer a guy building guitars I couldn't sell. My guitars now sold faster than I could make them. More significantly, I became a contributor to the support of my family.

The income created by David's belief in my work allowed Lucy to take a few years off from teaching and stay at home with our children. We now had our son Joseph, along with Natalie. I built guitars from a detached shop on our property while our children were in the house being taken care of by their mother. All in one place. We had lunch together as a family, we went to doctor's appointments, playdates, visits with grandparents, trips to the park, all together.

Lucy's parents, who I adore, also watched our children as often as they could. They cherished being the quintessential grandparents doting on Natalie and Joseph. This close family bond was so valuable to raising the most caring, intelligent and wonderful children I could hope for. Natalie and Joseph are now grown adults but have always remained deeply connected to their parents with a strong sense of family. Way beyond playing my guitars, David's friendship and support had a profoundly positive impact on my family and who we are today. This can't be underestimated.

Many people have a 'David Crosby story' and many are vastly different. But my story is of a dear friend and man who changed my life professionally and privately. I love him. I know David as a devout family man, loyal husband and father. David loves his wife, he loves his children, he loves his home, and he loves his friends. David loves dogs, he enjoys flying, sailing, and offering his time and resources to people in need. He remains deeply passionate about music and is the most driven and musically creative person I've ever met.

I got to know the guy who gets to create music for a living and he became my friend. Lucky me!

Bio: *Roy McAlister has been handcrafting high-end guitars for more than 30 years. After working at Santa Cruz Guitars, he set out as a solo builder and now makes a good living as a luthier, working out of his home in Gig Harbor. Priding himself in the ability to build custom guitars tailored specifically to the needs of individual players, he is one of the most prestigious guitar-makers in the world. His clients include Marc Cohn, Jackson Browne, David Crosby, and Graham Nash.*

FOREVER FRIENDS

by Lucien van Diggelen

When I was 16, I used to go to a friend's house during lunchbreaks, and it was there I began listening to Crosby, Stills, Nash & Young. I loved their music right away, so I bought *Déjà Vu* and listened to it for several weeks. The following year, on 26 March 1976, I attended Neil Young's concert at Jaap Eden Hall in Amsterdam and fell in love with his music too. The next day I went to buy all the CSN&Y records I could find and ran home to listen to their albums, which I still do today.

February 1, 2005: Graham Nash and Simon Posthuma in Amsterdam, The Netherlands. Photo by Lucien van Diggelen

I always had a feeling I wanted to know more about them, even beyond the music. So, when I found an ad in a music shop in Amsterdam, left by Tino Bekkering, another long-time CSN&Y fan, I sent a letter to Francesco Lucarelli, the editor of *Wooden Nickel*, a CSN&Y fanzine based in Rome, Italy, and we became pen-pals. A few years later, Herman Verbeke, a Neil Young fan from Belgium, contacted me, asking if I would like to help him write a Neil Young biography. My CSN&Y in-depth journey had just begun.

After we completed that project, it was only a matter of a few more years before we began working on a CSN&Y biography. In early 1993 we invited our Roman friend and his *Wooden Nickel* partner, Stefano Frollano, to join us. It was during the making of this project that I became friends with Graham Nash and David Crosby.

In January 1994, me, Herman and Francesco – along with singer-songwriter Stefano Fedele – flew to Los Angeles, having scheduled a bunch of interviews with Stephen Stills, Graham Nash and many of their musical partners. Eight years later, in London, we presented *Crosby, Stills, Nash and Sometimes Young*, a mammoth three-volume work on the story of the band, all their concerts, and studio sessions.

In 2005, Crosby and Nash were touring in Europe and scheduled to play the Paradiso in Amsterdam on 3 February. Graham told me he and the whole Nash family had been enjoying reading our books. They brought some good memories back and he asked if I could put him in touch with Simon Posthuma, a Dutch painter and singer-songwriter he spent time with in the late Sixties. I tracked down Simon and told him about Graham's request. He couldn't believe it but said, 'If Graham is coming, I will give a party to celebrate my birthday on 1 February. And I will invite some great people'. I am a chef and so I promised him I would take care of the food.

A few hours after Graham arrived at his hotel in Amsterdam, Simon called, but the hotel receptionist did not connect him to Graham. So, he phoned me in the middle of the night, worried my story was not true. I called Graham in the morning, and he confirmed he would arrive at seven o'clock in the evening. It took me some efforts, but I was able to convince Simon the party was going to happen. Finally, Simon's house in Amsterdam was where they met each other after more than 30y years.

At seven o'clock the doorbell rang and there was Graham. They hugged and danced for several minutes like little children and had so much fun during the whole evening. Later, Simon played a song on his piano and Graham followed him, playing and singing 'Cathedral'. At midnight, Simon's birthday was over, but it was Graham's turn now – he was born on 2 February and all the folks there started singing, 'Happy Birthday'. It was a very special night, one I will never forget. The following night, during the concert, Graham dedicated a song to Simon, there with his complete family.

It was a very moving moment after the memorable night spent at Simon's place.

A few years ago, Simon Posthuma moved to an elderly home due to his worsening illness. When I heard, I told Graham that if he wanted to see him again, he better not wait too long. When he came to Europe in the Spring of 2016 for a promotional tour, he made sure he had time to visit his old pal. Forever friends.

Bio: *Lucien van Diggelen was born in Den Haag, the Netherlands, and is married to Marleen Vromans, with two daughters, Karlijn and Janneke. He runs a catering company and loves cooking.*

Songs: 'Long Time Gone' (C); 'So Begins the Task' (S); 'In Your Name' (N).

March 5, 2005: Crosby & Nash live at Fillmore Live Club, Cortemaggiore, Italy. Photo by Francesco Lucarelli

A BIT OF SEX, DRUGS AND ROCK'N'ROLL

by Herman Verbeke

It was an honor and a pleasure to help organise and be at Simon Posthuma's birthday party in 2005. Me and Lucien van Diggelen met Simon when we interviewed him for the book we did about Neil Young. Before he became a musician, Simon made a name as the painter of John Lennon's piano, the Apple shop mural, and the cover of the Cream album *Disraeli Gears*.

First with artists' collective, The Fool, later as part of duo Seemon & Marijke, Posthuma recorded the albums *The Fool* and *Son of America* (which contains the 1972 hit 'I Saw You'). Both albums were produced by Graham Nash.

Shortly after the release of that book, me and Lucien planned to work on a new one, *Crosby, Stills, Nash and Sometimes Young* with Francesco Lucarelli and Stefano Frollano of CSN&Y fanzine *Wooden Nickel*. Thinking it would be wise to ask some kind of permission, I drove to Paris to attend a gig CSN were playing there. I wasn't sure if it would have been possible to talk to David or Graham (or Stephen) about our plans. I wanted to be smart and wrote our plan and wishes on a piece of paper. If I didn't get the chance to get backstage, I thought it could have been possible to give the paper to Graham through a roadie or someone on their staff.

When I arrived in Paris, I was able to park my car rather close to the venue. Getting out, I literally bumped into Graham, shooting pictures in the parking lot. I was so surprised I didn't know what to say, but I gave him my piece of paper. After a few seconds, I became myself again. Graham was very kind and invited me to come backstage and meet with him, David and Stephen. The seeds for the CSNY book and their invitation to go to LA for some interviews were planted there and then.

July 11, 2013: Graham Nash, Herman Verbeke and David Crosby backstage at Kursaal, Oostende, Belgium (CSN show). Photo by Marnix Allegaert

On 1 February 2005, Graham was at the Postuma party too. The vinyl releases of The *Fool* and *Son of America* were rather hard to find and - guessing Graham didn't have the records anymore - I thought it might be a good idea to find and offer him a copy. And it was. He was indeed pleased with the CD, LP and single I gave him before the party started.

Simon and Graham hadn't seen each other in more than 30 years, and it was fun to see how they 'got together' immediately. While Lucien took care of food and drinks, Graham kindly socialised with everyone in the room.

Of course, there was a piano at the Posthuma's. At the time, Simon's son Bob (who later became singer-songwriter Douwe Bob and played to more than 50,000 people at Pinkpop Festival) was about 12 years old and was already playing the instrument pretty well. That night he was kind of the opening act for Graham, who - after a while - got behind the piano and played 'Cathedral'.

Coincidence or not, at midnight Simon's birthday party turned into Graham's birthday party. Later that night, I drove Graham back to his hotel.

'Where's the sex?' I hear you thinking. Well, that's of course another little story. A few years ago, Crosby & Nash played in Belgium. A week before the gig, *Humo* magazine published a C&N interview by Serge Simonart. In his introduction, Serge wrote that when he shook hands with David and Graham, he was thinking, 'Oh, it's better not to wash my hands for some time, because both hands have caressed the tits of Joni Mitchell.' Backstage I told David and Graham about it, and they just couldn't stop laughing.

> **Bio:** *Born in Flanders in the Dutch speaking part of Belgium, Herman Verbeke lives in Waregem. He's a bank manager and loves music, sport, travel, and theatre ('not necessarily in this order!). He is the author of a couple of books in Dutch about Neil Young and the co-author of Crosby, Stills, Nash and Sometimes Young. For a moment, he was once …Stephen Stills, explaining, 'A few years ago, after joking with Graham and David backstage in Brussels, they took a picture of the three of us. It was only after I looked at the picture that I realised we kind of reshot the 'couch album' cover.'*
>
> **Songs:** *'Wooden Ships' (C); 'Carry On' (S); 'I Used to Be a King' (N).*

AM I FIRED NOW?

by Jeff Pevar

Back in 2005, when I was recording for the last Crosby Nash album, it was brought to my attention that David and Graham wanted to bring James Raymond and I into CSN to augment the touring ensemble. It was very important to them to be able to perform the new songs featured on the C/N record and play them live on that upcoming CSN tour.

It was also explained to me that Stephen didn't go way out of his way to prepare songs for tour, other than his own songs. Many of the new Crosby & Nash songs were very guitar specific songs, including 'Jesus of Rio', a song I co-wrote with Graham which featured a very specific, flamenco/acoustic finger-style guitar part. They wanted to bring me into the band to cover those specific guitar parts and guitar solos.

Admittedly, when they mentioned their interest, I truly didn't know how Stephen would feel about having another guitarist in the band, as my past interactions with him were not exactly as welcoming as I would have hoped.

My first encounter with Stills was when Marc Cohn and I opened for CSN around 1990. I was invited to sit in with Graham and David during those shows and Stephen would usually be off stage when I played. I remember the very first time I sat in with them. When I left the stage after a rather exciting performance which brought the house down, Stephen came back onstage, walked up to the mic and said, 'Ok, well, am I fired now?' I didn't know whether to feel complimented or embarrassed. I guess I felt a little of both.

David had mentioned to me Stephen's insecurities about his own playing, and competitiveness towards other guitarists, which I found hard to believe, being as talented as Stephen is. When this opportunity of being involved with CSN as an acoustic, electric and lead guitarist arose, I suggested to Graham that Stephen and I met up, just to hang out and get to know one another before the tour, so I could attempt to - for lack of other words - endear myself before working together.

This ended up being the absolute perfect thing to do. We met up at his place and it was wonderful. There was no posturing or competitive energy meeting up with him on his own turf. Stephen and I had a couple of guitars and were jamming at his house. The first thing we played together was some sort of blues tune. When we finished, his eyes lit up and he said, 'Holy shit, Jeff! I didn't know you could play blues like *that*!' It was that very moment I felt an actual friendship begin.

September 21, 2004: Jeff Pevar jamming with Stephen Stills at Les Schwab Amphitheatre, Bend, Oregon, USA. Photo by Tim Owen

We shared some wonderful moments together on those CSN tours and I remember us doing nightly, dual-lead solos that brought the house down every show! I was really pleased and honored to work with CSN those two tours and be of service to music that was such an important part of my musical history. Every night on tour we played our tune, 'Jesus of Rio', and I got to trade guitar solos with Stephen on 'Dig Down Deep' and 'Wooden Ships'.

It truly was a dream come true for a young lad who learned to play guitar listening to their music.

Bio: *Born in Springfield, Massachusetts, on 16 February 1957, Jeff Pevar currently lives in Ashland, Oregon. A composer, producer, performer, touring musician, arranger, and multi-instrumentalist, he works with a vast array of talented artists, and also composes music for film and television and independent releases of his own music. He adds, 'I'm not sure what I'm going to do when I grow up, as part of the reason I am a musician is one never has to entirely grow up when they are a musician. They call it playing music for good reason.'*

Songs: *'At the Edge' (C); 'So Begins the Task' (S); 'Lady of the Island' (N).*

RAY OF HOPE

by Allan Thomas

Somewhere in the middle of the year and a half it took me to complete my album, *Making Up for Lost Time*, released in October 2007, I often ran into Graham Nash while he was in Hawaii. Every time we met, Graham asked how I was doing and what I was up to, and the same thing happened in late 2006. I gave him the drift. He then said what I'd hoped he would, asking if there was anything he could do on the new recording. Not wasting a nano-second I gave him the affirmative that yes, I would be honored to have him sing on a track. Sometimes I have to kick myself for the amazing good fortune to have such great players on the record, and this was no exception.

Six or so months later, in May 2007, Graham was back in Hawaii and I drove up to his home and played him the song 'Ray of Hope'. He listened intently but said he didn't hear a part for himself. I asked him to hit play one more time and got up the nerve to sing him possible harmony parts over the

2011: Allan Thomas recording with Crosby & Nash in Hawaii, USA. Photos from Allan Thomas personal collection

vocal in both chorus and verse. Bobbing and weaving to the music in the usual Nash way he smiled and started making up his own parts and agreed the song would work for him.

The next day Graham met me at the Kilauea gas station and we begin the drive up to Ron Pendragon's studio. Every ten minutes or so Nash hit play on the pick-up's CD player and rehearsed his harmony parts with my lead vocal. Kind of mind blowing really when you hear your little creation begin to sprout wings.

Ron was totally prepared for us, having set up the tube Neumann U67, so we got right to work. Nash pretty much astonished both Ron and I with his near perfect pitch, great attitude and ease of effort. At one point I had a suggestion for a harmony part which Nash liked. He asked me to join him and sing it together, I started heading for the mic but stopped for a second and realized that as much as I wanted to sing and record with him, his groove might be in serious jeopardy if I were to slow down his workflow with flat notes or whatever, so I passed and just let him perform his magic, content to not have to sing or engineer, and just produce and enjoy the memorable session.

231

The whole deal was over in an hour and 15 minutes, and by the time we finished, 'Ray of Hope' had a new shine about it.

Bio: *Born in Manhattan, New York, Allan Thomas has lived on the north shore of Kauai in Hawaii for the last 35 years or so. He writes songs, performs regularly, records and produces other artists and teaches guitar, voice and songwriting. He says, 'My main achievement is still being an active performing musician and recording artist some 50 years from when I started as a doo-wop singer in Brooklyn.'*
He released his sixth album of original music in early 2018, featuring members of Steely Dan, the James Taylor band, and the Yellow Jackets, and surfs and windsurfs as much as humanly possible. To date, Graham Nash has sung on three of his records and Graham and David Crosby sang together on 2012's Deep Water album.

Songs: *'To the Last Whale'/'Wind on the Water' (C/N); 'Helplessly Hoping' (S); 'Liar's Nightmare' (N).*

DAVID CROSBY: ASSORTED REFLECTIONS

by Paul Zollo

David Crosby's a big man with big emotions. As those who know him already know well, when he's happy, his joy is infectious. It's that sparkle in his eyes, that laughing at the universe attitude which has drawn so many people to him. But in the same way, when Croz is unhappy, or - even worse – angry, that fire is also palpable, and undeniable.

I've seen both sides over the years. I've interviewed him many times over the years, from the first time in his Encino kitchen, when he still lived there before moving north, through subsequent other interviews, including one onstage at the Belly Up in beautiful Aspen.

I remember our first meeting in his big Encino kitchen, 1993. Wisely, I went with my secret weapon, my friend, the legendary writer-musician Henry Diltz. Back then, Henry would accompany me on all my big interviews, to take photos for *SongTalk*, the magazine of the National Academy of Songwriters, for which I was the editor. Henry would kindly take photos for me, and true to his generous spirit, would charge us what we called his 'Woodstock prices,' which is to say hardly anything.

Having Henry with me was always great, because he is such a lovable, funny and fun guy. Also, because he's maybe the best photographer of musicians ever, and certainly of those still alive. He taught me and all photographers a good lesson on how to photograph these authentic artists. Nothing phony or contrived. He would always make people feel happy, never uncomfortable. It's why those photos are all so great: those are people always looking with love to a friend. Smiling eyes.

And because Henry is so universally beloved, anytime I showed up with him, whether it be at the home of Croz, Tom Petty, Leonard Cohen, Graham Nash or anyone, that person's face would light up. Henry put people at ease, and nothing's better for an interview than an artist at ease.

Now knowing Croz as I do, he probably would have been at ease anyway. But on this day, I remember well that big, sunny, gregarious energy coming from him. Soon as we walked through the door, he exclaimed, '*Henry!*' and hugs and laughter ensued. I was an instant friend for being one of Henry's friends.

Soon came big mugs of good coffee, which Crosby poured while telling me the truth about Henry Diltz.

'People know Henry for all those photos of me and Young and Stills and Nash together,' he said, 'but those were really almost afterthoughts. Henry was there to take photos of our girlfriends skinny-dipping! Anytime Christine or Reine had their clothes off, you can be sure he wasn't shooting me.' Both he and Henry dissolved into laughter at this comment, Henry a tad sheepish for his legacy to be now tilted thus.

July 19, 1998: Crosby live at Testaccio Village, Roma, Italy (CPR tour). Photo by Francesco Lucarelli

On this day Croz was busy doing a multitude of creative projects at once. He had just returned, he told us, from Castle Rock, where he had pitched a movie idea. His mother-in-law arrived at the same time, and she got the same happy reception. It was like being at a great party of much joy. And there was no question in my mind that this joy derived from the fact that he'd been to the very bottom in every way - addiction, arrests, jail, illness - and had not only survived but had triumphed. Just being alive - at this moment - filled him with delight that was big and infectious.

Also he'd recently released a remarkable solo album, perhaps his best ever, *Thousand Roads,* on which he sang great songs by his pals like Jimmy Webb, and also the one song he wrote with Joni Mitchell, the wonderful 'Yvette in English.' That being alive joy permeates that track and the entire record.

He spoke of many things during this, our first interview of what luckily has turned out to be many. He said that unlike famous pals like Neil Young, who churned out song after song, he preferred to let them emerge slowly and organically, like leaves turning golden, and would wait years if necessary for those few he considered 'stunners.' Nothing else of his own composition was worth his attention. 'I cannot legislate a song into being,' he said. 'But I can create a space for it to happen, and sometimes a song will come and fill that space.'

The man is a Leo, and like other famous performers such as Mick Jagger, he embodies the sun-bright golden leonine pride distinctive to Leos. He is also big enough that he's unafraid to laugh at himself, something impossible for lesser men. He said that it was in jail that he performed for the first time ever completely sober. He also mentioned that it was about then that he made love straight for the first time, after which he quickly clarified that happened *after* serving his time.

'Yeah, I didn't mean I made love in prison,' he said with a laugh. 'That happened when I got out. I didn't have sex in prison. I was too old and ugly in prison for that, you don't have to worry.'

He's a man with a big voice, yet because so much of his career has been singing within groups - whether a rock band, quartet, trio or duo - and because he is such a remarkable harmony singer, the full power and soulful dynamic force of his own voice is often under-sung. Yet he has the presence, the songwriting genius, and vocal greatness to have been a beloved solo artist, as his pals Jackson Browne, James Taylor and Paul Simon were. His genius with harmonies was not only his cunning proclivity to create the perfect harmony part which united all others, but to sing it so that it blends perfectly with the other voices in every aspect: phrasing, tone, rhythm, and timbre. But because of this remarkable precision and blend, his voice disappears into the whole, which is the goal, to create a unified sound. His part becomes a ghost that perfectly merges with the timbre and phrasing of the other two voices so much so that it almost disappears, becoming, as Art Garfunkel described the secret magic of Crosby's harmony singing, the 'glue' that holds all three parts together.

Yet when the man sings alone, it is chilling. He has a seemingly unlimited well of power from which to draw when singing alone, and when he lets loose and taps into the full dynamic power inside him, the sound is truly awesome. As I learned up close when he was my guest at Lyrically Speaking, the songwriter-interview series I produced and hosted for the Aspen Writer's Foundation at the lovely Belly Up club.

It was after I had done a few of these that I was asked if I could invite Croz. So I did. Unsure if he would even consider it, he delighted me by saying he would love to, but with a few conditions. He wanted to come with wife Jan and son Django. He also wanted ski-tickets and equipment for Django, 12 then, to go snowboarding. This, he told me later, was the main reason he said yes. So Django could have a fun snow time vacation. The final condition was that he travel there and back on a private jet. Worried this requirement could be a deal-breaker, I nonetheless called the Aspen folks. To my delight, they said they had a friend with a private jet company who would handle it in style.

Croz told me I could fly with him if I met him in Santa Barbara. So that morning I took the train due north from downtown Los Angeles, to meet up with Croz, his wife and son. This was my first ever voyage on a private jet, and I immediately understood why he insisted on this. It was much more like riding in a limo, as opposed to the crowded bus that regular airplanes have become (although with smaller seats than buses). Not only did you not have to go through security, you didn't even have to go inside the airport. Croz and company were driven directly to the tarmac of the jet. He smiled a gentle smile. It was evident that being treated like royalty was second nature to him.

He and I spoke much along the way. Jan and Django sat behind us and were otherwise engaged. George W. Bush was president then, which he found appalling and we both felt (and now know we were wrong) was as bad as it could get.

A tremendously erudite guy with far-ranging interests, we spoke of politics past and present, and the evolution of his own thinking and that of our country as it's spanned the decades of his own lifetime. 'We were the first generation,' he said, 'to truly live each day with an existential crisis. That ever since we dropped the bombs on Japan, we live each day on the edge with the knowledge it all could end instantly. That knowledge, that edge, shaped our consciousness in a way people never had been, and led to the riots and revolutions and revelations of the Sixties, and beyond.'

We also spoke of music history. Of The Beatles, who he pointed to as the foundation stone of his entire career. He never wanted to be a folkie, and certainly never a solo musician. He wanted to be a Beatle. And he came close - he was a Byrd. It was electrified singer-songwriting, but born on these shores.

He also knew The Beatles, as he did Dylan and pretty much everyone else in the business. He, as is famously known, was the one who brought Joni Mitchell into the star-maker machinery, producing her first album essentially by letting her be free in the studio to be Joni unencumbered. We spoke of all of these and more. He spoke of a friend both close and famous, who actively stole songs for which he took credit. He told me other such stuff, much of which will remain off the record.

Except one comment which I so loved and will share here as it's so essentially Croz: funny and brilliant both. When discussing the spirit of free love in the Sixties, and its real impact on love and life then. Having long marveled at how his friendship with Graham Nash remained solid, even after both men, as well as other close friends, all had love affairs with Joni Mitchell. When I asked him about this, he answered immediately.

'Not *all* of my friends,' he said. 'Not Stills. Joni had to draw the line *somewhere,* you know!' Much laughter came after that one.

Sharing the stage with Croz, as I did on that one night in Aspen, was an absolute joy, and also one replete with much big Crosby laughter. The foundation always put these shows completely in my hands, so that I would plan completely my array of questions, interspersed with live performances by our guest artist.

It was also my job to discuss with each artist which songs they planned to do, so I could prepare questions. As Croz rarely does solo shows of any kind, there were some songs he simply refused to do alone. 'Almost Cut My Hair', he said, was impossible for him to do without a band, as was 'Déjà Vu'. Although he did discuss the origins of these songs, and occasionally picked up his beautiful 12-string or his six-string acoustic we had there. There was also a baby grand for him to play, which he did.

The show sold out as soon as tickets went on sale. They even sold many more tickets - something I was told they never did - than seats. So that people were standing all along the back, and in the aisles. It was *packed*.

To start the show, the director of the AWF spoke about their organization, and about this series - which was intended to show that songs are literature, and deserve as much attention. She then introduced me and left the stage as I took over.

I started by saying, 'Some people are way more talented than others.' I then mentioned how what he did used to take several people. 'There used to be one guy writing words, one guy writing the melody, a singer, an arranger, a producer, and a musician. That is used to take six different people. Crosby, as those in the know already know, did all.' I spoke about Croz a little bit, mostly his singular achievements as a songwriter.

Because the songs of David Crosby remain quite miraculous. Unlike Stills, Nash and most living humans except Joni Mitchell, Croz wrote his songs in open guitar tunings he devised himself. Those alone gave all his songs different colors than those used by everyone else. But to that came his ingenious and expansively brave freedom with song structure itself, often creating little suites closer to symphonies of many movements than a pop song. Something like 'Déjà Vu' is so freeform, it is unlike most anything in pop music, with the possible exception of some of Brian Wilson's most adventurous songwriting.

Yet his songs never seemed random. With words of naked candor merged with poetry, expanded consciousness and his ripe sense of humor, his songs were always so singularly his songs. The music, although usually founded on richly sophisticated harmonic progressions, was always poignantly melodic and perfectly ordered.

So that achievement with songs both singular yet tremendously appealing, most of which were discovered in the midst of embodying one of the first-ever supergroups, was the main focus of my introduction.

When I finished and spoke his name, an electric wave of love swept through the room. Everyone was on their feet. I was facing backwards, waiting as Croz emerged, smiling, and gently walking to his chair as if people stood and cheered for him always. And they did. He was accustomed to that outpouring of affection. I, however, had never felt anything like it. Sure, I'd been onstage thousands of times, but usually at my own gigs. And ever did I feel anything remotely like *that*. It was the feeling of real love. Or awe, admiration, respect, delight and deep, abiding love. David, like many of his peers, have been our musical friends for decades. Since we were kids. It's a love that is not taken lightly.

After he settled and the crowd stopped cheering and sat down and greeted them like the old friends they were: 'Hi guys,' he said. Acknowledging their ovation, I said, 'There's a lot of love in the room tonight. I can feel it.' To which they started cheering again.

I asked my first question. It was basically just a joke, designed to amuse him and also signal the audience that this was not going to be dry and academic. I mentioned that he'd been a member of Crosby, Stills & Nash, and also Crosby, Stills, Nash & Young as well as Crosby-Nash. 'How did you always get top billing?' I asked. To which he threw back his head and laughed openly. And then explained that having his name first simply scanned better rhythmically. He did acknowledge that CSNY would have been a better acronym had they given into Stills' urging to put him first at that point and Crosby last. 'He wanted to call it Stills, Young, Nash and Crosby,' said David, 'which spells out SYNC. But we didn't go for that.'

We spoke of his remarkable history, first with Les Baxter's Balladeers, and then The Byrds. He played many great songs he wrote himself, including 'Delta' on piano, which was stunning.

I made a joke which, like the best ones, was entirely true. Because getting to see and hear David Crosby perform these songs solo while sitting right there on the stage with him was tremendously electric for me, and inspirational. After he performed 'Delta,' I said, 'These are the best seats I have ever had at one of his shows. I am having a great time.' To which the audience cheered, showing their agreement as they, too, got to take him in at very close range. Though I was the closest!

He kept the audience - and this host - laughing the entire time. As this took place back when George W. Bush was still in office, he referred to the president's habit of pronouncing the word 'nuclear' wrongly, always as 'nu-cul-lar,' and said, 'I feel any President of the United States should be required to be able to pronounce that word.'

Afterwards, Croz was really excited, and suggested we go on the road together. A suggestion I so would have loved to take him up on. He said, 'That was *fun*. We were *funny*!'

Then there was the time in Orange Beach, Alabama - known by some as the 'Redneck Riviera', where I traveled with Henry Diltz and Jon Brewer, film director. We were shooting a documentary, which became *Legends of the Canyon*, about all the Laurel Canyon musicians, and were here on this ridiculously hot day to interview Crosby, Stills and Nash. Though it was not our intended goal, the history of CSN and also Y became the heart of our movie.

Because of timing, though, our only chance to interview Croz and his band members for this project was not in Laurel Canyon, which sure would have been more convenient for me, as I live off Laurel Canyon Blvd. in North Hollywood. But in Alabama, because CSN were on tour and could meet with us then.

Of course, the plan was to interview each of them separately. Not that there was ever any choice. Except for soundchecks and actual concerts, C, S and N rarely spent time together. To ensure the tour would work with a minimum of animosity, each of them traveled this tour on their own tour bus. Nash told me at the time he smoked no marijuana at all for the tour, the first drug-free tour he'd ever done.

Stills, whose guitar playing was more incendiary ever on this night, reminding one and all he was jamming with Hendrix long before he played with all these folkies, was unusually humble after the show. When I mentioned his lead electric guitar playing was greater than ever, he said softly, 'Thanks, man. Thank you. I appreciate that. And, you know, it should be better. I have been playing for more than 40 years now.' I mentioned he'd been writing songs that long as well and asked if songwriting got better for him. 'No,' he said immediately. 'That gets harder.'

Onstage in Orange Beach, their harmony was impeccable, and they put on a great show. Although, I could tell from the wings just offstage, Croz seemed somewhat weary. Graham did almost all the talking between songs, as Croz would slowly strap on the right guitar for the song. But once inside the song, he did what he always did. He sang the remarkable middle part, the oddest of harmonies that was the glue between Stills and Nash, almost imperceptible in the delivery as Croz is all about that perfect, dynamic vocal blend.

The concert was great, despite the exclusion of some of their most famous, and our most beloved, songs, such as 'Suite: Judy Blue Eyes.' We kept waiting for it, yet it never came. After the show, Jon, Henry and I went into the backstage bathroom. While doing our business, Brewer - a large Brit with a booming voice always heavy with condescension - complained about the concert, listing the songs they should have done and those they should have excluded.

What we didn't know was that Croz himself was in one of the stalls, with door closed, hearing all this. As Brewer was completing his lengthy anti-CSN tirade by stating he simply could not understand how they could make such obviously bad choices, the door to that stall swung open and Croz emerged, fuming. 'Maybe you can't understand,' Croz said, burning a hole into Brewer's sickly pale forehead with his eyes, 'because you're fucking down here and we're fucking *up there*! Nobody cares what the fuck *you* think!'

With that, he walked out of the bathroom. Henry ran after, saying, 'It wasn't me, David!' I'd never seen Henry, in my decades of knowing him, look scared like that.

I was left with Brewer, who was absolutely shaken to the core by this direct dressing down. His eyes were bulging, and he looked like a man who had just been condemned to a terrible fate. Later that night, after collecting Henry, we drove the long, empty way through nothing but dark marshland. It took over an hour. That entire time Brewer, who was driving, had his window down so that he could scream at the top of his lungs, 'I'm sorry, David! DAVID! I'm SORRY!'

The next time I saw Croz he was back to being the big sunshiny, happy guy. Just like he was the first time. I asked if he remembered what Brewer had said. 'You mean that fat Brit guy who looked like a stoned pirate who is a moron?' Yeah, I said. 'Nope,' he said smiling. 'Not that I can recall.'

Bio: *Paul Zollo is a singer-songwriter, music writer, and author of several books, including* Songwriters on Songwriting, Conversations with Tom Petty, *and* Hollywood Remembered. *Born in Chicago, he lives in California, where he is pursuing his main dream of having Willie Nelson record one of his songs.*

Songs: *'I love 'Suite: Judy Blue Eyes,' 'Wind on the Water' and 'Helplessly Hoping,' and, and, and ... But of all of them, I think of the wisdom in 'Carry On' a lot. That no matter what, we have no choice to carry on. 'Delta' makes me swoon ... it is so beautiful. He played it live when we did our Aspen thing and it blew me away. But every song Croz has written slays me. I love his songs maybe more than ever.'*

July 4, 2009: CSN live at L'Olympia, Paris, France. Photos by Francesco Lucarelli

July 25, 2015: Graham Nash live at Uptown Theater, Kansas City, Missouri, USA. Photo by Christine Bower

CROSBY, STILLS & NASH

10's

Music is worth all the pain

2015

CROSBY · STILLS · NASH
BEACON THEATRE
OCT. 16TH-22ND 2012

ALL ACCESS

BUS STOP	SET 1
MARRAKESH	
I USED TO BE A KING	
IMMIGRATION MAN	
SLEEP SONG	
MYSELF AT LAST	
THIS PATH	
MILITARY MADNESS	
WIND ON THE WATER	
WASTED	

Liberty Live presents
An evening with
Graham Nash
This Path Tonight Tour
Wednesday April 05 2017 7:30 PM
Center   Row Seat
LOBERO BOX OFFIC
Santa Barbara, CA
805.963.0761 - lobero.org

April 5, 2017 – Santa Barbara, CA

JL0815E TOM

A135.00   WI

AC21.00   CROSBY, STILLS AND NASH   ADULT

102   JIFFY LUBE LIVE   102

X SECTION 13X   NO CAMERAS/RECORDERS   X SECTION 13X

S 16   SUN AUG 15, 2010 7:00PM   S 16

ZPC1554   +$6 PARKING   55216

1APR0   102   S 16   135.00 CN 1APR0

DATE SOLD   SECTION   ROW/BOX SEAT   PRICE (TAX INCL)   DATE SOLD

ticketmaster

Get tickets at TICKETMASTER.COM

0021279011119

GRAHAM NASH
GS FOR SURVIVORS
JULY. 29. 2002
WWW.GRAHAMNASH.COM

MSA
SECURITY

The Ride
Pierc

CRO

CSKY2K
462-4000

Crosby Nash To

November 2, 2

TEATRO SIST

ROME, ITAL

Sound Check 4

Dinner: BU

Doors: 8:0

Show Time:

After Sho

RETURN T

Tomorrow: ALL

WILL PRO

DAVID
CROSB
AND FRIENDS

DAVID CROSBY
TOUR 2K16
MARCH 5, 2016
SEGERSTROM HALL
COSTA MESA, CA

OUND CHECK 4:00 PM
DINNER: 5:00 PM
DOORS: 7:00 PM
W TIME: 8:00 PM

SHOW TRAVEL:
THOUSAND OAKS, CA

VIP

phen Stills • Barry Goldberg
Kenny Wayne Shepherd

SHINGTON DC • MARYLAND • NORTHERN VIRGINIA

THURSDAY
NOV 29TH 8PM

WEINBERG
CENTER FOR THE ARTS

July 16, 2010: CSN live at "Milano Jazzin' Festival", Arena Civica, Milan, Italy. Photos by Mauro Regis

FAITH IN MUSIC

by Marcus Eaton

One of the most amazing milestones in my musical journey began as an e-mail I received in the fall of 2010 that would forever transform my life and career. It was an invitation from David Crosby to play on his forthcoming album, which would become *Croz*.

In the strange business of music, there are often situations which just do not work out. Plans fail, things fall apart, and despite our best efforts and highest hopes, we are left where we began. In this case, my hopes were very high, but I didn't dare tell anyone what was happening for fear that I would jinx it.

On Hallowe'en I arrived at Burbank Airport and stepped foot into the studio with Crosby and his son James Raymond for the first time. It was only then that I allowed myself the indulgence of calling my family and telling them where I was and what I was doing. I was on cloud nine and felt I was right where I belonged - in the studio with amazing musicians making real music. The following day, before we began recording, a slew of incredible guitars was dropped off at the studio. Normally I would feel shy about opening the cases to see which axes were inside, but I knew the guitars were there for me to choose.

Crosby and I met through mutual friend, Norm Waitt. Norm believed that we may get along musically, and he was right. He invited us to a dinner to meet one another and since Croz and I arrived before our host, we discussed our latest playlists and musical interests. I was amazed that we had so much in common, considering I am half his age and also that he is into very progressive music much like me. Before we parted ways, he gave me his phone number and told me we would speak again soon. We kept in touch and the next time we met, we made arrangements to have dinner and play guitar in Boise, Idaho, where I am from. He was traveling there a day early for his next show with CSN.

As we discussed the current situation with the oil spill off the Gulf of Mexico, I observed Crosby's intelligence, recollection of facts and vast knowledge of our world. He said to me, 'I have a guitar that you need to play.' 'What is it?' I replied. 'It is called a McAlister and it was made by a guitar-maker in Santa Cruz, named Roy McAlister. He gave me the guitar a few years ago, and it is one of the best guitars in the world.'

Obviously, I could not refuse an offer to play what Croz called 'one of the best guitars in the world'; he handed me the guitar and I played him one of my songs, 'Smile'. It was like butter; the neck and guitar disappeared in my hands. I began the two-handed tapping section of the bridge, and the song became more than a performance - a transcendent moment in time where I became recognized by a musical icon. With a look of happiness and awe, he said, 'You've got to play for my son!' Immediately he phoned James and told him, 'You need to come to my room and hear this guy play!'

That was how I found my way into this remarkable situation, and we worked on the *Croz* album over a period of three years between extensive tours.

Around February or March 2011, back at the studio, another guitar delivery arrived and this time I knew exactly what was in the case. I opened it, carefully pulled out the beautiful McAlister, and began to play.

Admittedly, I was lost for a while. This happens to me when I play: I go somewhere else. Croz walked in the studio door, and I snapped almost all the way back to reality. 'You really like that guitar, don't you!' I couldn't really muster up the words in my guitar trance, so I nodded yes. 'It's kind of strange ... it's sort of like someone *really* liking your wife,' he said. We began to laugh and realized I probably should put her back, since she did not belong to me. 'You need to get one of those guitars ... he's a friend of mine and will give you a great deal.' I said, 'I would love to when I can afford it!' Croz promptly left the studio and after a few minutes returned to make an announcement. 'I just spoke with Roy, and he's living near Seattle now.'

I was scheduled to be there for a solo performance and meet with Crosby while he was on his Crosby & Nash tour. 'He wants us to come by his shop ... are you available?' 'Absolutely, I can't wait!'

It was April, with Seattle as rainy as ever. I headed to Crosby's hotel to pick him up and start making the trek to McAlister's shop in Gig Harbor. We stopped at my favorite coffee shop, Lighthouse Roasters, followed by a dense breakfast that harmonized with the gloomy skies of the Northwest. It's about an hour to Roy's shop through the greenery of the I-5 and across the famous Tacoma Narrows Bridge.

We knocked on the door and were greeted by Roy and his wife, Lucy, who had baked fresh chocolate chip cookies for us. The smell permeated the air and again I felt I was right where I belonged: in the company of craftsmen and musicians.

Roy's passion is instantly recognized and as we began discussing guitars, he spoke about the diverse types of wood, the tree's cellular structure, density, reaction to climate, and the increasing difficulty in obtaining Brazilian rosewood: the most coveted wood for the back and sides of the guitar. I interjected, saying, 'I recently played a guitar that had a type of Cambodian wood for the back and sides ... and it sounded incredible!' Roy responded with an ambiguous but subtle look on his face. 'It's strange you say that, because I'm building one for a client right now who requested the ultimate tonewood ... it has Cambodian rosewood back and sides with a German spruce top!' 'Wow!' I exclaimed. 'I can't wait to see it!'

We walked to the shop tucked into the forest of Roy's backyard and as the doors opened, it was as if a chorus of angels began to sing. For a guitarist, especially one so passionate about acoustic guitars, the gates of heaven had opened. The scent of wood stirs the soul, and perhaps the art of constructing

September 11, 2018: Michelle Willis, David Crosby, Marcus Eaton and Jeff Pevar - soundchecking at Teatro Dal Verme, Milan, Italy. Photo by Francesco Lucarelli

something with bare hands and wood speaks to our genetic ancestry. Roy showed us a plethora of guitars in various stages of construction. The shelves were stacked with sets of backs and sides, including elusive Brazilian rosewood. The *Acoustic Guitar* magazine article that put McAlister Guitars on the map adorned one section of the wall above his chisels, with a two-page picture of Crosby playing the first guitar Roy made for him, the instrument Crosby first handed me in his hotel, the reason I was standing in Roy's workshop.

When Roy presented the guitar to Crosby many years before, he was very sceptical, and remarked, 'I have a lot of guitars, man.' Much to his surprise, it was the best sounding acoustic he ever played. Crosby set out to pay Roy, but he declined payment. So, Crosby made sure his guitar was featured not only within the article but also held it lovingly on the cover picture of the magazine. Within weeks, Roy was bustling with orders, and karma had been fulfilled.

I continued looking around and beheld an incredible guitar body hanging on the wall. The top was nearly white, and the back and sides were crimson red. Crosby picked it up and said, 'Is this the one you were telling us about?' 'Yes,' Roy said. 'It is the Cambodian rosewood and German spruce one!' Crosby tapped right where the bridge would be placed. The tone sounded and he scrunched his face with an excited smile. 'Oh! You hear that? That is right where the bridge will be!' It sounded like a resonant drum with tone, structure and depth. 'Yes!' I said in amazement. 'May I look at it?' He handed me the body. It was very curved with a tight waist, the same body as his guitar, and it did not have binding yet. I could not get over the wood, the construction and all of the subtle design elements. The grain was profound, and the guitar already had a soul: it was perfection.

I carefully placed the guitar back on its hook. I thought to myself, 'One day, you will have to have Roy make you a guitar.' I turned my back when Crosby said, 'Do you like that guitar?' 'The one I was just holding?' 'Yes, it is astounding!' He handed me a small piece of paper and said, 'Here is the label that is going to be inside of it.' It read, 'To Marcus Eaton from David Crosby'.

I nearly fell over. I didn't have the words to express how I felt, but we were all smiling, and he said, 'I *got* you!'

It was no coincidence that this unique guitar found me and I would have chosen the same rare woods. It was so peculiar that at one point Roy believed Crosby had ruined the surprise and told me all about the guitar. Roy and I have subsequently become great friends and he took me to Italy with him for the *Acoustic Guitar* meeting in 2012. This completely changed my musical trajectory, and I am very grateful.

Every time I play my McAlister, I feel absolute joy, connection, hope and faith in music. We can believe in ourselves, but often it takes another artist to reflect back to us who we really are. Belief and hope are essential elements to carry on in music and life.

Bio: *Marcus Eaton grew up in Idaho and currently resides in Los Angeles, California. He's been playing guitar, writing songs and singing since he was very young, his passion leading him to many incredible experiences throughout the world. He worked as a writer, singer and guitarist with David Crosby on the album, Croz, and toured in his band. He has shared stages with many wonderful and diverse artists throughout his career, including Bob Dylan, Derek Trucks, Seal, and Tim Reynolds, releasing six albums and an EP.*

Songs: *'Bittersweet' (C); 'Suite: Judy Blue Eyes' (S); 'Right Between the Eyes' (N).*

1 aaaaaaaa.

KIDS IN LOVE

by Daniela Wood

I met Carl Gottlieb a few years ago. Co-author of the screenplay of *Jaws*, he's known David Crosby for more than 50 years; they met in San Francisco in 1963, when The Byrds were playing as the house band at a go-go club up the street from where Carl was working as a stage manager at an improvisational comedy cabaret called The Committee. They've been friends ever since, good times and bad.

Illustration by Daniela Wood

Very soon after we met, Carl took me to see CSN play in Long Beach, California in 2011, and we went backstage. It was there that I met Crosby and his wife Jan. We four fit together immediately, and over the next five years we'd visit whenever the band or David played in Southern California, or on occasions when Carl and I would drive up to Santa Barbara and go to see David and Jan at home. I usually have my camera with me, so I've had the opportunity to take some wonderful pictures when everyone is relaxed and happy. Carl says their love and friendship is like a light shining inside them, and I agree.

One of the most beautiful memories I have belongs to the year after I first met David and Jan. I would travel with Carl to visit them in Santa Barbara County. We would often go to lunch or dinner in one of the picturesque towns near where they lived. On one occasion, Carl and I were walking behind David and Jan as they strolled back to their car, and I snapped a photo of them holding hands. When I printed that photo, I was so fascinated, I wanted to make a painting of it. Later, I added the wide-open horizon and sky in front of them, so it appeared as if they were walking towards a limitless future, which is what couples in love do.

It was sweet, how they always held hands, like they were kids in love. I guess they have always been kids in love. As Carl says, their love and friendship is like a light shining inside them and, when you look at them, you know he is right.

Bio: *Daniela Wood was born in Bulgaria, graduating from medical school there. But art in all its forms was always her first love. She moved permanently to the States in 2000 and now lives in Southern California, where she enjoys art photography and home-schooling her son.*

Songs: *'Déjà Vu' (C); 'Suite: Judy Blue Eyes' (S); 'Teach Your Children' (N) ('I always begin lessons to my son with this song').*

ONE BET, TWO WINNERS

by Mark White

I was diagnosed with cancer at the end of March 2011. This dreadful, world-shattering news was compounded by the fact that I had booked tickets to a number of Crosby-Nash concerts in the US in May. Organising this trip from the UK hadn't been straightforward, what with work demands, three kids at home and a wife who (still) doesn't understand the pull of C, S or N, in whatever combination. So, getting permission from my wife to go AWOL to the other side of the world for 10 days or so, when I was supposed to be preparing for my operation, was not greeted with - shall we say - a great deal of understanding. I even had to ask my astonished consultant if he could delay my life-saving procedure for a week or two, as the date he proposed for my operation clashed with a Crosby-Nash gig at the Wilbur in Boston. Get the picture? Fuck cancer. I'm not going to miss this trip, okay?

Anyway, cutting a long story short, myself and mates Graham and Buzz turned up in Portland, Maine, for a Crosby-Nash gig at the State Theatre. We stayed in the same hotel as the band, chatted with a few of them during the day, then headed out for lunch. That afternoon, I was due to interview Graham and Croz for a newspaper I work for back in London. After listening to the soundcheck, Crosby, Nash & White choose three comfortable-looking chairs in the theatre and started to chat.

Well, that was the plan. Crosby was resolutely unengaging. He sat there with his CSN cap covering most of his face so I couldn't see his expression, but boy, his body language was telling me all I needed to know. He did not want to talk. I know the guy was probably all done in what with schlepping across America in a bus, onstage for three hours every night, having to endure (as I heard in Boston only the previous day) witless questions from radio jocks opening every interview with, 'So ... you were at Woodstock. What was it like?' And he wasn't expecting much different that day.

But the fates were smiling on me, and a cheeky remark about Crosby's impersonation of Chris Rea sounding more like Rajiv Gandhi than someone from England's North-East brought the old boy round, and like the characters on the 'Group W Bench' in Alice's Restaurant we were suddenly great chums laughing and joking, swapping anecdotes, and exchanging confidences with Graham about his hush-hush forthcoming project, a boxset cataloguing the best of CSNY's 1974 tour.

Nearly two hours went by, my mates leaving the theatre to go for a beer and Crosby telling me this band he was playing with on tour was so good that they would just need a quick run-through of any song and they could play it live, that very night, no sweat, no big deal. I was ready to discuss the rehearsal process that such an undertaking would require, but dinner was now being served backstage. Graham asked me to join them. Well, might as well - I' wasn't doing anything else for a few hours.

We headed upstairs, where the rest of the band were helping themselves to chowder and bits of meat in a sauce of some description. 'There is a tradition', says Crosby, 'that dictates that the worse a pre-show meal is, the better the show will be.' Graham and I sat at a table and discussed books, England, and being on the road. After half-an-hour, despite assurances to the contrary, I said I must have outstayed my welcome and must be getting in the way, making to leave, saying my goodbyes.

As I came to the exit door, Croz was sat with James Raymond and guitarist Dean Parks, next to an array of expensive-looking acoustic guitars. I said thank you for having me and told Dean that Croz reckoned the band was so good that they could play any song with just one quick rehearsal. As there was a general murmur of consent, a devil popped up on my shoulder and whispered into my ear, and I found myself saying, 'I bet you can't play 'Dream for Him' tonight.' Crosby muttered something about the setlist and I rfound myself going further. 'Come on, I bet you. You've got to prove it. You can't back out.' I could see Stevie D rolling his eyes. Hmm. That might be the last time I get invited to take afternoon tea with the band backstage for a few years.

The first set went very well. The house was full and everyone was upbeat. I said hello to a few people I had met only electronically in e-mail group, the Lee Shore. I met one of the two ladies about whom 'Triad' was written. She was lovely, and we have a great chat. Quite a day.

As the lights went down for the final half of the show, Graham Nash came onstage and proceeded to tell the audience how, 'Crosby told a journalist friend of ours from England this afternoon that this band' (pointing to the group onstage) 'can play any CSN or CSNY song. Any song. Well, this guy had the nerve to say to Crosby, 'Well, I bet you can't play 'Dream for Him''

At the after-show, we hung around a bit and Crosby came towards me, a glint in his eye. 'Thank you,' I said. 'You won the bet.' He laughed. 'The odds were always stacked in my favour,' he replied.

And in mine, too. My operation was a success, and I have been clear of cancer for more than five years now.

Bio: *Mark White has followed CSN all over the world. Memorable concerts include David Crosby at The Troubadour, CPR in New Jersey (the night of Croz' arrest for firearms possession), Stephen Stills solo in London, and Graham Nash's 2017 homecoming concert in Manchester. Having worked as a national newspaper publisher in London for over 25 years, Mark changed careers after his fight with cancer and now teaches English.*

Songs: *'Rusty and Blue' (C); 'Haven't We Lost Enough' (S); 'Mississippi Burning' (N).*

I AM THE MAYAN

by Lane Gosnay

Some things are meant to be casually observed and released; others, to be experienced at the level of the soul and kept nostalgically preserved as part of either our own personal history or shared for a greater good.

Working as a harbor patrol officer at Santa Barbara Harbor in 1995, I would pass by Crosby's schooner, the Mayan, during patrols. She was not at a dock, but rather chained to a mooring inside the harbor. Her sails were down and her canvas covered for protection, her tall masts piercing the sky. I noticed her beauty and I felt her loneliness. avid was sick during that time, and I believe he was waiting for a liver donor. He wasn't sailing her anymore. I could imagine Croz laying in his bed somewhere in the hills of Santa Barbara, the Mayan beckoning him back to the sea.

David wrote many of his songs on the Mayan, and somehow his muse 'spoke' to me. I decided to write a song about the ship and - with the help of my friend, singer-songwriter Blenda Shipp - I cut a rough take of the song on tape. Somehow, the cassette tape was tucked away in a box, and I forgot about it for nearly two decades.

Shortly after recording the song, I moved back to Texas and worked as a state game warden on the South Texas coast. After sustaining an injury during a water rescue, I eventually founded The Bugle Boy, a non-profit music venue located in La Grange, Texas.

In April 2012, in the age of Google, I discovered the Mayan was for sale. Remembering those days spent on the California coast, I was again confronted with the passion I felt for this beautiful, iconic sailing vessel.

While hosting Grammy-winner Ruthie Foster at The Bugle Boy, I shared the Mayan story with her and at her encouragement, I decided to 'dust off' the cassette and revive the song. I felt an overwhelming compulsion to get the song re-recorded and gifted to David. All the logical reasons to not do so had zero chance of stopping the process. Not being a professional songwriter or recording artist, I was humbled to have three individuals make an honest, concerted, heartfelt effort with this project. Along with award-winning music producer Mark Hallman at the helm, I was supported by the talented vocals and arrangement expertise of Elizabeth Wills and ever-popular Woody Russell, who agreed to add electric guitar and back-up vocals. Together, we all worked to express the voice, personality and power of the Mayan in the most genuine of ways. Though neither Elizabeth, Woody nor Mark had ever seen the Mayan, they, indeed, now know her. They have taken a most memorable journey with her.

251

David Crosby sailing. Photo courtesy of the Wooden Nickel archives

After 'I Am the Mayan' was recorded and printed on a CD, it was tucked into a beautifully-crafted teakwood case with a brass inlay. I sent two copies to David's boat broker, whom then gave David his copy. It was just a gift to David. I really didn't expect a response or even know if he would like it. I have to admit that when I got an email from him, I was very surprised.

'Lane … thank you for the beautiful song … wish me luck on finding a good home for her … I have loved Mayan and sailed all over the world … lived on her … written many of my best songs on her … I very much do not want to sell her … I love her … but she is in near perfect shape and I can't afford to keep her that way … neither can I bear to let her go downhill on my watch … Croz.'

I felt like David's email was a gift back to me. A gift I will forever treasure because I knew I actually got what I so strongly felt was the voice of the Mayan in his hands. The circle was complete.

Bio: *Born in Orange, Texas, Lane Gosnay spent half of her growing up years in Dallas. A graduate of Texas A & M Maritime Academy in Galveston, she has worked as a Scuba instructor and dive guide in Florida and the Cayman Islands. She also worked as a harbor patrol officer for the city of Santa Barbara, California, and is a former Texas state game warden. Since college, as 'kind of a hobby,' she has worked with musicians writing songs, booking gigs, supplying rehearsal space, and organizing small tours. In 2005, she founded The Bugle Boy listening room in La Grange, Texas, where independent artists perform original music. In 2008, supporters of The Bugle Boy created The Bugle Boy Foundation, a non-profit organization, to 'elevate and sustain original live music' through the* *operation of the listening room and a variety of other music-based community outreach projects. Lane is currently an executive director of The Bugle Boy Foundation. On further contact with David, he gave permission to use photos of the Mayan, put together in an online video to share 'I Am the Mayan' with the world. Lane added, 'As a music lover and presenter of singer/songwriters, I am very aware of the gift of the often-elusive muse. The Mayan should forever be remembered as the muse of all time. My hope is that somehow, some day other artists will have the opportunity to be inspired by her.'*

Songs: *'Wooden Ships' (C); 'Southern Cross' (S); 'Teach Your Children' (N).*

VAI SER UMA BOA NOITE!

by Gustavo Wornunk

In early 2012, Crosby, Stills & Nash announced a South American tour, including dates in Brazil - São Paulo (10 May), Belo Horizonte (12 May) and Rio de Janeiro (13 May). An anxious wait began. When the big day finally came, I managed to find out that they were staying in a hotel near my workplace in São Paulo. I decided to try my luck and went to the hotel to try to meet them.

I was wearing a CSN shirt, so - when Shane Fontayne saw me - he came over to talk. We chatted for a few minutes, then I saw Graham Nash leaving the hotel. I asked Graham to pose for a photo and he agreed, with great kindness. Someone took a picture of us and Nash wanted to check how the image came out. He thought about it for a moment and, believing it was too dark, suggested taking another with a flash. We only talked for a few minutes, but it was a very pleasant and exciting experience. I told him The Hollies were one of my favorite Sixties bands, and he obviously enjoyed it. I asked if The Hollies ever recorded 'Marrakesh Express', and he replied that there was a version by them, but it was never completed.

He had to go to the soundcheck and so, as he got on a small bus, I said, 'See you later at the concert!' Inside, I could see Crosby and some others. A moment later, Nash opened a window, leaned out and said to me in Portuguese, 'Vai ser uma boa noite!' – 'It will be a great evening.' Shortly thereafter, I also spotted Stills, driving away to reach the Via Funchal theatre.

At the concert, I was in the front row, and a funny thing happened. I knew the lyrics of all their songs, so I sang them all. Crosby saw it. At one point, they started playing 'Lay Me Down', a lesser-known song, and during the instrumental introduction, David started looking at me, as if thinking, 'Now, let's see if you know this too.' When I started singing the lyrics to that as well, Crosby laughed, nodding his head, as if to say, 'I can't believe it!'

To complete that wonderful day, during 'Bluebird', Stephen threw me a pick. Unfortunately, another guy escaped me and took it. Stills noticed and threw me another! The concert was incredible, a magnificent setlist including songs by Buffalo Springfield and Manassas, and songs such as 'Jesus of Rio' and 'The Lee Shore'.

Graham was definitely right: it was a really great night!

October 17, 2012: Beacon Theatre, New York City, New York, USA. Photos by Francesco Lucarelli

Bio: *Born in Ribeirão Pires, Brazil, Gustavo Wornunk currently lives in Muswell Hill, London, working in the graphics department of a Christian charity. When he was younger, he played bass in some bands. He doesn't play live anymore but is recording some of his songs, inspired by British rock from 1966/67/68. Since adolescence, in Brazil, he has really liked The Hollies, especially songs sung by Nash. Consequently, he ended up discovering CSN. When he travelled to England for the first time, finding out they would be touring Britain, he bought tickets to see them at London's Royal Albert Hall and in Liverpool. He also bought a ticket to see Paul McCartney in Hyde Park and, to his surprise, sometime later it was announced that CSN would also feature on that bill in what became his first CSN and first McCartney show. Years later, he had the opportunity to see them twice in Brazil. In 2016, he attended a Nash solo show and the recording of the BBC Mastertapes radio show, where he played some songs and shared several stories.*

Songs: *'The Lee Shore' (C); 'Johnny's Garden' (S); 'Mama Lion' (N).*

MY ANGEL

by Nancy Moore

I didn't get to meet the band or anything like that, but this is still special to me. I live in Tuscaloosa, Alabama, a college town. I am 62 and have loved CSN since I was 15. We got many great concerts, but they eluded me. Then on 11 July 2012, they came to the Tuscaloosa Amphitheatre in Tuscaloosa. I had just got a job after being out of work for months and frankly wasn't sure I could afford a ticket. I thought about it all day and finally decided I would go and buy the cheapest ticket I could get. At least I'd see them.

By the time I got there, it was raining, and they were already on to their first song. There were about 100 people milling around outside. I got in line to buy a ticket. While waiting, there was a tap on my shoulder. I turned around to find a total stranger. He asked if I was buying a ticket. I said yes. He replied, 'Not tonight. I have an extra ticket and a voice said to give it to you.' There were a hundred people out there, and he picked me! He told me to enjoy, then walked off.

I never saw him again. I am pretty sure he was just an angel, for I *truly* believe God cares for the desires of our heart and He knew how much this meant to me. God has done many things like this for me, things I would not have thought possible. When I entered, I found out it was a $100 ticket, so close to the stage. I sat in the rain right by myself, sang, and cried.

July 19, 2013: Stills on stage at "Luglio Suona Bene", Auditorium Parco della Musica, Rome, Italy (CSN show). Photo by Filippo de Orchi

255

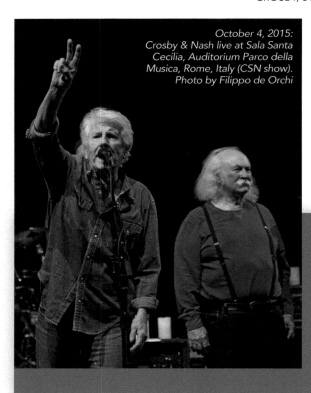

October 4, 2015:
Crosby & Nash live at Sala Santa Cecilia, Auditorium Parco della Musica, Rome, Italy (CSN show). Photo by Filippo de Orchi

Exactly one week later I was sat on my couch, about to go to bed. I was on Facebook, and something popped up on a fan page. It said they were about to be on a national radio talk show, and they gave an 800 number to call and interact with them live. I took a chance and called.

I was the first caller. I got to talk to David and Graham and tell them my story from a week before. They were so sweet and friendly, and loved my story. I could have died happy that night.

Bio: *Nancy Moore, from Tuscaloosa, Alabama, fell in love with Crosby, Stills & Nash when she was 15, listening to them for hours with her high school sweetheart. They remain her favorite group.*

Songs: *'Guinnevere' (C); 'Carry On' (S); 'Lady of the Island' (N).*

WHEN CSN WENT JAZZ

by Jody Goldman Daddio

The year was 2013. The dates were 1 and 3 May. CSN performed two very special concerts with Wynton Marsalis' Jazz at Lincoln Center Orchestra, called *The Crosby, Stills & Nash Songbook*. The venue was the Rose Theatre, a specially designed theatre built to provide the very best acoustics available.

The first show was a gala concert, completely out of my price range, but 3 May was more affordable. I grabbed a ticket at the last minute, it was a very good seat, and I was excited! The show would be a jazz format, completely different for CSN. Their music was being rearranged with the help of James Raymond and Wynton Marsalis and would be performed with an orchestra backing their vocals. David Crosby was quoted on *jazz.org* regarding performing with the orchestra, saying, 'These are musicians who have spent their whole lives becoming the very best in the world at what they do. We are excited and fascinated with this merging of musical streams and looking forward to a night to remember.'

On Friday 3 May I arrived in NYC early, bringing my camera in the hopes of taking photos in Central Park before heading over for the show. I never did get around to that, as I was invited by a friend who works for CSN to join him for dinner, an offer I could not refuse.

I found myself backstage, in the dining area where David Crosby was talking with Mark Quinones, a percussionist for The Allman Brothers Band. After a quick bite to eat and some catching up, we went to the stage area. Stephen Stills, Wynton Marsalis, David Crosby and Graham Nash were trying to look casual for a photo shoot happening on the stage before the audience came in. After a stretch of time, some people started taking photos of this historic moment in time. I asked if I could take a few and got the thumbs up. I was so glad I had my camera!

There was a mutual admiration and respect between CSN and the musicians in the orchestra. It was actually tangible; you could feel it in the air. CSN had such respect for these musicians that they wore suits, not the normal attire for these guys.

I thought I knew CSN's music, but it sounded quite different performed as jazz. It was difficult to figure out what the next song was when I could normally tell by the first few notes. The horn section was stunning. It replaced the harmonies on 'Critical Mass', the magnificent vocal intro to 'Wind on the Water', then reverberated sublimely the flow and breath of the vocals on 'Helplessly Hoping'. Some of the most successful moments happened when the signature of the songs moved to different areas, like with the jazzy writing of 'Déjà Vu', or Stills' Latin up-tempo numbers like 'Love the One You're With'.

May 3, 2013: Wynton Marsalis and CSN - preshow photoshoot at Lincoln Center's Frederick P. Rose Hall, New York City, New York, USA. Photo by Jody Goldman Daddio

I was fascinated, and the audience loved the show. When the concert was over and the house lights came on, the standing ovation did not end. It went on and on, no one leaving the theater. Finally, after ten minutes, Wynton Marsalis and CSN returned with members of the orchestra, and they launched into Nina Simone's 'Li'l Liza Jane', one of the standards of the New Orleans brass band tradition. Everybody was having a great time, on stage and in the audience. What an amazing night.

Bio: *Jody Goldman Daddio was born and remains in New Jersey, with husband Frank and often grandkids Angie and Anthony. For 18 years she's worked as a graphic designer, loving music, specifically CSN, adding, 'Their music makes my spirit soar, touching my soul to the core! I love the people I've met through music.'*

Songs: *'I love The Beatles' 'Blackbird' performed live by CSN. Their harmonies bring tears to my eyes, giving me goosebumps! Crosby's 'Carry Me' and 'Delta' have a similar effect. I love 'Déjà Vu,' 'Wooden Ships,' 'Woodstock' (live), 'Shadow Captain,' 'Carry On/Questions,' 'Long Time Gone,' 'Turn Your Back on Love,' 'As I Come oOf Age,' '4 + 20,' 'Pre-Road Downs,' 'Delta,' 'Marrakesh Express,' 'Cathedral,' 'Teach Your Children,' 'Our House' ... I'm going to pause here. I'll try to trim this list back one day.'*

THE CROSBY, STILLS & NASH OFFICIAL IPAD APP

by Terri Haram

In the Fall of 2012, CSN published their official CSN iPad app, a really great app regarding the history of the band. When I started using it, I had difficulties, so emailed tech support. The person responding was none other than James Raymond. I told him my issue, and he said he could either refund my money or send a signed Crosby picture.

I was extremely shocked, so said, 'Sure, I'd love a signed Croz print, but really I would like the issue fixed.' He replied that they would also take care of the issue. Time went by, the issue was semi-fixed, and no print showed up. So, one day I decided to send another email, letting him know the issue really wasn't fixed, and I never received the print. He apologized and invited me backstage to one of the shows, also offering a signed CSN poster. We ended up going to the Charlotte concert in North Carolina.

On 19 May 2013, we left our car in the parking lot of the Ovens Auditorium and began walking up to the arena. Suddenly, among the parked cars, we heard somebody playing a guitar. My sister and I walked up to see what was going on and who was in the back of a station wagon playing an acoustic guitar with a crowd of about ten or so people around him? Yep, none other than David Crosby!

There was a gentleman there who apparently makes guitars, and he was showing Croz one or two of his guitars. Croz fell in love with them and was just sat in this car playing free as a bird, happy as a clam! I pulled out my phone and videoed it. Unbelievable. After a while,

May 19, 2013: Crosby playing in the parking lot of the Ovens Auditorium, Charlotte, North Carolina, USA. Photo by Terri Haram

he started talking about dogs and their hearing. It was time to go to the ticket window and yep, James Raymond had left me two backstage passes to meet the band after the concert.

We enjoyed the concert as usual, singing every song, word for word. After the encores, we had no idea what to do but stayed in our seats. There were about 20 others doing the same. They had the same type of pass as us. An usher took us backstage to a room where there was a bunch of food, telling us we could have what we wanted. After some time, the band came in, James Raymond came over, and handed me this poster that the guys had signed, saying, 'You are Terri, right? Here's the poster, I hope you enjoyed the show.'

I was blown away. Why in the world would this guy do all this for me? How special was that. Unbelievable. I thanked him about a trillion times, we chatted for a while, then we met Croz and Graham and talked with them too. I thanked them as well and they were like, 'Oh, you're the one who got the poster.' They would sign this poster to make a fan happy. What a wonderful gesture. I was elated. What a night, what a memory!

Bio: *Terri Haram resides down on the Gulf of Mexico on Venice Island, Florida. She loves to garden, play guitar, birdwatch, travel, walk the beach, and still believes music can change the world. She adds, 'I was raised on CSN music from the age of five. It touched my heart so many years ago, and 50 years later continues to do so. Music is love!'*

Songs: *'To the Last Whale' (C) – 'a provoking tune that resonates even more today, still bringing a tear to my eye'; 'As I Come of Age' (S) - 'a beautiful song about reflecting on life; Stephen's voice just mellows my heart.'; 'Cathedral' (N) - 'spiritual yet confirms my disbelief in any organized religion.'*

A PORTRAIT OF GRAHAM NASH, OBE

by David, Ian and Tim Bingham

We are three artist brothers who have worked together since the early 1990s. Painting the human form has always been our preferred art form, particularly inspired to paint a series of portraits of some of the most interesting, creative people of our time.

We've admired and followed Graham Nash since the mid-1960s, so he was high on our list of people we would like to paint. We have also been inspired by Graham's work as a photographer and contacted him through Nash Editions. Crosby, Stills & Nash were touring Europe in the summer of 2013 and Graham kindly agreed to do a portrait sitting while CSN were in the UK.

We like our portraits to evolve spontaneously, so it was great that Graham was wearing a Crosby, Stills, Nash & Young t-shirt, as they appeared in *The Simpsons.* We're sure this was a conscious decision by Graham, giving the portrait an added dimension. Photographers and artists often use the juxtaposition of different forms of visual language to create a more interesting image. By contrasting a formal portrait with cartoon imagery created a strong visual tension. Our portrait of Graham is certainly one of the most popular in the series.

We spoke with Graham about painting and photography. He said he always visits galleries while in London. He's very knowledgeable and has a real passion for the visual arts.

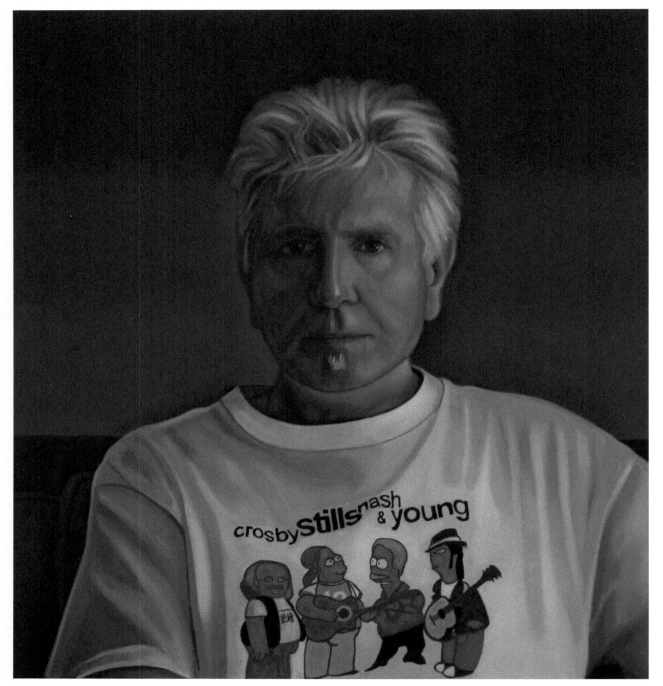

Oil on canvas by David, Ian and Tim Bingham

We had a wonderful time and particularly enjoyed walking with him through London, taking photographs. We were laughing about the class system in the UK but agreed that art transcends limitations of any such system. We were also laughing about the way time goes so quickly. He said, 'Life seems more like a virtual reality. When we're young, life seems like a long road ahead, but looking back it's more like looking into a little cul-de-sac!'

Summer 2013: Graham Nash in Hyde Park, London, England. Photo by David Bingham

Bio: *David, Ian and Tim Bingham were introduced to art at an early age. Their father, Bill Bingham was born in Belfast and posted to England while serving in the RAF. In the 1950s, their uncle Jimmy Bingham introduced Bill to painting. Jimmy was a close friend and shared a studio with prominent Irish painter, Daniel O'Neill (1920-74). Jimmy too became a recognised Irish painter. Developing their work independently, David, Ian and Tim then worked together from the early 1990s, in the mid-Nineties painting portraits of Hollywood actor Charlton Heston, singer/songwriter Paul Weller, and England cricketer Neal Radford.*

Songs: *'Long Time Gone' (C); 'Love the One You're With' (S); 'Marrakesh Express' (N).*

MEMORIES FROM THE ROAD

by Crook Stewart

The very first show I did with CSN was a private date for an insurance company located in Cincinnati, Ohio, 3 August 2007, and I flew out the day before. Told to keep the identity of the performers secret, as the insurance company liked to surprise their employees every year, we were under strict order not to tell anybody who we were there with.

The day before the show I decided to go across the street to a fast-food restaurant to get a little lunch. When I walked in the door the place was packed and one of the guys behind the counters looked up and said, 'Hey, look! It's David Crosby.' To which everybody in the restaurant turned around. I thought I was going to be fired before I even got to do my first show with them, because I had blown their cover. As a matter of fact, I bear a passing resemblance to David Crosby and these days Crosby loves it when I play body double for him. I regularly got mistaken for him, and sometimes it works to his advantage.

Luckily, I didn't get fired and I kept my job with CSN. In the summer of 2013, the boys were touring Europe and on 16 July they were supposed to play the Théâtre Antique de Fourvière, the oldest Roman-built theatre in France, situated on a hill above Lyon. The manager of the venue informed us that locals showed appreciation for good shows by throwing seat cushions at the stage on the last song of the regular set. So, in the afternoon when soundcheck was over, we had a meeting with the road managers and informed them about this particular habit.

July 16, 2013: CSN onstage at Festival Les Nuits de Fourvière, Théâtre Antique de Fourvière, Lyon, France. Photo by Giorgio Baratto

Stills' road manager neglected to pass the word along to Stephen. So, at the end of the show, a couple of thousand seat cushions came flying up to the stage and Stephen had no idea it was going to happen. He was pretty surprised, not knowing what to think at first. It was quite a funny situation. Later, when he came off and it was explained to him, he got a big kick out of it.

Working with CSN, I've learnt there's never two shows alike. On 15 May 2015 they were on the bill at Kings Theatre, an historical venue in Brooklyn, New York, newly restored after a 40-year closure. The place was stunning. Crosby, Stills & Nash knew some big guns of the Nederlander Organization would have been there, because they were considering the idea of producing a Broadway show based on the CSN story.

I've known David, Stephen and Graham for a bunch of years, working on hundreds and hundreds of their shows, and that night they put on the best show I have ever seen them do. Many people who were on tour with them that have been there much longer than I also thought it was one of their greatest ever shows. They were on fire. It was a great experience.

Bio: *Crook Stewart III was born in Panama City, Florida, and has tour managed legendary artists for almost 30 years, including CSN since 2007. Other artists he has worked include Joan Baez, Jackson Browne, Bonnie Raitt, Art Garfunkel, and the Rolling Stones. When not on the road, Crook and his wife Victoria host musical events at their home in Panama City, affectionately known as The Ghetto Palace. Crook and Victoria also founded Music Matters, in order to bring live music to their hometown.*

Songs: *'Long Time Gone' (C); 'Suite: Judy Blue Eyes' (S); 'Teach Your Children' (N).*

THE TRIPTYCH

by Luciano Viti

Many years ago, I think it was 1972, a girl I'd just met on vacation invited me to listen to some Californian music, of which I knew little or nothing. At the time, I was an avid Zeppelin fan. When we got home, she put an LP on the turntable and handed me the cover. Inside, opening its gatefold sleeve, there was a photo of Stephen Stills on top of a mountain at sunset, his arm outstretched and a finger pointing towards infinity.

Some 40 years later, on 19 July 2013, I was backstage at the Auditorium Parco della Musica in Rome for a daring photo session with Crosby, Stills & Nash. Actually, only two of them arrived for the appointment: David and Graham, who started leafing through the portfolio I brought for the occasion. Initially out of curiosity, then with growing interest.

Impressed by the portraits of Miles Davis, they took the opportunity to ask for a print.

While I finished setting up the set, Crosby smoothed his moustache and commented ironically, 'How come you photographers never have beautiful girls as your assistants?' After ten minutes taking portraits of David, Nash arrived, then stopped and looked with interest at my cameras. I was still using film. Graham is a great photographer and his compliments arrived as I started shooting.

At this point, only Stills was missing. Will Nash, tour manager and son of Graham, looked for him to remind him of the appointment but he was nowhere to be found. Unfortunately, time passed, and it was showtime. While my assistant disassembled the equipment, I walked towards the audience with the regret of not being able to complete the trio. The concert began, CSN putting on an excellent show. We were almost at the end of the first set when a technician came off the stage and walked towards me. 'Mr Viti! Mr Stills said he too would like to be photographed and wants to do it during intermission.'

July 19, 2013: Luciano Viti taking a portrait of David Crosby backstage at "Luglio Suona Bene", Auditorium Parco della Musica, Rome, Italy. Photo by Francesco Lucarelli

The deadline was tight, bringing on a cold sweat, looking for my assistant in the audience and quickly assembling the photo set again. I set up the cameras, loaded the films, and waited with anticipation.

Here they were. After a brief stop in the dressing room, Stills approached me: 'We have to do it quickly. We'll be back on stage soon.' I used a 35mm camera and started shooting, while Nash suggested the best poses to his friend. I didn't have time to finish the reel before a roadie arrived to take them back to the stage. I could finally relax, my goal achieved. The triptych was complete!

Tired, sweaty and with a lot of adrenaline still in my body, I don't know why that distant summer and that photo of Stills on the mountain suddenly came back to mind. With a melancholy smile, I thought of the girl who handed me that cover and without whom I probably wouldn't have been there that night. Unfortunately, we lost Rita many years ago, but I was pleased to dedicate that triptych of Crosby, Stills & Nash to her, with heartfelt affection.

Bio: *Born in Rome in 1955, Luciano Viti is a music photographer, one of the very few in the world to have portrayed both Miles Davis and Chet Baker. His photos have appeared on the covers of at least 100 albums of both Italian and international artists. Among a vast archive, a large section is dedicated to Pino Daniele, whom Luciano photographed from 1980 to 2014. He produces and sells limited-edition fine art prints, and has produced four photographic books, but adds, 'I was not born in London or in Los Angeles. If I had been, it probably would have been a whole other story!'*

Songs: *'I fully love CSN's first two albums, and CSNY's Déjà Vu.*

DOWN BENEATH MY FLOATING HOME

by Dena Mintz

Over the course of 25 years and thousands of dives, I've had a handful of diving experiences that really stand out. Being in Fiji with David, Jan and Django Crosby was one. Fun, funny at times, memorable, and - for me - momentous.

Here I was, getting to dive with a true rock legend, someone whose music had touched me deeply since I first heard *Déjà Vu* at the age of 14. Pretty amazing, and a perfect opportunity to photograph divers on the reef.

It was December 2013 in calm, clear water, with tons of colorful soft coral. I asked the family to feel free to get into my photos whenever they liked, giving them a 30-second primer on underwater modeling over lunch, our first day at the resort. The next morning, I just started doing my thing, taking pictures underwater.

Jan and Django - a real natural, underwater - were at first more hesitant to get in front of the camera. But David was not shy. He saw me set up a scene, adjusting my settings and lighting, and after a few test shots swam into the picture, making the scene happen.

People relate differently underwater. There's no talking, and hand signals are pretty basic. Sometimes, just a look or smile says it all. Swimming one more time in front of my camera, his face lit up, his eyes smiling behind the mask. David's love for the ocean and amazement at the beauty around him was *so* apparent. It was wonderful to see.

Bio: *Born in Los Angeles and currently living with husband Rick in Newport Beach, California, Dena Mintz retired from optometry after 30 years to become a full-time dive bum. Underwater photography has been her hobby and passion for 28 years.*

Songs: *'Long Time Gone' (C); 'Suite: Judy Blue Eyes' (S); 'Carry On' (S).*

December 2013: Fiji waters, Melanesia, Oceania. Photos by Dena Mintz

CSN AT THE PALEY MEDIA CENTER

by Leslie Brophy

I was 20 or so and when summer rolled around would get this feeling like I needed to see a show. I would call up Atlantic Records and get the tour dates over the phone. I remember the excitement building as summer approached, because I knew the boys would be back at Jones Beach and Pier 84.

July 19, 2013: CSN interviewed by Ron Simon; Paley Media Center, New York City, New York, US. Photo: Leslie Brophy

My first concert was The No Nukes Concert in Battery Park. I was there with my friend, Avra. We were in the third row or something, and also in the movie. It was the first of more than 300 CSN shows I have attended, in each and every combination.

One of the most amazing was Crosby & Nash at Westbury Music Fair, Long Island, 3 December 1986. It was David's first tour after he was let out of prison. The show opened with Graham alone on stage, then out of the darkness David Crosby walked into the spotlight, his hand up, waving slightly, like, 'Yes, I'm back.' It was amazing: the crowd stood up, cheering and filled with emotion. It was so cool to be a part of that and to have him back.

At Westbury Music Fair, the stage revolves very slowly and one night David Crosby said, 'Am I having flashbacks or is the stage moving?' I've seen a bunch of shows at Westbury, being a native New Yorker, mainly seeing shows nearby. One night the crowd was wishing David a happy birthday, and he was like, 'Thank you very much. When you get to be my age, you don't have birthdays anymore. Ask your parents!'

Then they proceeded to ask the audience what song they wanted to hear. The crowd was going wild, shouting out titles, and you couldn't hear any one particular song. David was like, 'Wait! You have to realize that when you all shout out songs like that at the same time, it arrives up here like ... Bablinababushkinf!' He started picking people, pointing to fans: 'You!' And one at a time people requested songs. Then someone shouted out 'Delta' and David quickly said, 'We haven't done 'Delta'. I wanna do 'Delta'.'

CROSBY, STILLS & NASH

David started with those sweet opening piano chords, and 'Delta' unfolded. It was amazing. Then Graham came into the spotlight with his harmony. It was probably the best night ever at Westbury. Everybody loved it. Then somebody shouted out, 'Southbound Train'!' and Graham said, 'Southbound Train'? David's 'Southbound Train'? Legit call. We gotta do it.' They found the right chords and Graham opened with country style harmonica and they harmonized into 'Southbound Train'. Amazing. They did all the best, obscure Crosby & Nash. I think they did 'Magical Child', 'Laughing', 'Carry Me'. It was a great night.

They played an amazing couple of sets. 'Laughing', 'Simple Man', Crosby's new song 'Compass', 'Wind on the Water', 'Teach Your Children', 'Long Time Gone'. Before 'Almost Cut My Hair', which he used to sing when he was making time in Texas because 'it pissed the guards off', David went into a rap about prison, said, 'If you're going to get busted, don't do it in Texas!' and everybody cheered. He added: 'When in prison, I worked in a mattress factory. If you're ever out there in America and come across the worst mattress you've ever been on, I'm probably the guilty party.'

I also remember going down to the Westchester County Center in late August 1989. At the last minute I realized I needed to be there, although I didn't have a ticket. I was listening to this tape of old Jug Band music from the Twenties that my boyfriend at the time gave me, and I thought Graham Nash might like to hear it. I hopped on an Amtrak train to Westchester from NYC and got down to the venue, scored the last seat in the venue and got to see the boys. Everybody was so well behaved at this concert, and nobody was really moving or standing or anything. It was cat quiet. Then I realized the last train back to NYC was leaving in 10 minutes, so I had to run, else I would be stranded in Westchester. I literally started running up toward the stage, took the tape I made out of my pocket and slid it across the stage to Graham while he was playing guitar. He stopped while the other guys were jamming, picked up the tape and put it in his shirt pocket, watching me run out of the venue like a bat out of hell. Everyone else was watching too, but I had to go ... I made the train and listened to whatever music I had recorded from the show when I got on the train back to New York.

Fast forward. The Paley Media Center in New York was great. On 7 July 2014, CSN were all there, being interviewed by Ron Simon. I was taking pictures and the boys were in great spirits, talking about everything, about their careers and how it truly had been a long, strange trip. A great trip. Four nights later, CSN played a stellar performance at the Beacon Theatre.

The great thing about Crosby, Stills & Nash is how they interact with fans. I think it keeps them coming back. I've been to about 300 shows, just for the music, art and stories they tell. They have very good interaction with their fans that makes them feel like they're important and there's not a glass bubble around them, separating them from the audience. There's a real sense of community and camaraderie, reflective of the peace movement from the Sixties and their true hippie ways.

I've brought my friends and family to many shows, but I prefer to go alone. I become at one with the music. I've seen a lot of bands, but none of them really speak to me and connect with me on a musical level the way Crosby, Stills & Nash do. As Graham once said, 'The music is just strong enough to pull out of us a better self.'

Bio: *Leslie Brophy is a New York City artist: painter, photographer and videographer. A Bachelor of Fine Arts from the School of Visual Arts in NYC, he currently studies under US-born painter Pat Lipsky at The Art Students' League and looks forward to having a gallery show of his work. He also worked for MTV Networks on VH1, Nickelodeon, Comedy Central, and MTV Studios.*

Songs: *'Déjà Vu' (C); 'Everybody I Love You' (S); 'Pre-Road Downs' (N).*

EDIBLE ART

by Heather Sherman

Having made a cake for Blues Traveler in July 2012, I was invited to make one for CSN when they came to Red Rocks Amphitheater the following month. It was requested I use low-glycemic (30) coconut sugar, both the cake and buttercream icing made without any refined sugar at all. It was unbelievably tasty - like dark brown sugar. I would recommend it heartily. The decorations were made from marshmallow fondant and sugar gumpaste. No internal supports were used, only cardboard under the cake itself - even in guitar necks - solid sugar.

I chose the iconic image of the beat-up couch from the cover of the first album, plus sugarpaste portraits in guitars, along with

Heather Sherman, the cake, and CSN. Photos: Heather Sherman

2012 and 2014: CSN and Heather Sherman backstage at Red Rocks Amphitheatre, Morrison, Colorado. Photos courtesy of Heather Sherman - Art2Eat Cakes (www.art2eatcakes.com)

their logo (also unsupported solid sugarpaste), Wooden Ships, the Alien Ships over the Citadel ('Daylight Again'), and a nod to their good work with the Bowl of Guacamole (Guacamole Fund).

The gents seemed to truly enjoy the piece, which was music to me after all the art they have given. Graham Nash shook my hand and told me I was amazing. I told him I was so glad the feeling was mutual! Stephen Stills played with the whammy bar on the sugar miniature replica of his guitar and said he could hardly believe all the accurate detail. He insisted on taking a picture with his own camera. After an amazing show, we served it to fans, crew and staff, and everyone loved it.

Two years later, in 2014 I was lucky enough to bring the band another cake when they returned to Red Rocks Amphitheater. This time I wanted to go gravity defying and chose 'The eagle flies with the dove', as 'Love the One You're With' is a song which means so much to so many, and indeed they loved it. David Crosby smiled broadly when he saw this art of mine, and it was an amazing moment to provide a small bit happiness in his.

Graham Nash was very interested in the edible art, and I broke off a piece later to show him the sugarpaste and plastic-wrapped structure beneath. He spoke to me for several minutes and asked several thoughtful process questions I might have expected from a cake student. Incredibly thrilling! This cake was made with an internal inedible food-safed structure covered with sugarpaste, like a cake topper. Vanilla pound cake and buttercream fill the clouds below the birds, covered with more marshmallow fondant and cotton candy. Once again, we served it out to fans, crew, and staff, and it was enjoyed by all.

It was incredibly sweet for me to be able to bring joy to those who have brought joy to so many. Their art brings wonder, amazement, thrill, and meaning to so many. It was a defining moment as an artist to be able to bring that Sweetness to them. I have listened to them for years, pored over those album covers, pondered lyrics, and was inspired endlessly in ways I cannot count. To this day they continue to re-invent themselves, and continue to amaze me with their independent, individual pursuits.

Bio: *Art is Heather Sherman's thrill, and cakes are her medium. A Colorado near-native, she's been creating cake art since 2008, living where she was raised in the Rocky Mountains of Colorado, experiencing many media - paint, graphics, photography, illustration, kids, and more. She adds, 'Naturally, my first cakes were for my children. One of my most famous, the Rainbow Pegacorn Mama and Baby cake, went viral in 2009 with over a million shares, and continues to be circulated. I have since made cakes for some very wonderful folks, also including Cirque du Soleil, Jackson Browne, and Icing Smiles. My work has been published in Cake Masters magazine more than once and I have won multiple awards at Cake Shows in Austin and Denver. The original thrill that still fuels my fire are the oohs and aahs that continue into yummms and smiles whenever people see and eat my cakes. Sculpted cake is truly performance art.'*

Songs: *'Wooden Ships' (C); 'Love the One You're With' (S); 'Our House' (N).*

ABALONE AND MOTHER OF PEARL

by Paolo Sussone

In December 2014, one Monday afternoon, I received an unexpected phone call from a voice with an American accent, and the next day, armed with guitars, I was in Lucca, a meeting with David Crosby waiting for me. The reason: he wanted to try out my latest Concerto acoustic guitar.

It was a very strong, electrifying, somewhat surreal experience: being in front of such a musician, seeing him hold my guitar, hearing him sing one of his most famous tunes, and has more to do with the dream world than the real one. However, it was all true. It's hard not to get excited. Impossible even. A musician of his talent, with his history, who at 73 still has the grit and power of an inspired 20-year-old.

I waited for him inside the theater, where he was due to perform an acoustic show that evening. I met Crook Stewart, his tour manager. We chatted. I showed him some tools. Then I relaxed in a dressing room, waiting for Croz. His voice came first, powerful vocalization from the corridor, unmistakable and very clear. Then he appeared, flesh, bone and moustache. A short introduction, a handshake, and his abrupt, 'I want to try your guitar. A friend told me it sounds nice.' Then he went away.

Still stunned, I just had time to recover, understand where I was, and after a few minutes he came back. A stern and determined look, then: 'Let me try it.' I opened the case and handed him the instrument. He looked at it, weighed it, and said, 'Nice wood, I like it.' He also looked at the abalone and mother of pearl rosette. Then immediately he played the first notes, which are irregular, and searched for the first chair within arm's reach, to really start playing.

A change of tuning, and off he went. The fingers slid on the keyboard. Precise, safe, the sound that came out unmistakable. The right hand marked the pace and the voice harmonized with the guitar. Then a change of pace, and off with another riff. And another. And yet another.

The voice followed the notes and created atmospheres I know well which took me back to glorious vinyl LPs. I was in front of him and listened carefully, with open eyes and ears, determined not to waste a single moment of that time.

Then the sentence was passed: 'Excellent. Nice harmonics. I really like this wood; I also like its color. Where did you get that? A really nice guitar. What kind of spruce did you use?' We began to talk about wood, research, the passion guiding me in the construction of instruments. Then, suddenly, a gift: 'Tonight I'll start the concert with this song.' And the notes of the beautiful 'Everybody's Been Burned' filled the air, with its irregular gait, embroidered by his voice, warm and powerful, which had not lost its enamel, despite the sore throat of the last few days. The last harmonics vanished, and as from a dream, the awakening. 'Good. Now I have to go to work. Can we see you later? I want to play it again after the show.'

Bio: *Born in Genoa in 1979, raised between the docks and the worst inns in the historic centre of the city, Paolo Sussone has always loved the guitar and singer-songwriters' music. He also loves being with friends and good wine. He considers himself a low-grade guitarist, but at almost 30 he approached lutherie and discovered his true passion, which led to him opening a shop in 2013, building instruments for some of his favorite musicians, without understanding why.*

Songs: *'Everybody's Been Burned' (C), 'Southern Cross' (S).*

March 29, 2017: Stephen Stills and Kenny Waybe Sheperd - The Rides live at Ryman Auditorium, Nashville, Tennessee, USA. Photo by Tom Davis

December 9, 2014: David Crosby's soundcheck at Teatro del Giglio, Lucca, Italy. Photo by Francesco Lucarelli

February 9, 2015:
Graham Nash live
at San Francisco Art
Exchange, California,
USA. Photo by Tom
Davis

April 21, 2018:
Stephen Stills and
Neil Young live at
Light Up The Blues
Autism Speaks
Benefit - Dolby
Theatre, Los Angeles,
California, USA.
Photo by Tom Davis

TRUTH, EQUALITY, JUSTICE

by Mike Finnigan

It's nearly impossible to share any specific story including all three guys which is also dear to my heart. But I can talk in general about what I admire about the guys: their political activism and their music, ground-breaking contributions in sound, recording techniques, three excellent writers, three excellent singers. I think that's important.

The thing that impressed me most was how their dedication to the music always managed to override their worst instincts. By that, I mean some of the quarrels, personality clashes, and resentments - big and small. At their best they made great music together. They had a sound that was unique to them.

They are all excellent singers and together they were fantastic. They are all songwriters, and all wrote unforgettable songs. Stephen, in his prime, produced a stunning explosion of compositional genius in the Sixties

December 9, 2014: David Crosby live at Teatro del Giglio, Lucca, Italy. Photo by Francesco Lucarelli

and Seventies. He wrote some very good songs after that period, but (in my humble opinion) nothing as fine as his output in the early years. Stephen was the most accomplished musician and perhaps the most talented of the three, but also the most personally and professionally erratic. The exception was, of course, Crosby's period of near-fatal drug addiction, subsequent criminal conviction, and incarceration. Of course, both David and Graham also wrote songs that were part of the American soundtrack of the late 20th century. The common thread was that most of the great songs had the benefit of being performed by CSN.

As for any moment that stands out in terms of the creation of the music, there were far too many to select one. As with other musicians, the moments when all is right, when the result exceeds the abilities of the individuals and the sum of the parts, when magic happens, these are the moments an artist lives for. The moments that are close - or even do not come remotely close - aren't too bad, either. I was in the room or onstage with CSN for many such moments. I played with them for 28 years, so you can see the difficulty in picking one moment!

In Spring 2017, *Variety* published a story headlined 'Crosby, Stills, Nash & Young could reunite - because they hate Trump more than each other.' This was amusing, and likely true. CSN (and CSNY) were a big part of the cultural and political revolution of the Sixties and Seventies. The political rightward drift really picked up steam with the ascension of Reagan and was a reactionary convulsion to the cultural and political revolution that scared middle America and the power brokers. The interesting thing is that CSN and other artists of the period (Dylan, Beatles, Hendrix, et al) were only giving voice to the values and social principles that our elders had taught us were the things that mattered.

Autumn, 2014: CSN supporting HeadCount.org. Photo courtesy of Mollie Farrell at HeadCount.org

Truth, equality, justice, and most important, love - manifested through respect for one another, for the earth, and all living things.

It would be difficult to overestimate the influence and impact of CSN in carrying this message. Interestingly, not all the guys who worked with them during my tenure were on board with their politics, but I sure as hell was. It felt good to play music that often contained what I believed to be important social commentary.

Finally, I must say that playing with those guys, and counting them as friends, has been a privilege. They always treated me fairly and each of them has been extremely helpful and supportive to me and my family.

Bio: *Born in Cleveland, Ohio, Mike Finnigan grew up in a musical family, in a home where all kinds of popular American music was heard constantly. His Hammond organ featured on Jimi Hendrix's Electric Ladyland, after which he was high in demand, contributing to dozens of recordings and tours by a wide variety of artists: CSN, The Manhattan Transfer, Etta James, Dave Mason, Joe Cocker, Dan Fogelberg, Ringo Starr, Tracy Chapman, Rod Stewart, John Hiatt, Leonard Cohen, Buddy Guy, Sam Moore, Curtis Salgado, Keb Mo, Taj Mahal, Bonnie Raitt, and many others.*

SOUL LEGACY

by Sara Sugioka

The first time I heard their music was in a house located in a deep valley in Canada. It was during my long solo trip. I wanted to set my soul free. I wanted to get back to nature. I was drifting some places while working on a farm.

I left Japan for Canada because I had been wanting to live in a new country since I was a teenager. I lived in Vancouver for a year with a working holiday visa and went to school to learn English, working at a restaurant and design studio. After that, I switched to a visitor visa to extend my stay and begin my trip to discover that country.

My amazing hosts, a couple who moved there in the Sixties following the 'Back to Land' philosophy of the time, had a copy of the first Crosby, Stills & Nash album on a shelf. It was music I had never heard before. The more I listened, the more I loved and appreciated it. Nothing has changed since. Their music truly keeps giving me different emotions every time I listen to them.

My most significant connected event happened later, back in Japan, at a concert in Tokyo, March 2015, an encounter with Graham Nash changing my life. I wore a vintage skirt from the Sixties. Before the show, I tried to see them, waiting in front of the exit they would use at the venue. Surprisingly, Graham came out. I approached him and spoke to him for a little while. I was extremely happy and nervous, almost speechless. Nash, always the gentleman, reacted so kindly. I don't remember much more than telling him, 'I love you so much' but clearly remember his gentle eyes.

When CSN showed up on stage and started playing, I got the feeling that I was witnessing a moment of legacy. I got shaken by their voices and their sound. I will never ever be able to forget that experience forever in my life.

We all stood and sang 'Teach Your Children' together, the last song of the show. During that moment, I thought of my dad, who passed away exactly one year before. 'Teach your parents well, their children's hell will slowly go by.'

It's like their music has helped my soul to grow up, and I'm going to live with their music for the rest of my life.

Bio: *Born in Japan and in love with music, travel, the Sixties and Seventies, Sara Sugioka works in IT. Her respect for indigenous people in North America led her to being a writer, occasionally dedicating herself to writing to make the world a better place. Since listening to CSN&Y for the first time, her life has never been the same.*

Songs: *'I'd Swear There Was Somebody Here' (C); 'Helplessly Hoping' (S); 'I Used to be a King'(N).*

TRAVELLING TWICE THE SPEED OF SOUND

by Ravi Srinivasan

In 2010, a friend who worked for Absolute FM radio in the UK invited me to visit him, trying to piss me off with a list of concerts scheduled for London that summer. To his surprise, I refused the invitation, prompting him to ask if

March 19, 2015: Ravi Srinivasan with Graham Nash, backstage at The Star Theatre, Singapore, Singapore. Photos by Aloysius Lim / Alvin Ho for LAMC Productions

there was any artist for whom I would make the trip. I answered without hesitation, 'Crosby, Stills & Nash, of course!' I was blown away by his reply, 'CSN will play at the Royal Albert Hall on 4 July.'

Unfortunately, the concert quickly sold out, but by then our four tickets to London – with my wife and two children - were booked. Help came in the form of a few people who had extra tickets, so we set off, travelling at twice the speed of sound.

Getting to London was very easy. British Airways operates a direct flight from Chennai, India. We booked a hotel near Hyde Park and took a walk in the park to overcome jetlag, unaware of what to expect. Without knowing it, we arrived close to the area where the Hard Rock Calling festival was being held, and I thought I could hear the music of Crosby Stills & Nash in the air. It was them! They were on the bill that day, 27 June. We didn't have tickets but sat outside to listen, a sort of aperitif ahead of the Royal Albert Hall show.

That week, we visited Stonehenge and Winchester Cathedral. Then, finally, the big day came. We were thrilled and when we entered the Royal Albert Hall it felt like we were in a dream. I had been waiting for that moment ever since I saw them in the *Woodstock* movie. My brother-in-law, another CSN fan and avid concert-goer, was there with us to share my enthusiasm. I cannot describe in words what my feelings were when the 'Gods of my Parthenon' arrived on the stage, greeted by warm applause. It was a magical moment.

Nash seemed not to have changed, Crosby took some time to warm up, and Stills had some difficulty with his vocals but made up for it by playing the guitar in an extraordinary way. I was happy to attend one of those concerts in which they also offered some covers. I liked the stories between songs, the dialogue with the audience, and Crosby's voice joining Nash's on 'Cathedral'. Magnificent!

Their version of 'Behind Blue Eyes', one of our favourite songs of all time, was an unexpected bonus. The only minor disappointment was not hearing 'Suite: Judy Blue Eyes', perhaps the No.1 song of the ten I would take to a desert island, and one of my wife and children's favourites too.

March 19, 2015: Graham Nash live at The Star Theatre, Singapore.
Photos by Aloysius Lim / Alvin Ho for LAMC Productions

As that beautiful evening drew to a close and we were taking the edge off, it still did not seem true to me that I had listened to the songs of these artists live. Musicians who have had such an extraordinary influence on me and on my vision of life. It had been a long time coming.

There is a small tail to this story. In 2015, just turned 60, with the belief that it should have been the year of my life, I landed in Singapore with a copy of *Wild Tales* in hand. I had recently read that book and was struck by the words of Nash, who spoke of the importance that fans have for him and how much he always tries to find time for them. I was firmly determined to meet him, and wherever I went, the book was with me.

Come 19 March, the day of the concert, I still hadn't been able to meet him. But at 11 am, my daughter - who lives in Singapore - sent me a message, telling me there would be a small event before the show and some fans would get to meet CSN. After an afternoon spent in spasmodic anticipation, it was finally time to head to the Star Performing Arts Centre. I left my name for the lottery and went to the bar for a drink, trying to take it easy. After the first sip, the phone rang. I was among the lucky ones! As they say, the rest is history, my photo telling a lot more than my words.

> **Bio:** *Born and raised in what was Madras, now Chennai, in the southern part of India, Ravi Srinivasan studied in a premier engineering school, the Indian Institute of Technology, and has been involved in running a company with interests in water-saving products for bathrooms and in waste-water recycling, pioneers in that field in India.*
>
> **Songs:** *'Guinnevere' (C); 'Love the One You're With' (S); 'Cathedral' (N).*

A MAN'S A MAN WHO LOOKS A MAN RIGHT BETWEEN THE EYES

by Lorenzo Conci

I've always had a soft spot for Crosby and Nash. I remember when, in my teens, people enthralled by *4 Way Street* would enquire about their favorite members of CSN&Y. Young and Stills were the most popular, with Crosby coming third. I mostly loved the camaraderie of the group and the living room atmosphere of their acoustic sets and, of course, the harmonies that were Crosby and Nash's signature. 'The Lee Shore', 'Chicago', 'Right Between the Eyes' ... What a sequence! And I fell head over heels with the first Crosby Nash album, still one of my favourites.

I was waiting for their second effort, even though in the early Seventies everybody was longing for another CSNY masterpiece.

Wind on the Water came out in October 1975, and I listened to it several times a day. I was an exchange student in High School in Chico, California and was to graduate in '76. I remember everything: from buying it at the small record shop downtown, to the billboards advertising it and the reviews in *Rolling Stone*. From the cover to the sound, everything was so California, and I was there, albeit not in LA or Frisco, but still ...

The hills of the Central Valley were so yellow and dry, and I loved everything about being there. More importantly, I could finally appreciate the words, if not their meanings, the phrasing. When I grew up and could travel, I started following them, like a pilgrim. And having had the chance to know them personally added all kind of nuances and flavour to my trips.

So, it's with a hint of melancholy that I remember their last show, 11 April 2015, San Francisco, Nourse Theater, a benefit for SEVA, the foundation started and promoted by Wavy Gravy, a comedian well remembered for his MC-ing at the Woodstock festival.

I got there early and noticed something strange. It seemed that David and Graham were ignoring each other. I couldn't really tell, because Graham pretty much kept himself to himself, so I'd spent more and more time with David. Somehow this time it was even more awkward. Croz and Wavy Gravy had a press interview and David brought me along. It was in the foyer, and I found it strange that Graham was not there with them. I'd seen them at benefit concerts many times before and it was always a very relaxed and casual affair.

After the interview was over and the pictures taken, Croz called me over and asked if I minded taking a walk. 'Let 's go,' he said. Well, of course. It was springtime, a nice Saturday evening in San Francisco, the Nourse near the City Hall. Families with kids were strolling or about to go to restaurants. I tried to read his mind, but I couldn't tell if there was anything bothering him. We stopped for a coffee at a stand. People recognised him and came close, asking for pictures or autographs. He kindly obliged and I stepped aside. Along came Django, looking for him, seemingly upset, David having forgotten another engagement with press, and late.

Croz turned to me with his famous grin and said, 'Don't know why ... sons become such a pain in the ...' Afterwards, we had dinner with Jan and Django. It felt strange we were not with Graham and the crew. Maybe the Nourse was not providing a catered meal. Anyway, I was elated to be part of such restricted family and stopped worrying about my ramblings.

Back at the Nourse, David retreated to his dressing room for some rest before the show and I casually ran into Nash. We talked briefly and he asked me my plans. When I told him that the next day I was driving down to Santa Barbara, where David was playing a solo acoustic gig, he coldly turned his face. He did not know and didn't really want to know about

November 2, 2011: Crosby & Nash live at Teatro Sistina, Rome, Italy. Photo by Francesco Lucarelli

David's plans. It sounded so weird to me. In the past he would have been the first to tell me about such an event, emphasising that it had been a long time since Crosby's last solo show.

I got a bad feeling and it only got worse when Rance Caldwell, CSN's monitor tech, came looking for Nash to ask for help to complete the setlist. He wanted to know what number they would play solo. It was going to be 'Myself at Last'. As for Croz, Graham shrugged and

November 2, 2011: Crosby & Nash live at Teatro Sistina, Rome, Italy. Photo by Francesco Lucarelli

dismissed him saying, 'Probably 'What Makes It So', and I detected a touch of disrespect to mean he surely hadn't written anything newer. Croz would actually play 'Somebody Home'.

The show itself lacked any camaraderie. They hardly looked at each other, there was no comedy, no jokes. It made me wonder how they could stand singing *'Guinnevere'*. I don't think the crowd realised any of this. They were very professional and wouldn't let anybody down. They have always been generous, and this was the tenth time they'd played for SEVA. Probably their last commitment. Loud cheers called them back. It was 'Teach Your Children', one more time.

As the crowd left the venue, I overheard happy and satisfied comments, but personally I felt deep sadness and was melancholy inside.

THE YEAR OF CSN

by Monika Falkenberg

The year 2015 was officially declared my CSN year, trying to catch up with all the times I had missed them live before. I flew to the US to see them together and to see Stephen Stills solo, as well as David Crosby and also Judy Collins, the woman who inspired my favorite CSN song, if not my favourite song ever.

When I decided to celebrate the music of CSN that year, I commented about it on the Stephen Stills Facebook group. I was surprised to receive a private message from a man I hadn't even interacted with before, offering a spare ticket for the King's Theatre, Brooklyn concert. Second row! I had only been able to get 11th row. 'How much?' I asked. 'Is free a good price?' was the reply. It seemed so strange, but I have that same spirit: I like to share my joy. I thought, 'why not?' In addition to this extremely kind and generous offer, it turned out we would also have backstage passes, provided via Graham Nash, which seemed just too good to be true. It turned out to be nothing but the wonderful gesture of a man who thought 'shared joy doubles it up'. Thank you, Dave!

The night I arrived in NYC to see CSN's two concerts at Brooklyn's beautifully restored King's Theatre, Judy Collins was performing the last show of her residency at the famous Carlyle Café on the Upper East Side. I thought, 'Stephen Stills will be in NYC already, and I'm pretty sure he's going to be at the Carlyle to see 'Sweet' Judy and her incredibly blue eyes.' 'Nonsense,' I was told. 'That's just your wishful thinking.'

Our flight was delayed, my cab having to get through rush-hour traffic. We checked in at the hotel at 30th/6th about an hour and a half before our reservation time at the Carlyle. Shower, quick make-up, dressing up: all done in less than an hour. Tickets grabbed, 23 floors down, standing traffic on 6th Avenue, no cab and a door man, shaking his head 'from here to 76th in half an hour? Forget it!' A rickshaw taxi stopped and offered a flat rate: 'I'll get you there at 7 pm. It's gonna be tough, but I promise.' It was a hell of a bumpy ride.

I guess we were the first ever formally dressed guests arriving at the Carlyle in a rickshaw. What a start! We could even choose a table with a nice view to the stage. The house was almost full. I was studying the menu when I caught a glimpse of a man entering the intimate 60-seat venue, going straight to the back door: Captain Manyhands! I was right. Seconds later he came out and sat three tables away from where I was.

I took my phone and all my courage in my hands, went to his table and decided to sit in the chair next to Stephen Stills. I knew he would have to be able to hear what I was saying. 'Excuse me, Sir. Stephen, this is my dream come true. Please, send me away if I am bothering you. I'm Monika from Germany. Would you mind if I take a photo of the two of us as a memory?' He was smiling like he thought it was funny that a 'girl' my age was blushing and so excited. He was very warm, like he was enjoying this heartfelt devotion. He said, 'No, I don't even mind that we're sitting here. Let's take a pic!'

A kind gentleman, who turned out to be Judy's friend, offered to take a few pics. I thanked Stephen and told him I came from Germany to see CSN over the next two nights in Brooklyn. He seemed honestly pleased, and when he took my hand I said, 'Would there be a chance to make me incredibly happy and play 'Suite: Judy Blue Eyes' at one of the shows?' He was grinning, that charming, impeccable smile I knew from photos. 'I cannot promise. We decide the setlist together, always on the day.' They hadn't played that song a lot during recent shows, but at least I had asked. And Judy Collins was brilliant: entertaining, storytelling, emphatic. Just her crystal-clear voice and the piano. What a prelude that was!

The first night at the King's Theatre was amazing: 11th row, centre, perfect view, perfect sound, just sublime. I rushed to the stage for the last songs and the encore. I was right in front of Stephen, who came forward for his solo on 'Almost Cut My Hair'. He surely recalled me from the night before. After 'Teach Your Children' they were about to leave. Stephen talked to Graham and gave a sign to his guitar technician. He was handed a Martin and was grinning at me. I stood, paralysed, and when the first chords resonated in the hall, I jumped and screamed and teared up ... there it was, that beauty of a song - the song I had listened to in all its different versions together with my music soulmate. I was in heaven!

Bio: *Monika Falkenberg was born in a small town near Düsseldorf, Germany, where she lives again now. Her main interest is music, especially live music, preferably singer-songwriters, rock, blues and any combination of that. She adds, 'I love all kinds of contemporary art, visual art, performance, land art. Yves Klein is my favourite artist of all time, looking at his genius paintings is like swimming in a deep blue ocean a meditative, sensual experience to me. Listening to live music is not just listening to music to me: it's being in a state of deep inner peace and happiness. I love good food and wine, as well as traveling and historic cars, especially racing cars. And most of all I like people.' And a special achievement in her life? Her pumpkin soup with black truffles, 'the best soup on this planet!'*

Songs: *'Wooden Ships' (C), 'Spanish Suite' (S), 'Cathedral' (N).*

THE MASKS

by Sergio Boldrin

About 20 years ago, during the Venice Carnival, I was in my small Mascareri (a mask-making workshop) at the foot of the Rialto Bridge, busy working, and had put on a Joni Mitchell record. It was cold and there was torrential rain. Suddenly, the door opened, and a person peeped in, and - with a very nice smile printed on his face - asked if he could come in to shelter from the rain and dry the bags with his photographic equipment.

Hearing the music, he asked if I liked Joni. 'It's one of my favourites,' I replied. His face lit up. He entered and introduced himself, telling me he was one of the photographers of the artists of that time. I was surprised. He knew Joni, Crosby, Stills & Nash, Neil Young, Jackson Browne, Jim Morrison, and many others. It was Tom O'Neal, the author of the photograph that CSN&Y used on the cover of *Déjà Vu*.

Tom is a very open guy, innately likeable. It was natural to start talking about music, records, and art, and we quickly became friends. A friendship that did not stop at that meeting, since - having to go to Los Angeles from time to time for work - we also met in California and over time, through him, I got to know some of his friends, including Cree Miller, of CSN and Jackson Browne's management.

It was also thanks to her that, when Crosby, Stills & Nash played in Piazzola del Brenta in July 2013, the opportunity arose to go backstage and meet them in person. For that occasion, my brother Massimo and I prepared masks to pay homage to them. We reproduced the symbol of peace, painted with stars and stripes and the colours of the American flag, a mask with a somewhat tragic face coming out of the centre. We gave one to each of them, individually named.

In June 2016 I had the pleasure of seeing Nash again in Trento when he came to Italy for a solo tour. We started talking about the possibility of organising an exhibition together, since he is also a photographer, and we were fascinated by the idea of combining my masks with his photographs. Graham loves to take portraits, as evidenced by many of his photos with faces of his friends and artists, and – as a matter of fact – even the mask is essentially a face. With his shots, Nash captures the soul of whoever is photographed, while I try to give a soul to papier-mâché. It would be nice to combine these two disciplines, and I'm working on trying to make this exhibition at a Venice gallery.

Knowing I was meeting Graham, I was pleased to be able to give him a mask. I wanted to create something personal, and I was looking for inspiration, thinking about what or who his face could represent, as a character, to bring him into the world of masks.

Knowing his history, his battles against nuclear power, his environmentalist spirit always ready to fight for ideals, I created a mask with a slightly elongated face, a little beard, and a helmet to protect the face.

I liked the idea of imagining him as a modern Don Quixote.

Bio: *Sergio Boldrin was born in Venice, where he lives and works. For about 40 years he has created and decorated papier-mâché masks, sharing this activity as a mask-maker with his passion for painting. One of the highlights of his career was creating masks with his brother for Stanley Kubrick's film, Eyes Wide Shut, and the brothers' participation as artists at the 55th Venice Biennale.*

July 20, 2013: Sergio and Massimo Boldrin backstage with CSN at Hydrogen Festival, Piazzola sul Brenta, Italy. Photos by Alberto Sarria

Songs: *'Guinnevere' (C), 'Helplessly Hoping' (S), 'Southbound Train' (N).*

October 4, 2015: Graham Nash live with CSN at Auditorium Parco della Musica, Rome, Italy.
Photo by Francesco Lucarelli

October 3, 2015: Stephen Stills live with CSN at Gran Teatro Geox, Padua, Italy. Photo by Francesco Lucarelli

MAN IN THE MIRROR

by Dallyn Pavey

I grew up with Crosby, Stills & Nash. In 1969 my mother was young and beautiful and on the fringe of being a hippie. She turned me on to some of the best music ever created, Crosby, Stills & Nash never leaving the turntable.

Fast-forward 15 years, I was working at radio station WMMR in Philadelphia. Afternoon personality, Pierre Robert and I had bonded over the music of CSN. So, when Nash was scheduled to visit the station, we were excited with anticipation. That visit was the beginning of a long friendship between Pierre and Graham, and I have happily been along for the ride over the last 30-plus years.

One of my funniest memories of Graham was from the mid-Nineties. I wanted to do something special for Pierre's birthday. I knew Graham was creating pieces of art with his handwritten lyrics. I sent an email to his publicist, asking if Graham would write a song out for Pierre. I left my mother's phone number, because I was going to visit her for a weekend at the beach, and no one really used cell phones for anything but emergencies back then.

The anticipation of waiting for a phone call from a music legend was pretty exciting. He could call at any time. But, wouldn't you know it, soon as I got into the shower the phone rang. My mother knocked on the

August 9, 2015: Graham Nash and Dallyn Pavey backstage at the Grand Opera House, Wilmington, Delaware, USA. Photo by Graham Nash

bathroom door and said, 'Graham Nash is on the phone! Do you want to talk with him?' 'Yes, of course,' I said. 'Give me the phone!'

'Hi Graham, you caught me naked in the shower!' We both laughed and I think he said, 'How nice!' He asked what Pierre's favorite song was. I told him, 'Cathedral'. A week later, Graham FedEx'd the handwritten lyrics to me. I had it framed and presented it to Pierre for his birthday. It hangs proudly on his wall to this day.

Another great memory I have was at his concert on 9 August 2015 at the Grand Opera House in Wilmington, Delaware. I had become very interested in photography over the last few years. I knew

Graham was a prolific photographer. In fact, I have a copy of *Eye to Eye* on my coffee table and refer to it often. I asked Graham if it would be possible to photograph him at his show that night. He said yes and allowed me to photograph his entire show, instead of the usual first three songs. The photos from that show are some of the best images I have ever captured.

From following Graham's work, I knew he had created some beautiful self-portraits. So, I thought it would be cool if he would turn the tables, so to speak, and take a photo of me. I got the idea from my father, who asked Andy Warhol to take a Polaroid of him at one of his art openings. Then Graham's son Will suggested he do a self-portrait through the mirror and included me in the photograph. What a great idea … and here is the result.

August 9, 2015: Graham Nash live at the Grand Opera House, Wilmington, Delaware, USA. Photo by Dallyn Pavey

Bio: *Born in New York City, Dallyn Pavey lives in Philadelphia, Pennsylvania. A publicist specializing in restaurants and rock'n'roll, his company is Dish Public Relations.*

Songs: *'Carry Me' (C); 'Change Partners' (S); 'Our House' (N).*

ATLANTIC CROSSING

by Franco & Maureen Pietoso

Maureen:

We were on our honeymoon on the Queen Mary II on a voyage to England that began on our wedding day, 4 September 2015. Unbeknown to us, the coming together of our lives coincided with what may have been the last time Crosby, Stills & Nash toured together as a band.

Fresh from our wedding ceremony at Strawberry Fields in Central Park, New York City, we were transported to a majestic boat in our fancy wedding garb. Soon as we boarded the ship and were headed to our state room, we ran into Michael Jensen, CSN's publicist. Michael knew we were coming but seemed surprised we were still in our wedding clothes.

Crosby, Stills & Nash.

More than four decades since Crosby Stills & Nash (CSN) first harmonised in Laurel Canyon and played their first-ever concert as a trio at the legendary Woodstock festival, its members continue a creative partnership that is one of the most influential and enduring in music. David Crosby, Stephen Stills, and Graham Nash have each been inducted into the Rock and Roll Hall of Fame two times–once with Crosby, Stills & Nash, and a second time with The Byrds, Buffalo Springfield, and The Hollies, respectively. They have also been inducted into the Songwriter's Hall of Fame, with the honour recognising both CSN as a group, and each member as individual solo artists.

CSN's music first became a cornerstone of rock 'n roll with the self-titled 1969 debut LP, one of Rolling Stone's "500 Greatest Albums of All Time." Ever since -- through changing times, various configurations, and acclaimed solo careers–Crosby, Stills & Nash have continued to tour and record as "three together".

Date	Time	Activity	Location
Sun 6 Sept	11:00am	Autograph session	Grand Lobby Deck 3
Mon 7 Sept	8:30pm & 10:30pm	Crosby Stills & Nash in concert	Royal Court Theatre
Tue 8 Sept	10:30pm	Crosby Stills & Nash in concert	Royal Court Theatre
Wed 9 Sept	11:00am	Q&A session	Royal Court Theatre
Wed 9 Sept	3:00pm	Autograph session	Grand Lobby Deck 3

Times may be subject to change. Guests will be automatically allocated a ticket for one of the three concert performances which will match their dining arrangements. These will be delivered to your staterooms on 6 September.

Crosby, Stills and Nash.
Please respect the artist's privacy during this voyage. Arrangements have been made for our guests to coincide in an Autograph session with the group on two occasions during the voyage. We kindly ask that guests refrain from taking photographs. Autograph signings will be restricted to one item per guest in order to ensure as many guests as possible have the opportunity to meet the band.

We checked into our room, but before we could even change an announcement came over the loudspeaker that there was a mandatory emergency drill. After the drill we got in an elevator to head back to our stateroom. Filled to capacity, strangers wished us luck and oohed at my wedding dress. Suddenly, I noticed Franco bent over, speaking with a stranger in the corner. As I looked closer, it was evident that this was no stranger. It was David Crosby! Franco – who had known David since the Nineties - was telling him we had just got married.

David was next to his wife Jan, trying to remain unnoticed. The people around him seemed so taken by having newlyweds in their presence that the Crosbys remained unrecognized until they left the elevator when they reached their floor.

Franco:

Despite not having worked with CSN since 2005, I still manage to catch up with David and Graham and their great road crew when they tour the East Coast. In fact, we spent time with Graham and girlfriend Amy Grantham a few weeks before the cruise, attending a photography exhibition Graham and Amy were participating in along with Elliot Landy and Joel Bernstein up in Woodstock, New York. Graham expressed some trepidation about the long transatlantic voyage, joking that he hadn't forgotten about the Titanic. Amy was looking forward to it, as it would be her first cruise. Graham mentioned that his sister Elaine would also be on the cruise.

Our original idea was to get married by the Captain on the QM2 on the way to England, asking Graham and David to be witnesses. Our children didn't want to miss the ceremony though, so we changed our plans and decided to get married at Strawberry Fields in Central Park just before we set sail instead. Maureen and I were prepared for seven wonderful days of CSN followed by another week of Beatle history in Liverpool and London. The cruise was wonderful, but a bit different from what we expected.

September 2015: CSN crossing the Atlantic onboard Queen Mary 2. Photo by Michael Jensen

Maureen:

Franco and I, high from love and getting married, tried to settle down at dinner, where we were seated with CSN fans Wade and Dr Mary Kreig, who became good friends. It was at dinner that we realized the entire cruise was not made up of CSN fans. About 50% of the passengers were well-to-do conservative, elderly travelers, making for a decidedly odd clash of cultures during the voyage.

The next evening was one we were really looking forward to, the first CSN concert. There was some sea turbulence that nearly made Nash lose his footing onstage. The theatre was packed, the songs all the classics you could hope for, Nash also doing a couple of new songs.

Franco:

The guys sounded great, and the audience loved them, even the older, conservative people there purely out of curiosity were on their feet applauding by the end. Maureen couldn't resist getting up and dancing. We ran into David and son Django backstage after the show. I introduced David to Maureen. He said, 'We already met in the elevator, remember?' I laughed because David was so low-key then that he just quietly nodded. I wasn't sure he heard me. Still, David seemed more subdued than his normal animated self. I chalked it up to possibly being tired after an hour and a half performing.

Night four marked another concert. By this time the ship was in pretty rough waters, the boat noticeably rocking from side to side. This didn't stop the guys from putting on yet another stellar show, nor Maureen from getting up and dancing with sheer enjoyment. Later, Graham told us how seasick they all were when the ship was rocking big time.

After the show, we got word from the crew that they were meeting in the Golden Lion pub, the place to be for late-night fun. They had some great music trivia with audio clues for an hour or so followed by an hour or two of karaoke. We headed down to this large dark pub and formed teams. Rance, James, their wives and others were in the centre. We joined Crook, Victoria and a few others, maybe CSN merchandiser Mike Murphy. Rance joked that they could use my music expertise. Graham quietly came into the pub with Amy, looking uncharacteristically serious. They took position at the other side. The first audio clue saw me off to a great start. I was the only one on our team that knew it was 'Under the Bridge' by Red Hot Chili Peppers. It was all downhill after that, the audio clues mostly rap and techno songs, not my strong suit. Rance and James's team came first, Graham and Amy's team second, us a distant fourth.

The next day involved a meet-up with the band. I gave Maureen a heads-up not to be surprised if Stills was a little quiet. In all the time I'd spent backstage after shows, I think Stephen and I have had about four conversations. He was never stand-offish, just seemed to like to relax in his dressing room after the show and unwind, while Graham and David schmoozed with friends and fans. Of course, Stills made a liar out of me. We hadn't even reached him when he pointed to Maureen, gave a big smile and said, 'Hey! I remember you! You were dancing to all my guitar solos!' I looked at Maureen, laughed and shook my head. So much for keeping to himself.

The next day we were up early so we could clear customs when we docked in Southampton, back in England. We were heading up to Liverpool by train from there, while the band and crew were heading to London for a show the next night that would kick off a month-long European tour ending in Oslo, Norway on 11 October.

At that time, I doubt that either us or any of the audiences on that tour realised it may have been the very last chance to see these three guys play together as CSN.

Bio: *Franco Pietoso went to his first rock concert (complete with backstage passes) at the tender age of six, thanks to older sister, Diane, national president of the Ricky Nelson Fan Club. He went on to become a session drummer while still in his teens, working primarily with iconic R&B producer Teacho Wiltshire (The Platters, The Drifters, Dion, etc.). Franco worked with veteran producer and engineer Stephen Barncard on various CSN&Y*

websites from 1997-2005. He also worked in partnership with legendary music promoter Sid Bernstein. Franco is currently president of Laurel Canyon Records, an independent label focused on folk-rock, power-pop and singer/songwriter genres.

Songs: *'Page 43' (C); 'I Give You Give Blind' (S); 'Cathedral' (N).*

Bio: *Maureen Pietoso began her career as a journalist covering the political scene in Washington, DC. She returned to her native New Jersey to become a reporter for several New Jersey newspapers, covering news and entertainment stories. Maureen went on to work in public relations for various New Jersey politicians, then returned to the entertainment field. A personal publicist for legendary music promoter Sid Bernstein, who brought The Beatles and other British Invasion acts to the US in 1964, it was through Sid that she met Franco. And it was in Sid's honour that Maureen and Franco were married at Strawberry Fields, Central Park, NYC, before embarking on a honeymoon cruise to England with Crosby, Stills & Nash.*

Songs: *'Capital' (C); 'Suite: Judy Blue Eyes' (S); 'Teach Your Children' (N).*

THE SINGER INSIDE

by Steve Silberman

David Crosby's 'If I Could Only Remember My Name' was not just my favorite album in high school, it was my soul-guide, my sacred touchstone and talisman, a map of my inner landscape. I played it constantly and used it to check in with myself when I was feeling lost or despairing. I had never heard any music that sounded more personally relevant, like my own soul would sing if I could write songs.

As I got older, I came to realize the music on that album had been an education for my ears. It prepared me to hear and appreciate the modal meditations of Miles Davis, the poignant reflections of pianist Bill Evans, and much more. The album was like a doorway that I stepped through, into a whole universe of music. Then something amazing happened. In the early 1990s, after being nourished by David's music for a couple of decades, we became friends, close friends, through a chain of events that felt like destiny but could easily have never happened. So it was that I found myself sitting across a table from David eating breakfast in a hotel in Boston in December 2016, when he told me something about that album that I'd never known.

On 12 December I was in Boston to attend a show at the Wilbur Theatre, one of the concerts on the *Lighthouse* tour. David's bandmates were out visiting friends and playing a house concert, leaving us alone at the hotel with plenty of time to relax, listen to music, and talk. By that point, I knew David well enough to know that despite the fact that 'If I Could Only Remember My Name' had been an inexhaustible source of joy for me and many other people, it was recorded during one of the saddest times in his complicated life - after the sudden death of his first great love, Christine Gail Hinton, who was killed in a car crash while driving her cat to the vet.

David's response to this tragedy had been to hole up at Wally Heider's studio in San Francisco for months with members of The Grateful Dead and the Jefferson Airplane - the so-called 'Planet Earth Rock and Roll Orchestra' - developing moody instrumental passages that became the hallmark of the album. But what I didn't know was how David's illustrious friends supported him emotionally during this terrible time.

August 2016: Crosby and Steve Silberman at David's 75th birthday. Photo by Stacia Raymond

It was their contributions to David's album that turned me on to The Grateful Dead - a parallel musical adventure I had pursued through at least 300 Dead shows, my 1994 book *Skeleton Key: A Dictionary for Deadheads*, and co-producing the band's career-spanning boxset, *So Many Roads (1965-1995)*. I had spent enough time with the Dead family and road crew, including a conversation with Jerry Garcia, to know they were a salty, sarcastic, and supremely cynical bunch; not at all the soft-hearted sentimental hippies their younger fans often assumed them to be. And I'd hung out with David enough to know he was exactly the same way. Hanging out with David, particularly on the band bus, is basically an exercise in learning to enjoy scathing witticisms at your expense and give them right back. That's how you know he *cares*. But I wondered how all that went down when David was simultaneously grieving the first love of his life and making some of the most incandescently beautiful music of his career.

'Jerry and I never talked about it,' David told me over breakfast. 'We never mentioned the pain I was going through after Christine's death. That wasn't his style. Instead, he did something better. He came down to the studio, night after night, for months, and played so well that it lifted me up and gave me something to reach for.'

And by doing so, I thought, the two men had made music together that would be lifting people up, and giving them something to reach for, long after they were both gone.

A few months later, listening to the final mix of *Sky Trails*, it struck me that David resembled Miles Davis as a bandleader in one particular way: though he hired the greatest musicians of his era to play on his records - including John Coltrane, Bill Evans, Wayne Shorter, and Herbie Hancock - they always sounded unmistakably like Miles' records. Even when *In a Silent Way* sounded nothing like *Kind of Blue*, which sounded nothing like *Birth of the Cool*, there was some essential thread running through them all that made them great, and that thread was Miles' uncompromising musical sensibility.

David, too, had played with some of the best musicians of his generation - some superstars, like Neil Young and Joni Mitchell, and some that deserve more attention, like his own gifted son, James Raymond, and the other members of CPR. But they always sound like David's records. No one else's. *Croz*, *Lighthouse*, and *Sky Trails* sound nothing like *If I Could Only Remember My Name*, but they're all unmistakably David Crosby records, providing a set of moods and feelings that can only be found in his music.

Shortly after having this thought, I called David up to compliment him on a tiny, graceful aspect of one of his vocals on *Sky Trails* that I suspected would sail right past most listeners. On *Capitol*, he sings, 'visiting the Capitol and the national parks' in a voice that sounds rather like a tour guide ticking off items on a list - which is absolutely perfect for the meaning of the line and the feeling of the overall song. He was surprised and happy that I'd noticed, which I suppose explains why we became friends in the first place. And David replied with a perfect Crosbyism, 'I have a good singer inside me,' he admitted. 'I think somewhere in my big toe.'

Bio: *Steve Silberman was born in Ithaca, New York and lives in San Francisco with husband Keith Karraker. The author of NeuroTribes: The Legacy of Autism and the Future of Neurodiversity, a New York Times bestseller, translated into 14 languages, he won the 2015 Samuel Johnson Prize. He has also written liner-notes for various CSNY compilations and The Grateful Dead, and appears in the Dead documentary, Long Strange Trip.*

Songs: *'Guinnevere' (C); 'Go Back Home' (S); 'Another Sleep Song' (N).*

ACRYLIC ON CANVAS

By Ian Olito.

Bio: *Ian Michael Olito created in 1955 - An easy going, globally sold visual artist in recent years, music aficionado, culinary creator, avid hiker, cycler, kayaker and past horse trainer, Ian at age 67 is a very sensitive, relaxed, fun loving, adventurous guy and a tremendous fan of CSN. Ian has seen them 43 times in all variations of the three. Ian's artwork can be further explored on ianscryptoart.com*

Songs: *The Lee Shore (C); Helplessly Hoping (S); Cathedral (N).*

*July 2, 2018:
Graham Nash live
at Casa del Jazz,
Rome, Italy. Photo by
Francesco Lucarelli*

*November 1, 2011: Graham Nash live at Teatro Verdi, Florence, Italy (Crosby & Nash tour). Photo by
Francesco Lucarelli*

October 4, 2015:Stephen Stills live with CSN at Sala Santa Cecilia, Auditorium Parco della Musica, Rome, Italy. Photo by Francesco Lucarelli

WILL THERE BE MORE STORIES TO TELL?

by Lorenzo Conci

It must be my lucky day. It's about six in the evening, 7 April 2017, and I'm trying to negotiate access backstage at the Fox Theater in Riverside, California, Graham about to exit the building with his girlfriend Amy. He approaches me casually and affectionately, 'Hi, we are going out to dinner, wanna come?'

Wow, the relief warms me up. I can relax and take in the scent of flowers in the dry Southern California air. There is only one small restaurant nearby and they are heading to this Mexican food joint. I'm not very familiar with the menu, I try to be quick, and Graham very kindly treats me to my order. In a few moments, we are joined by guitarist Shane Fontayne, becoming a small family going through a daily ritual. I sit back and listen to their conversation, as I don't have anything to ask or add. I feel privileged to hear the sound of a voice I've always loved to listen to while singing beautiful songs. The topic is Trump, the news not good, same as over in Europe with Brexit and all the rest.

Then Graham, a little intrigued, asks if we heard that David is rehearsing for a tour with a band in LA, 'and he won't be able to break even. I know how these things go...' he adds, and it sounds like he would want to alert his former partner against ill advice, rather than wishing him bad luck.

I jump at the news, because I had seen the dates, but dismissed them as a continuation of the *Lighthouse* tour I had seen last Fall. I press Graham into saying more - Who's in the band? Where are they rehearsing? Nash only knows about Pevar and Raymond, and that's enough for me, because they were not part of the *Lighthouse* tour, so it must be a different combination. Wow! I need to get more information.

Back at the theater, Graham excuses himself and I find myself as Cinderella at the stroke of midnight, just one of many fans waiting in line to enter the venue. I look at the posters with Graham's face

September 11, 2018: David Crosby and band sound-checking at Teatro Dal Verme, Milan, Italy. Photo by Francesco Lucarelli

advertising 'An evening with Graham Nash'. I walk around, admiring the prestigious facade of the old theatre, finally forcing myself to do what I have never done so far: call Crosby on his cell. I have always rather sent a SMS. Phone ringing … no answer yet … a few more seconds … then the answering machine kicks in. I tell myself, 'What did you expect?' I don't give up. I wait for a while, then give it another try. This time David answers, excusing himself, 'Hi Lorenzo, sorry I didn't make it. I was stepping off a taxi.'

It's great to hear his voice. 'I'm in Riverside for a Nash show', I say. 'He told me you are rehearsing with a band. I was kind of wondering whether I could … erm … come and listen to you guys …' I can't believe it's really me talking. I really dared ask him. Now what 'Of course you can!' is his warm answer, reassuring me like if I didn't even have to ask. 'We are at CenterStaging in Burbank, near the airport, starting at noon.' Wow, great! Done deal.

On 8 April, Burbank, California, I go the wrong way close to my destination. I waste a few minutes and when I park, I can already hear 'Cowboy Movies' seeping through a door left ajar. They are here! I don't know what to expect and I'm a little nervous. Nervously I make my way in. The studio is not too big. The band sounds great. It's Jeff Pevar, Steve D, a girl I've never seen before on bass, plus Michelle Willis – who I know from the previous *Lighthouse* tour - and James Raymond on keyboards.

When 'Cowboy' is over, I step up to Croz. We embrace. He is so welcoming, and I feel so grateful. Beside them it's only Django, working the teleprompter, and two sound technicians, one of whom is Rance Caldwell.

I sit on a couch not more than 10 feet away. I still can't believe I am here like this. Between songs, Croz comes over and talks to me, asking if I like what I hear and telling me he's super-happy with this combo. I feel like I'm on cloud nine. 'Map of Buried Treasure', 'In My Dreams', 'Delta', 'At the Edge', 'Sky Trails', 'Luck Dragon', 'Homeward Through the Haze', and 'Low Down Payment' are some of the songs they are working on. Each musician had practised the set-list at home and now they go through all the songs together.

James acts as musical director and David looks like he is at the same time one of the subjects

July 5, 2018: Shane Fontayne, Graham Nash and Todd Caldwell harmonizing on stage at Villa Arconati, Milan, Italy. Photo by Francesco Lucarelli

of his son's coaching and the final decision-maker. They have fun going through different arrangements, exchanging views. Croz appreciates all of them and eventually decides.

A break is called around mid-afternoon. It's burgers for everyone and we sit at a table outside. I'm the guest and get to sit right next to him. He introduces me to the girl playing bass. Her name is Mai Agan. She is from Estonia and is Greg Leisz's girlfriend. She is young, cute and a terrific player. David asks about Graham's show last night and I answer it was very good, but the set-list could be more adventurous. I kind of expect him to cut him up, instead - to my surprise - he adopts a very sympathetic look, showing affection to the friend he has broken up with, wisely telling me, 'You know, Lorenzo, you play what you feel most comfortable with.'

It feels like maybe something is changing. Last year any reference to the old partner, on both sides, would have produced a cold reaction at best, or given way to mean comments. This time it is different. Yesterday it was Nash telling me about Croz rehearsing with a new band, today it's Crosby finding kind words of respect and affection toward his former partner. It warms me inside and makes me feel good. Maybe, I think, this is what happens to children of divorced parents. You see them separately, but you miss seeing them together.

These thoughts keep following me on the freeway while I skirt LA north to south on 405. There's a beautiful sunset and it touches me. When we hugged goodbye, it was hard to leave. I struggle to get a grip, to go back to reality after this dreamlike afternoon. I feel kind of lonely. I fear I intruded myself a little too much into somebody's else life and feel a bit unsettled.

At the same time, I think how big the role these artists have played in my life. How they feel like family to me. They have gone their separate ways for reasons which - to me - don't look like unsolvable problems. They both have told me their own version of the story and I keep thinking that fences could be mended. Or maybe it is just that, the arc of a lifetime is too long even for a deep and meaningful friendship, and in the end you grow apart. Who knows ... But this time their behaviour and reaction has been different. I felt more understanding towards one another.

What lies ahead? Will they work together again? Will there be another CSNY reunion? Graham has told me that Neil has been calling him and that this is a good sign. The sun is sinking into the ocean and in this moonless night everything takes on a more mysterious look. Will there be more stories to tell?

TEACH YOUR CHILDREN

by Erik M. Richardson

I have been a fan of CSN for a quarter-century. There is something very special about their music and their harmonies that have kept me listening all these years. Whether it's been all three of them together, or watching them solo, it's been a magical experience.

I am very blessed to say I met Graham Nash a few times while attending his solo shows. Graham is a very humble, genuine human being, and it's obvious that he appreciates his fans.

In April 2016, I heard Graham was going to be at Barns & Noble in Manhattan to have a signing session of new album, *This Path Tonight*. Without a second thought, I took a bus from upstate New York to New York City to get my album signed. While in line, I thought to myself I'll have him sign my arm, then have a tattoo made out of his original signature. After he signed my album, I held my arm out and he signed it for me. I got back on the bus and got home later that night. The next day I had my tattoo completed. I was very happy with it, and it was such an unusual original piece.

Exactly one month later, 14 May, I went back to New York City to attend Graham's solo performance at The Town Hall. I arrived early, so went to a bar down the street to have a couple of pints before the show. When I stepped, looking to my right, I saw Graham and girlfriend Amy Grantham walking up the street, holding hands. As he walked by, I showed him my arm, and he smiled. Amy took a picture of Graham and myself, Graham pointing at my tattoo. That was a unique moment.

One more special CSN experience included Graham Nash. My four-year-old son Nolan would listen to the songs I would play at the house and eventually memorize the lyrics. And I could find him alone in his room playing with his toys, singing 'I Used to Be a King'. Sometimes we would get home and he would say,

May 14, 2016: Graham Nash and Erik M. Richardson, New York City, New York, USA. Photo by Amy Grantham

'Daddy, let's listen to Graham Nash.' In a short time, he became a big Graham Nash fan as well. As a result, I knew Nolan's first concert should be Nash.

We got tickets to Graham's show in Pennsylvania at the Sherman Theater in Stroudsburg on 21 September 2017. I even made him his own concert shirt that said 'NASH' on the front. Because of his t-shirt and his young age, Nolan received a lot of attention. It was unusual to see such a young guy so much into the music: he loved the concert and clapped after every song. After the show, we ran into Graham at his tour bus, and he was so sweet to stop and sign Nolan's shirt. What a night for this young fan!

Bio: *Erik M. Richardson lives in Binghamton, upstate New York and works in mental health at a local hospital. His main pleasure in life is spending time with son Nolan, his main hobby attending concerts and music festivals.*

Songs: *'Long Time Gone' (C); 'You Don't Have to Cry' (S); 'Just a Song Before I Go' (N).*

IN MY DREAMS

by Davide Pusiol

When you play music with someone, a hard to describe mechanism is triggered which goes beyond friendship and sharing a passion. Energies, life experiences, different cultures come together in a common language, which involves and elevates the spirit, whatever the result.

That's why I've always dreamed of being able to play at least one song in my life with David Crosby. I don't feel like a hardcore fan exactly, but I think I share a lot of things with him, besides the music of course. Humble guitarist, luthier for 20 years, I wish I had written every single note and word of his songs, especially 'In My Dreams'.

A dream made its way into my mind long ago of me ringing the bell at David's doorway to say, 'Excuse me, do you have five minutes to play 'In My Dreams' with me?' Seriously determined to make it happen, I found out his address and booked flights and rental cars, then left with my wife for our second visit to California, convinced that Crosby would open the gate to his ranch for me, and make my dream come true.

Once landed in San Francisco, we arrived at our destination after a spectacular journey through green valleys. I recognized David's wife in front of the house. Jan came towards me smiling, accompanied by a beautiful dog. I told her where we had come from and asked if David was home. Jan's smile faded. 'I'm sorry,' she told me. 'He left about ten minutes ago. He went to Los Angeles to record a new album.'

I thought I had seen him in a car in the opposite direction, but my mind did not want to accept the fact that my dream had not come true. Maybe I should have stopped that car, in perfect stagecoach attack style of the Far West, to have an 'In My Dreams' session on a lawn by the side of the road.

We couldn't help but hug and thank Jan, and head to Santa Barbara Marina, where David's schooner, the Mayan was moored. Sailing was another passion I share with Croz. Confirming that it was not my luckiest day, I discovered that the boat of my dreams had just been sold.

About ten years later, in February 2017, I was in the Florida Keys when the first edition of the Ground Up Music Festival was held in Miami. Crosby was the mentor of the event, with extraordinary artists on the bill: from Jacob Collier to Esperanza Spalding, to Michael League's Snarky Puppy, from the producer of David's *Lighthouse* record.

The collaboration between Crosby and Michael League was not accidental: David has always kept an eye on people who create new and interesting music. Furthermore, unlike other colleagues who have sat on their laurels, he has continued to explore, to seek new harmonic solutions, to search for new energies by collaborating with new generations of incredible musicians. David Crosby's musical evolution is astounding.

To cut a long story short, as soon as I read the news, I rushed to Miami. The concert was incredible. At one point, I found myself a few metres from the stage, Crosby by my side! We practically spent the whole day listening to the entire concert next to each other, eating mandarins, sharing music, emotions, glances and smiles, while I continued to fuel my dream.

I wanted to tell him a million things, but I'm not the type to bother famous people. So, I just gave him a short note, a sort of 'artistic' declaration of love, adding that I was a luthier - building acoustic, archtop and electric guitars - and I had built a guitar in his name. That day we didn't play 'In My Dreams'. 'Time will come,' I thought.

In September 2018, Jeff Pevar was on tour with David Crosby's band and was also scheduled to play some gigs in Italy with his wife, Inger Jorgensen. We wrote to each other, and he asked if I would allow him to use some of my guitars during his concert in Venice. Francesco Lucarelli and Jeff Pevar invited me backstage at David's concert in Milan to let Jeff try one of those guitars. After the soundcheck, the backstage atmosphere was friendly. The band was relaxing and talking to friends. Crosby lingered in the large room hosting us. He was calm and comfortable. Suddenly he saw my guitar resting on an armchair and asked if he could try it. He played it for a while. 'Not too many basses,' he commented. 'You can't expect the bass of a D-45 from a 000 model,' I replied. He smiled at me, hugging me with affection. Again, I wasn't able to play 'In My Dreams' with Crosby, but I felt elated. 'Time will come,' I thought.

Bio: *Davide Pusiol was born and raised in Venice at the same time as the Beatlemania explosion, which he fed on at all levels. He strummed the guitar as a professional for more than 20 years and after having traded, repaired and restored more than 1,000 instruments he decided to create them from scratch too. For 20 years he has been running his own workshop of stringed instruments. And like David Crosby, he has a great passion for sailing boats.*

Songs: *'In My Dreams' (C); 'Suite: Judy Blue Eyes' (S); 'Carried Away' (N).*

CSN star on Hollywood Walk of Fame, Los Angeles, California. Photo by Monika Falkenberg

ACKOWLEDGEMENTS

When the time came to put together this section, I knew I had to deal with the most difficult part of the project, especially when that project took so long to be completed. Over the past seven years, I talked and corresponded with hundreds and hundreds of people. Each page of this book was made possible by the contribution of many different individuals and each of them deserves a special mention here. I have tried to remember them all. Many beautiful people generously contributed to this project, sending visuals of all kinds.

There wasn't enough room for all the items I received but I'm pretty sure you will like the selection chosen. Thanks Shirly Ambrose, Fred Arellano, Shari Avenius, Graham Baker, Luc Bezemer, Dick Boak, Kathy Boyer-Shick, John Bowman, Christine Bower, John Braun, Leslie Brophy, Suzanne Cadgène (*Elmore* magazine), Paolo Carnevale, Ernesto Juan Castellanos, David Champagne, Andy Clearfield, Lisa Clemmer, Nick Dowsett, Marcus Eaton, Bill Evans, Monika Falkenberg, Chris Field, Mike Finnegan, Gary Goltz, Jochem Groeneveld, John Hartmann, Thomas L. Hagan, Ray Haley, Matthew Helminski (*Elmore* magazine), Cathryn Hendel, Paul Higham, Margaret Jackson Graeff, Beth Jordan-Kroll, Gabriëlla van Karsbergen, John Keller (audiovisual archivist, National Archives and Records Administration, William J. Clinton Presidential Library), Ross Knudson and Lauretta (LAMC Productions), Frank Lafaro, Hugh Lalande, Pete Long, Marc Maingard, Rochelle Manson, Roy McAlister, Gareth McNair-Lewis, Randy Mills, Susan Miller, Scott V. Oxman, Franco Pietoso, Christine Plumeri, Giovanni Pompili, Herbert Ragan (National Archives and Records administration, William J. Clinton Presidential Library), Roberto Ragonesi, Erik Richardson, Christine Holm Rubin, Daniel Ruiz, Pamela Schreckengost, Heather Sherman, Rod Sims, Annie Sollinger (visual archivist, Robert S. Cox Special Collections and University Archives Research Center, University of Massachusetts Amherst), Allan Thomas, Emily Vincent (director, University Media Relations, Kent State University Communications and Marketing).

And thanks to Giorgio Baratto, Paolo Palù and Agostino Viglione for all the beautiful concert recordings they shared with me, my soundtrack for endless hours in front of the computer screen.

Over the years, CSN have backed many organisations and their beautiful projects. Tom Campbell (Guacamole Fund), Mollie Farrell, Aaron Ghitelman (both Headcount.org), Tamara Klamner, Aaron Simon (both Seva Foundation) helped track down information and some precious images. Please take a moment to visit their websites and learn more about how to support them.

This book features the largest collection of CSN images ever put together and this was possible thanks to all those souls who made their art available: Photographers: Ramiro Agredo, Dana Africa, Marnix Allegaert, Ian Astle, Giorgio Baratto, Melinda Bates, David Bingham, Dan Birman, Emily Boak, Leslie Brophy, Lorenzo Conci, Mauro Coscia, Michael Curcuru, Tom Davis, Filippo de Orchi, Nicola Pietro de Rienzo, Henry Diltz, Richard Dowdy, Jeremy Dowson, Raymond Foye, John Ferrentino, Jody Goldman Daddio, Paolo Golini, Amy Grantham, Tom Gundelfinger O'Neal, Susan Haley, Tom Hambleton, Terri Haram, Guido Harari, Alvin Ho, Randy Hylton, Michael Jensen, Lorraine Kaczorowski, Mark Kelly, Lisa Law, Donald Leary, Aloysius Lim, Francesco Lucarelli, Dena Mintz, Graham Nash, Neri Oddo, Ernie Osborne, Tim Owen, Franco Paissan, John Partipilo, Dallyn Pavey, Geraldine Peters, Stacia Raymond, Mauro Regis, Alberto Sarria, Rowland Scherman, Bob Sheridan, Crook Stewart, Talitha 'Tai' Stills, Marco Tomassetti, Lucien van Diggelen, Joe Vitale, Paolo Vites, Luciano Viti, Anna Webber, Dan Wilson, Charlie Wine, Paul Wultz.

Visual artists: David, Ian and Tim Bingham; Gerri Winchell Findley; Alfonso Federici; Phil Hartmann; Gerard Huerta; Bani Kinnison; Ian Olito; Malleus (https://www.malleusdelic.com/); Simon David Smith; Daniela Wood; Stanislaw Zagorski. An extra special thank you goes to Gary Strobl (Henry

Author Francesco Lucarelli with a canvas by Alfonso Federici from his The Front Side of Rock project

Diltz's archivist), for spending countless hours digging into Henry's archives and bringing to light some incredible images.

A very special thank goes to Mark White and Katie Jane Wood, who made my translations shine, and to Malcolm Wyatt for honing the final text. A number of folks made me feel part of the CSN&Y family, since the very beginning. Thanks for putting up with me when I was in the way backstage and sometimes even on stage. You made all my CSN&Y moments precious and unforgettable. The ride would have not been the same without you: Doug Breidenbach, Rance Caldwell, Todd Caldwell, Jan Crosby, Paul Dieter, Henry Diltz, Steve Distanislao, Craig Doerge, Bridget and Candy Finnigan, Shane Fontayne, Frank Gironda, Glenn Goodwin, Bob Glaub, John Gonzales, R. Mac Holbert, Michael Jensen, Inger Jorgensen, Russ Kunkel, Bonnie Levetin, Cree and Donald 'Buddha' Miller, Ralph Molina, Mike Murphy, Will Nash, Kenny Passarelli, Jeff Pevar, Chris 'Hoover' Rankin, James Raymond, Mike 'Coach' Sexton, Leland Sklar, Bill Siddons, Crook Stewart, Chris Stills, Billy Talbot, Joe Vitale, Ken Weiss. Thanks also to the extended *Wooden Nickel* family for all the memorable times: Lorenzo Conci, Mauro Coscia, Stefano Frollano, Arie van Steen, Lucien van Diggelen, Herman Verbeke.

This book would not exist without a number of people, who I would like to thank with deepest gratitude: Eleonora Bagarotti for introducing me to Alberto Tonti, who had the original idea behind the book; Isabella Ferretti and Tomaso Cenci for helping me sailing rough waters; Debbie Meister for opening the door in the first place and for still supporting me, even after 30 years; Gareth McNair-Lewis, for an unlimited supply of CSN goodies, and for keeping the lamp trimmed and burning even in the darkest hour; Luciano Viti, photographer extraordinaire, for being such an inspiration; Adolfo Galli, for bringing a piece of California to Italy; Ian Astle for always making his photo archive available to me; and Marco Martella, the original spark behind this long journey. Extra special thanks to Neil Cossar, Liz Sanchez, Gary Bishop and all the folks at This Day In Music Books for embracing this project and helping me craft it with so much passion. Love to Graham Nash, for supporting the book with so much enthusiasm and generosity from the very beginning.

And to my family: Isabella, Andrea and Filippo. Our house is a very, very fine house but it wouldn't be *so* fine without Perry and Lola, our two cats in the yard.

This book is dedicated to the memory of Mike Finnigan, Bani Kinnison, Joe Lala, Pete Long, Elliot Roberts, Giancarlo Susanna.

There are a dozen different versions of how David Crosby, Graham Nash, and Stephen Stills first sang together, but on one point all versions agree: whether it was at Mama Cass's house, some studio, at Joni Mitchell's house, or somewhere else, everyone agrees, the minute those three voices blended in song, it was unmistakable to any listener with ears, and inevitable that they would make great music together.

The management team of David Geffen and Elliot Roberts convinced Ahmet Ertegun, president of Atlantic Records, to sign the trio and finance the production of their first album. Atlantic Records stepped up, put down the money for a studio to record the trio, and soon after that, Crosby, Stills, and Nash had their first hit, 'Marrakesh Express'. The album and most of the songs on it dominated top 40 radio airplay, clearing the way for concerts, touring, and the eventual hook-up with Neil Young, for the first American super-group to do stadium tours. CSN and CSNY were a global phenomenon.

Looking back on those early days, it seemed so easy: form a group, make some demo cassette tapes of original material, find a sympathetic record company to finance an album, release the album, make a billion dollars. What no one realizes is that there were thousands of young musicians with the same idea. But CSN was in the enviable position of having savvy managers, a solid work ethic, and an overwhelming devotion to the music. They were in the middle of a rapidly expanding music scene, in which tens of millions of young men and women experiencing the exploding new technology of cassette recorders, FM stereo radio, stereo broadcasts of popular music, and a concert scene that encouraged enormous numbers to come out to hear their favorite bands play live.

CSN (and sometimes Y) rode that rocket as far as it could go. Today, they are more apart than together, with some public animosity that makes any sort of reunion problematic, but in pop music and politics, never say "never."

Carl Gottlieb

May 2017

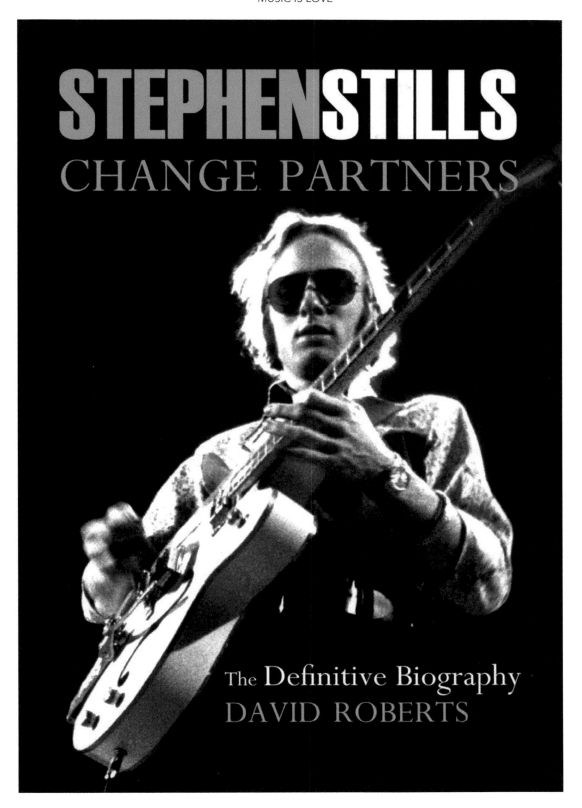

www.thisdayinmusicbooks.com

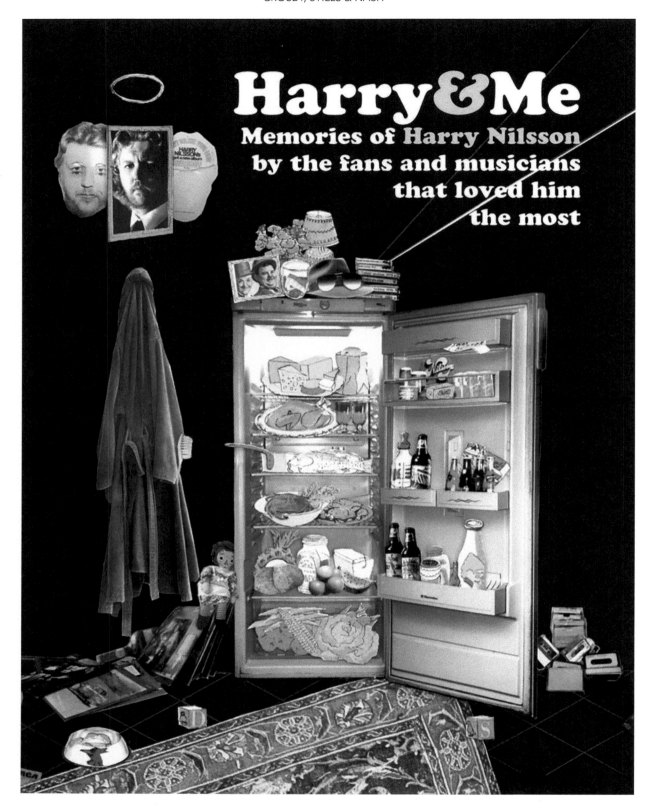

BOB DYLAN
THE DAY I WAS THERE

www.thisdayinmusicbooks.com